"It is said that great crises create great leaders, but that does not happen magically. Some succeed and many fail the heroic tests of superhuman adversity. When leaders across sectors and industries face genuine personal risk in triumphantly completing their worthy missions, they have never had the road map to guide their preparation nor real-time decision making—until now. Kolditz seamlessly blends the priceless "battle-tested" systemic and psychological insights to prepare anyone to lead others confidently through highly risky situations. It is rare to find a book packed with such useful tools and inspirational examples."

—**Professor Jeffrey Sonnenfeld,** senior associate dean, Yale School of Management, author of *Firing Back: How Great Leaders Overcome Career Disasters*

"West Point's mission is to produce leaders of character to serve as career Army officers; lives depend on the ability of our graduates to lead. Our Department of Behavioral Sciences and Leadership is committed to research and teaching on leadership in combat—but the lessons they have developed carry forward as examples for all leaders. With *In Extremis Leadership*, Tom Kolditz has successfully linked leading in dangerous contexts with the requirements of everyday leadership. This book is exciting to read, and makes the point that we should all lead as if lives depend on it."

—**Lieutenant General Franklin L. Hagenback,** superintendent of the US Military Academy

"Colonel Tom Kolditz is a visionary in the field of leadership training and development. With this work he has pushed into an area of leadership that has not yet been fully explored. His unique insights and wisdom offer the reader a fascinating view into the role of leaders and the leadership ethos of groups who will face in extremis conditions and how this drives the cohesion and sense of shared mission among these groups. Any student of leadership who aspires to be a worthy combat leader, SWAT team leader, or who will be involved in a critical incident leadership role should read this book."

—**David S. Corderman,** head of the Office of Leadership Development, FBI Academy, Quantico, Virginia

"Whether used to train public servants for dangerous roles or to take university students to the next level of leadership science, the concepts in *In Extremis Leadership* are novel, exciting, and chart a path to better understanding of leadership in the real world. This is a must read for leaders in emergency services organizations. Tom Kolditz knows how to lead and how to write. This book is a great example of a soldier-scholar making a difference in the art and science of leadership."

—**Brigadier General Howard T. Prince II,** U.S. Army, Retired, director, Center for Ethical Leadership, University of Texas

"West Point Professor Thomas Kolditz gives new meaning to the phrase "hanging on every word." His riveting book moves leadership into new and previously unexplored frontiers—where human lives, including the leader's, are literally on the line every day. But you don't have to be a skydiver, mountain climber, or special operations soldier living dangerously to appreciate this book. Anyone in a leadership role can learn much from what it means to live—and lead—in extremis."

—**John Alexander,** president, Center for Creative Leadership

For Kay, and Jenna, and Kerry

JB JOSSEY-BASS

IN EXTREMIS
LEADERSHIP

LEADING AS IF
YOUR LIFE DEPENDED ON IT

THOMAS A. KOLDITZ

foreword by
Joseph W. Pfeifer
deputy assistant chief
New York City Fire Department

John Wiley & Sons, Inc.

Other Publications from the Leader to Leader Institute

Leadership Lessons from West Point, *Major Doug Crandall, Editor*

The Leader of the Future 2, *Frances Hesselbein, Marshall Goldsmith, Editors*

Be•Know•Do: Leadership the Army Way, *Introduced by Frances Hesselbein,
General Eric K. Shinseki (USA Ret.)*

Hesselbein on Leadership, *Frances Hesselbein*

Leading Organizational Learning: Harnessing the Power of Knowledge,
Marshall Goldsmith, Howard Morgan, Alexander J. Ogg

Peter F. Drucker: An Intellectual Journey (video), *Leader to Leader Institute*

The Collaboration Challenge, *James E. Austin*

Meeting the Collaboration Challenge Workbook, *The Drucker Foundation*

On Leading Change: A Leader to Leader Guide, *Frances Hesselbein,
Rob Johnston*

On High Performance Organizations: A Leader to Leader Guide,
Frances Hesselbein, Rob Johnston

On Creativity, Innovation, and Renewal: A Leader to Leader Guide,
Frances Hesselbein, Rob Johnston

On Mission and Leadership: A Leader to Leader Guide, *Frances Hesselbein,
Rob Johnston*

Leading for Innovation, *Frances Hesselbein, Marshall Goldsmith,
Iain Somerville, Editors*

Leading in a Time of Change (video), *Peter F. Drucker, Peter M. Senge,
Frances Hesselbein*

Leading in a Time of Change Viewer's Workbook, *Peter F. Drucker,
Peter M. Senge, Frances Hesselbein*

Leading Beyond the Walls, *Frances Hesselbein, Marshall Goldsmith,
Iain Somerville, Editors*

The Organization of the Future, *Frances Hesselbein, Marshall Goldsmith,
Richard Beckhard, Editors*

The Community of the Future, *Frances Hesselbein, Marshall Goldsmith,
Richard Beckhard, Richard F. Schubert, Editors*

Leader to Leader: Enduring Insights on Leadership from the Drucker
Foundation, *Frances Hesselbein, Paul Cohen, Editors*

The Drucker Foundation Self-Assessment Tool: Participant Workbook,
Peter F. Drucker

The Drucker Foundation Self-Assessment Tool Process Guide,
Peter F. Drucker

Excellence in Nonprofit Leadership (video), *Featuring Peter F. Drucker,
Max De Pree, Frances Hesselbein, Michele Hunt; Moderated by
Richard F. Schubert*

Excellence in Nonprofit Leadership Facilitator's Guide, *Peter F. Drucker
Foundation for Nonprofit Management*

Excellence in Nonprofit Leadership Workbook, *Peter F. Drucker Foundation
for Nonprofit Management*

Lessons in Leadership (video), *Peter F. Drucker*

Lessons in Leadership Workbook, *Peter F. Drucker*

Lessons in Leadership Facilitator's Guide, *Peter F. Drucker*

The Leader of the Future, *Frances Hesselbein, Marshall Goldsmith,
Richard Beckhard, Editors*

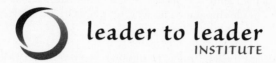
leader to leader
INSTITUTE

ABOUT THE LEADER TO LEADER INSTITUTE

Established in 1990 as the Peter F. Drucker Foundation for Nonprofit Management, the Leader to Leader Institute furthers its mission—to strengthen the leadership of the social sector—by providing social sector leaders with the wisdom, inspiration, and resources essential for leading for innovation and for building vibrant social sector organizations. It is the social sector, in collaboration with its partners in the private and public sectors, that is key in changing lives and building a society of healthy children, strong families, decent housing, good schools, and work that dignifies, embraced by a diverse, inclusive, cohesive community that cares about all of its members.

The Leader to Leader Institute provides innovative and relevant training materials and resources that enable leaders of the future to address emerging opportunities and challenges. With the goal of leading social sector organizations toward excellence in performance, the Institute has brought together more than four hundred thought leaders to publish over twenty books available in twenty-eight languages and the award-winning quarterly journal, *Leader to Leader*.

The Leader to Leader Institute engages social sector leaders in partnerships across the sectors that provide new and significant opportunities for learning and growth. It coordinates unique, high-level summits for leaders from all three sectors and collaborates with local sponsors on workshops and conferences for social sector leaders on strategic planning, leadership, and cross-sector partnerships.

Building on our legacy of innovation, the Leader to Leader Institute explores new approaches to strengthen the leadership of the social sector. With sources of talent and inspiration that range from the local community development corporation to the U.S. Army to the corporate boardroom, the Institute helps social sector organizations identify new leaders and new ways of operating that embrace change and abandon the practices of yesterday that no longer achieve results today.

Leader to Leader Institute
(formerly the Drucker Foundation)

320 Park Ave., 3rd floor
New York, NY 10022 USA
Tel: +1 212-224-1174

E-mail: info@leadertoleader.org
Web: leadertoleader.org
Fax: +1 212-224-2508

Published by Jossey-Bass
A Wiley Imprint
989 Market Street, San Francisco, CA 94103-1741   www.josseybass.com

Jossey-Bass books and products are available through most bookstores. To contact Jossey-Bass directly call our Customer Care Department within the U.S. at 800-956-7739, outside the U.S. at 317-572-3986, or fax 317-572-4002.

Jossey-Bass also publishes its books in a variety of electronic formats. Some content that appears in print may not be available in electronic books.

Library of Congress Cataloging-in-Publication Data
Kolditz, Thomas A., date.
  In extremis leadership: leading as if your life depended on it/Thomas A. Kolditz; foreword by Joseph W. Pfeifer.—1st ed.
      p. cm.—(Leader to Leader Institute series)
  Includes bibliographical references and index.
  ISBN 978-0-7879-9604-8 (cloth)
  1. Crisis management. 2. Leadership. I. Title.
  HD49.K65 2007
  658.4'092—dc22

                                                                      2007013438

Printed in the United States of America
FIRST EDITION
HB *Printing*   10 9 8 7 6 5

Contents

Foreword

Most forms of leadership, whether in the public or private sector, pose some type of risk. Traditional leadership is usually illustrated by risking power, money, or position. But what happens when people choose to exercise leadership in environments that could potentially kill them? *In Extremis Leadership* examines those high-risk environments and provides a new understanding of how to lead not only in life-and-death situations but also in everyday situations.

Thomas Kolditz defines those who elect to lead others during times of imminent physical danger as *in extremis leaders*. Under extreme conditions, leadership and life are placed on the line so that others may live. As Kolditz examines the concept of in extremis leadership, you begin to understand that exercising leadership in life-threatening environments requires instilling in others a confidence to succeed, a promise for survival, and a sense of resilience, while simultaneously performing almost impossible tasks. These principles are similarly applied to business, government, sports, or whenever else teams must perform under challenging conditions.

More than ever before, we see in extremis leadership in the public service of firefighters, police officers, and military personnel. On September 11, 2001, many watched as firefighters entered the burning towers of the World Trade Center. As fire units arrived, we were faced with enormous fires ninety floors above ground level and with the daunting mission of rescuing an estimated twenty-five thousand people. Fire officers led their firefighters up the narrow stairs of the 110-story office building in the hope of saving those who were in their greatest moment of need. Each firefighter at every level of command was in extreme risk while carrying out this daring life-saving operation.

In just over an hour from the start of the terrorist attacks, the South Tower of the World Trade Center collapsed, and orders were given for firefighters to evacuate the North Tower. In the process of leaving, one lieutenant stopped his engine company at the ninth floor to direct other fire units to safety. At the same time, a captain directed his ladder company to assist a woman who was unable to walk down the stairs, delaying their exit from the building. These stories of exercising leadership, along with countless similar accounts from that day, inspire us and cause us to wonder about the characteristics of in extremis leaders. What we observed on 9/11 were people doing ordinary things at an extraordinary moment in history. The aim of this book is to teach how to apply these traits to the daily workplace.

Kolditz takes a close look at the dangerous environment of the combat military officer and at the extreme sport of free-fall parachuting to explain the transformational character of in extremis leadership. These hazardous conditions magnify the role leadership plays in accomplishing basic and even insurmountable tasks, which gives us a new perspective on the meaning of authentic leadership. Kolditz's research offers a firsthand glimpse of the essential element of leadership under conditions of grave risk. Such research is rarely done because of the danger that is presented to the researcher, but it is essential to understanding the dynamics of leadership within hostile environments.

Every day fire, police, and military organizations respond to dangerous situations with leaders who personally direct perilous operations. Individuals within public service need a greater understanding about leading in this choice of profession. Kolditz's research reveals that the most experienced individuals often exercise leadership by placing themselves at greater risk in order to protect the safety of the less experienced. Such service, along with countless other demonstrations of selfless leadership, contributes immense public value to our communities. This book defines in extremis leadership and examines the emergent pattern of behavior when leading in both extreme danger and during ordinary routine events.

Within extreme conditions, Kolditz observes four requisites for in extremis leadership. These distinctive activities are first observed in the extremis context, where those who lead are self-motivated to not only master the fundamental execution of their jobs, but also to rapidly scan the environment and make sense of new information. Effective leadership requires rapid decision making by learning from a constantly changing environment of danger. Second, the danger or risk is equally shared between those who are leading and those who follow. This shared responsibility produces a profound trust in those who lead. The third element that Kolditz observes is the minor disparity in lifestyle among those who lead and those who follow. Pay differences are minimal and most often take a back seat to other values. Finally, Kolditz asserts that followers demand a level of competence from those who are in leadership positions. For those who exercise leadership under dangerous conditions, all outcomes are personally related to their level of competence and ability. These same requisites are essential to successful leadership in every profession.

Kolditz examines what most other leadership books seldom witness: the moment when a person's true character is called on to lead. Leadership in the face of danger usually takes place within a few tense moments. There is little time to look inward to complain about conditions, point fingers, or feel self-pity. Such negativity is a luxury one simply cannot afford. Instead, Kolditz argues that leaders possess a calm demeanor and look outward to make sense of a shifting environment and find solutions for resilience. In these moments, leadership is demonstrated by providing purpose, motivation, and direction to others. At its core, Kolditz explains, leadership is really about the success of your people.

There are many experts on leadership. However, there are few who can combine academic credentials with military and extreme sports experience to provide readers with a personal insight into leading when it counts the most. Whether you are an emergency responder, military officer, or business professional, you will be required to exercise leadership within a high-risk environment at some point in your career. Tom Kolditz's extraordinary stories will inspire you and educate you on the characteristics you need to provide effective leadership under challenging conditions. He also explains the important emotional and physical skills you will need to survive these extreme events. *In Extremis Leadership* provides a practical guide of how to lead at the most important times in your life.

March 2007   Joseph W. Pfeifer
                                                     Deputy Assistant Chief
                                                     New York City Fire Department

Introduction

The many people you will read about in this book placed their lives at genuine risk—some as part of living their own exciting lives and some specifically for the purpose of researching this book. The lessons you learn from their sojourns to the edge of life and death will forever change the way you lead.

This book uncovers new leadership lessons from firsthand experience in dangerous places. I say "new" because the principles described in this book haven't been put forth in other books you might have read about leadership. That's because this book gets at leadership as it is practiced at a peak of intensity: by watching leaders in circumstances where lives can be lost.

In situations where followers perceive their lives are threatened, leadership literally defines the promise of future life, and those at risk desperately seek capable leaders. Such high-risk situations are ideal settings to seek and find great leaders, assess how they might differ from other leaders, and glean invaluable insights for extraordinary leadership in our everyday lives. This book is a way for you to gain those novel insights without having to put your own life at risk.

For the past three years, I have committed myself to a greater understanding of authentic leadership in circumstances where the injury or death of followers must be actively avoided. I collected experience at extreme sport coaching, leadership in combat, and the ways that people respond to death. I originally set out to learn about leaders in dangerous settings because I thought I was going to find a form of leadership that would apply only to military, police, and firefighting—in other words, critical response organizations. It turns out that I discovered much more. I discovered that the unique leadership principles that emerge in life-or-death settings offer profound lessons for leadership in all settings.

I, and others who have worked with me, assumed risk firsthand in places that few people go and from where even fewer return. We refer to such places as *in extremis* settings, and the leadership found there as *in extremis* leadership. The leadership insights we've uncovered are bold, unmistakable, and novel; they are gems of understanding for professional life savers and life takers. Yet we never found a leadership lesson or principle in evidence in dangerous settings that didn't also inform or apply to leading in business or everyday life.

The opposite, however, was definitely true: there is much that poses as leadership in business, politics, and everyday life that is not really leadership, fails immediately when applied in dangerous settings, and, ironically, often doesn't work very well in routine settings either. What you learn from this book will help you cut through faddish, bogus leadership approaches and make you better at leading and being led.

You're About to Take an Exciting Ride

There are many reasons you should read about, experience, and think through in extremis leadership, and first among them is that in extremis leadership is quite exciting. Enjoy the ride. Whether the leaders you'll read about have conquering a mountain or an enemy battalion as their goal, whether the followers are at 15,000 feet in a free-fall at 120 miles per hour or poised to ram the door of an inner-city crack house, in extremis leadership promises high-risk, high-payoff outcomes. This book takes you to a world where adrenaline courses through the veins of people who live extraordinary lives and do extraordinary things. You're about to enter a world of extreme settings where "average Joe" (and even "above-average Joe") is only a spectator.

The more that I looked at leaders in dangerous places, the clearer it became that these leaders, in doing their work, could teach much about the more routine challenges of organizations, and even of political leadership. For example, in the context of the 2004 presidential election, an editorial in the *New York Times* cited the value of developing leadership characteristics under the threat of death: "People need to feel that the President is not going to be fazed by life-and-death decisions. And the only way you can demonstrate that is by showing that you've made some."[1]

A tour through in extremis leadership also gives a new look at public servants to whom we all owe so much. The vast majority of in extremis leaders spend their lives protecting ours, and we need to know more about the nature of their bravery and willingness to sacrifice their own safety. When danger threatens in our towns and cities, we have neither the time nor the resources to put the problem up for contract bid. Instead, a fire department lieutenant leads peers into a burning home, or a special-tactics police sergeant positions his team outside a bank full of hostages. Across the world, in cities now embroiled with anarchy or worse, military leaders thunder down nameless streets with their platoons and companies, barking orders that carry the promise of survival and victory for some and most certainly death and defeat for others. By and large, neither the leaders nor their followers who risk their lives in the public service are paid more than an average wage. All citizens should come to understand such a remarkable phenomenon.

And if you happen to be in public service, you may find that this book reads like a textbook for how to train and act in dangerous settings—whether they are common to your work or as rare as an instance of workplace violence.

The real value to most readers, however, will be in their role as organizational citizens—filling roles in teams and groups that cocoon us in our everyday lives. Most of us won't be a hero on the side of a mountain—but maybe we can be ordinary heroes and lead better in our families, workplaces, and communities. All of the information presented here offers information that can be applied to any organizational context, and to make it even easier to consider those lessons, I've added indicators along the way in sections labeled "Why This Is Important for All Leaders." In addition, I've concluded each chapter with a summing up of the key in extremis leadership lessons presented in that chapter. Both features are intended to be helpful guides.

Learning from In Extremis Leaders: Retracing Pathways in the Shadow of Death

The pathways you'll take in this book are actual experiences. Several individuals have helped with the effort to understand in extremis leadership, including at least eight who deployed to combat zones for research purposes. Most of the work, however, I had to do myself, either because of the inherent danger of the setting or because of my ability to take advantage of circumstances that developed because of my military credentials or abilities developed as a skydiving instructor. Thus, I learned a lot about in extremis leadership by watching, and sometimes living, in extremis contexts.

I define in extremis leadership as giving purpose, motivation, and direction to people when there is imminent physical danger and where followers believe that leader behavior will influence their physical well-being or survival. In extremis leadership is not a leadership theory. It is an approach that views leader and follower behaviors under a specific set of circumstances—contexts where outcomes mean more than mere success or failure, pride or embarrassment. Outcomes in in extremis settings are instead characterized in terms of hurt or healthy, dead or alive.

Defined in this way, in extremis leadership differs from the popular concept of crisis leadership. In crisis leadership, the focus is on how leaders react when thrust unexpectedly into an extreme challenge, disaster, or circumstance. It is based largely on military history vignettes and corporate case studies that seem to support rec-ommendations for leaders to communicate better, care more, and try to stay calm in the face of calamity. In contrast, in extremis lead-ers routinely and willingly place themselves in circumstances of extreme danger or threat and, more important, lead others in such circumstances as well. These leaders are professional and self-selected; crisis leaders are not. Wouldn't you rather learn from pros, especially when the stakes are high?

This is a reality book. Here is how I learned, and you can learn, from the reality lived by professional, self-selected, in extremis leaders:

- Two cadets, a sergeant, and I went as participant-observers to the Special Operations Command Military Freefall School in Yuma, Arizona, to conduct observation of in extremis leaders participat-ing in high-risk military training. We successfully completed all aspects of the course, including nighttime group free-fall jumps with oxygen and more than a hundred pounds of equipment.

- One research associate and I conducted more than 120 in-depth interviews across a range of both leaders and followers. Among the leaders (and many of them are listed by name in the Conclusion), we interviewed SWAT team chiefs from the New York City and San Francisco offices of the FBI.

- We interviewed mountain climbing guides from three states, including elite guides from the highly respected Exum Mountain Guides in Jackson Hole, Wyoming. Established in 1926, the school is touted by *Outside* magazine as having some of the best and most experienced mountain guides in the world.

- We interviewed leaders of unique, dangerous teams: for exam-ple, a leader of jungle photographic expeditions to India, unarmed and in search of tigers, and a leader of large-formation skydiving events to link hundreds of people together in 120-mph free-fall.

- I studied the U.S. Military Academy's national champion parachute team. The thirty-member coeducational team operates as a three-year, high-risk leader development laboratory. In the past six years, it has produced the academy's upper-tier student leaders, including four pinnacle cadet first captains in command of the Corps of Cadets and, equally remarkably, two Rhodes Scholars. As a comparison, we completed interviews with team leaders of conventional men's and women's college sports teams like football, softball, wrestling, swimming, and rugby.

- We talked to special operations soldiers, both live and over online chat or satellite telephone.
- And we interviewed the first armored cavalry commander to roll his tanks into the burning streets of Baghdad the day the United States invaded the city in April 2003.

Quotations from these interviews and detailed case studies of some of these exemplary people are featured in every chapter.

Our sample of leaders was rich and diverse and 100 percent in extremis. But to understand leadership, the analysis must go beyond the leaders and the context. The followers also hold an important viewpoint that too often is overlooked. So to talk to followers, three colleagues and I went to war. We talked to thirty-six Iraqi prisoners of war, interviewed by a translator in field settings in Um Qasr, Iraq, during the initial hostilities there in April 2003, and more than fifty U.S. soldier and Marine interviews done in breaks from the fighting on the outskirts of al Hillah and Baghdad. In these one-hour, in-depth interviews conducted prior to President Bush's May 1, 2003, announcement of the end of major combat operations, soldiers spoke openly of the strengths and failings of their leaders.

The greatest challenge in getting to know these incredible leaders and followers has been remaining true to the definition of in extremis leader: we had to dodge administrators who perhaps once led exciting lives but were no longer routinely in dangerous settings. We had to avoid the temptation of interviewing rear-echelon military leaders or followers, even when they were in Iraq during active combat operations. Every soldier and Marine we interviewed had had a peer killed in his or her unit in the past thirty days. We ensured that our mountain guides took clients on challenging climbs, that they were not simply climbing-school staff working with inexperienced beginners. This book taps a pure sample of truly unique individuals.

An Overview of the Lessons Ahead

In order for the unique character of in extremis leadership to take hold in everyday life, it has to be recognizable. In Chapter One, I describe the key characteristics of in extremis leaders. These characteristics paint colorful, sometimes exciting individual portraits. Although the totality of the work over the past few years points to these characteristics, some of the most compelling evidence comes from the words and deeds of followers who accompanied the leaders into combat or other in extremis settings. This opening chapter features follower comments, along with comments from leaders themselves, to complete the characterization of in extremis leadership.

With the basic characteristics of in extremis leaders established, Chapter Two focuses on the ways that in extremis leadership applies directly to the conduct of business and leadership in everyday life. To be honest, I never intended this work to be broadly applicable; I simply wanted to understand leaders who live and work in dangerous settings so that I could do a better job as chair of the Military Academy's leadership, psychology, and management programs. But in that role, I routinely talk to executives and the visiting public. I took the time to describe the in extremis work to these visitors in detail. Their reactions were powerfully illuminating: these diverse leaders drew the parallels for me, and they insisted that the lessons from the in extremis work were of value to them personally and professionally. Thus, Chapter Two is my interpretation of many comments and critiques provided by executives and leader developers from companies like GE, Goldman Sachs, Citigroup, Anheuser-Busch, and others who visited West Point, discussed in extremis leadership with me, and taught me through our dialogue.

Once it is established that in extremis leaders are useful people, it is valuable to discuss how to create them. Chapter Three discusses how to develop such characteristics in others. The chapter may be useful in curriculum established for public service jobs such as first-responder training and police, fire, and military training applications. Far from a cookie-cutter training solution, the chapter challenges trainers to think about how to apply in extremis developmental techniques in their own work. Such an approach also enables the chapter to be of value to academic or business leaders who want to review their leader development programs from a perspective never before articulated in the leadership literature.

The challenges of dangerous environments are not simply physical; they are psychological and emotional as well. Chapter Four addresses how emotions operate under conditions of high physical threat, and it debunks the myth that controlling emotions is necessary in order to lead in dangerous settings. Fear is the emotion featured prominently in the chapter. It also serves as a proxy for a variety of feelings experienced when lives are at risk.

Sadly, our worst fears are sometimes realized. In extremis settings always encompass the risk of grave physical injury or death. Chapter Five describes how in extremis leaders cope with the tragedy of death in the organization—an all-too-frequent occurrence in public service, and especially in the Army and Marine Corps, although all of us, sooner or later, will find ourselves in an organization that has to face the death of a respected or beloved member. Lessons learned from in extremis leaders can help all of us cope with the tragic inevitability of death.

In teaching leadership, it is often worthwhile to develop a complex example or case study to show some of the principles in action. Chapter Six describes a case of developing teams using dangerous contexts, and it draws on the specific practices used to develop young people on a collegiate skydiving team. When teams practice, learn, and bond in dangerous environments, levels of leader development occur that are remarkable when contrasted with development under routine conditions. The purpose of the chapter is not merely to show how amazing leaders emerge from dangerous circumstances—though they in fact do. Instead, the real purpose is to provide a detailed description of the ways in which high-risk teams are built, so that other team builders, whether challenged with danger or not, can draw on these same techniques.

My own developmental path, and this book is a way point, has everything to do with the people who developed me along the way. Most of my thinking about in extremis leadership has been heavily influenced by mentors, colleagues, acquaintances, and of course the subjects of the interviews and activities that led to the book. It is therefore important that you understand a bit more about these people beyond my merely acknowledging them. The Conclusion is a series of brief biographies about the in extremis leaders and followers who influenced the development of the concept beyond mere anecdotal observations. Learn from these people as I have. Many have sacrificed their lives or their livelihoods by leading in dangerous contexts. Their legacy continues to pay dividends when we learn from their experiences. Honor their commitment and sacrifices by serving the people around you, and leading as if your life depended on it.

Finally, the Resource at the end of the book articulates the unique physical demands of dangerous settings. It describes the danger of incapacitating injuries and explores how in extremis leaders can exercise in ways that reduce the likelihood that they will be incapacitated in the face of danger. The parallel for leaders in business and other less threatening settings is that there is tremendous cost—financial, interpersonal, managerial—when a leader is struck by a debilitating injury. This useful resource explains how all of us can benefit from activities that don't simply make us physically fit but that prevent injury. Employers who pay worker compensation may find it particularly worthwhile.

How This Book Can Help All Leaders

I have been told by former military leaders who are now leadership consultants that although the context may change, leadership is leadership. From their perspective, based largely on cold war experience, there is nothing particularly special about the threat of death in the context of leading. The conventional wisdom is that good peacetime leaders also make good wartime leaders. This perception is understandable, because it is the mission of the military services to train and prepare ordinary people in peacetime to fight and win our nation's wars. I know of no one, however, who has systematically investigated the assumption that leadership is leadership or has tried to characterize leadership in life-threatening circumstances. In addition, even if no unique patterns were to emerge from the study of in extremis leadership, the stakes are simply too high not to question and examine assumptions.

A universal comment from experienced warriors is that it is quite difficult, perhaps impossible, to describe the effect of being in a war to those who have not experienced it. War is serious business, and those who have engaged in the grisly matter of killing, even killing for politically, socially, or morally justified reasons, are usually quite hesitant to be forthcoming and descriptive. It's traumatic to kill, and certainly traumatic to be the object of lethal attack. Veterans solemnly admonish, "You have to have been there to know what it was like," and then fall silent.

The veil is lifted, however, by a twenty-year-old college student bubbling with excitement over her first solo free-fall with a parachute or by a mountain climber freshly returned from the summit of Everest or K2. People whose experiences are unique, exciting, and dangerous also often warn, "You have to have been there to know what it was like," but unlike the more silent and reserved combat veterans, these survivors gush for hours about the excitement and challenges that they overcame.

Their candor represents a window of opportunity for students of leadership. All leaders can learn from those who lead or work in an array of life-threatening contexts.

West Point, New York   Thomas A. Kolditz
March 2007

Key Characteristics of In Extremis Leaders—

and How They Are Relevant in __All__ Organizations

The key characteristics that in extremis leaders display are common among many types of good leaders. For example, competence, trust, and loyalty are leadership imperatives that span a variety of contexts. Nevertheless, when it comes to matters of life and death, leadership assumes a recognizable form: the in extremis pattern. This chapter explores this pattern and describes the key traits that comprise it, drawing on interviews with parachutists, SWAT teams, soldiers (both American and Iraqi), firefighters, and even a tiger hunter. We'll take a look at what they have to say about what constitutes great leadership in high-risk situations, which often has important implications for leadership in any situation.

Getting Started: Ranking In Extremis Leadership Competencies

One of the simplest yet inherently scientific ways to learn about the nature of leadership in dangerous contexts is to directly compare in extremis leaders who are actively engaged in dangerous activity with more ordinary leaders who are not operating at risk. One group that I interviewed included the most experienced members of the U.S. Military Academy (USMA) sport parachute team, who at the time were parachuting six days a week and served in leadership roles on the team. I then compared what I learned from these interviews with identical interviews that I conducted with senior athletes on other USMA sports teams. The athletes I talked to fell into one of three categories: team sport athletes, individual sport athletes, or competition parachute team members. I was most interested in comparing high- and low-risk sports teams. The rank-ordering of the leadership competencies was intended to represent the athletes' personal strengths in the context of their particular sport.

This simple comparison revealed powerful findings about the characteristics of good in extremis leaders. During the interviews, I asked the West Point athletes, who were mostly team captains and other leaders, to rank-order nine leadership competencies that are endorsed by the Army in its leadership doctrine, as shown in Exhibit 1.1. The rest of this chapter describes the results of this survey, which are substantiated by interviews with people working in other high-risk situations.

Exhibit 1.1. Leadership Competencies Ranked in the USMA Survey

Communicating: The leader displays good oral, written, and listening skills for individuals and groups.

Decision making: The leader employs sound judgment and logical reasoning, and uses resources wisely.

Motivating: The leader inspires, motivates, and guides others toward goals and objectives.

Planning: The leader develops detailed, executable plans that are feasible, acceptable, and suitable.

Executing: The leader shows proficiency, meets standards, and takes care of people and resources.

Assessing: The leader uses assessment and evaluation tools to facilitate consistent improvement.

Developing: The leader invests adequate time and effort to develop individual followers as leaders.

Building: The leader spends time and resources improving teams, groups, and units and fosters ethical climate.

Learning: The leader seeks self-improvement and organizational growth and envisions, adapts to, and leads change.

In Extremis Leaders Are Inherently Motivated

As you might expect, for leader athletes in both team and individual sports, the competency "motivating" was at the top of the list. After all, winning is about farther, harder, faster. One might assume that in sports with risk to life, motivation would be powerful, even more important. Astonishingly, however, among the members of the national champion competition parachutists, "motivating" ranked second from the bottom—a very significant difference. "Learning" averaged number one on the parachutists' list.

Using interview data to explore this counterintuitive finding, I inferred two characteristics of the in extremis pattern:

- In extremis contexts are inherently motivating. The danger of the context energizes those who are in it, making cheerleading much less necessary.

- The potential hostility of the context means that those who work there place a premium on scanning their environment and learning rapidly.

It is important to distinguish between the in extremis concept of inherent motivation and the more commonly cited concept of intrinsic motivation. People who are intrinsically motivated are internally driven. Consider these definitions of *intrinsic motivation* taken from popular books about the commitment of educators:

> "*Intrinsic motivation refers to motivation to engage in an activity for its own sake. People who are intrinsically motivated work on tasks because they find them enjoyable.*"[1]

> "*Intrinsic motivation is the innate propensity to engage one's interests and exercise one's capacities, and, in doing so, to seek out and master optimal challenges.*"[2]

> "*Intrinsic motivation is choosing to do an activity for no compelling reason, beyond the satisfaction derived from the activity itself—it's what motivates us to do something when we don't have to do anything.*"[3]

The inherent motivation of in extremis contexts is different from intrinsic motivation: rather than occurring for no compelling reason, it occurs as a result of the most compelling reason, and that's the consequence of death. Inherent motivation is externally derived from the in extremis context, not the internally derived intrinsic motivation. It is a new way of viewing the leader-follower dynamic in dangerous settings and is the conceptual portrayal of how the environment demands the total focus of the in extremis leader while at the same time motivating the follower.

Powerful motivation is inherent in dangerous contexts. This means that in extremis leaders don't need to do a lot of cheerleading; they're not the motivational speaker or high-pressure sales type. People need to be motivated to endure misery or physical challenge, but not through in extremis circumstances where threat of death or injury is high. Drill sergeants sometimes have to yell and scream to get trainees to function. This is usually not the case among combat leaders, because followers are inherently motivated by the grave circumstances of combat.

In Extremis Leaders Embrace Continuous Learning

In extremis situations demand an outward or learning orientation, and this orientation is also heightened by threat. This is a new variation, but is similar in some ways to a well-established concept in the management literature. In a widely cited article in the *Journal of Management Studies*, noted author Karl Weick refers to an outward focus on crisis as enacted sense making. Weick recognized the dynamic between the excitement people feel in crisis and the need for the leader to add further excitement to the crisis: "Sensemaking in crisis conditions is made more difficult because action that is instrumental to understanding the crisis also intensifies the crisis." Therefore, it is more important for people in in extremis contexts to focus outward and learn than it is for them to add excitement to the situation through motivation. Weick goes on, "People enact the environments that constrain them. . . . Commitment, capacity, and expectations affect sensemaking during crisis and the severity of the crisis itself."[4]

Thus, in extremis leaders need to focus outward on the environment to make sense of it and can actually make matters worse by intensifying people's fear by trying to motivate them. To Weick, this phenomenon was evidenced in crisis. In extremis leaders are routinely and willingly in circumstances that novices would label as crises, and my findings suggest that Weick's earlier work may help inform leadership in dangerous settings as well as in organizational crises. Such a parallel will be particularly important in Chapter Two, which directly compares leadership in dangerous situations with conventional business settings.

In Extremis Leaders Share Risk with Their Followers

Another characteristic that sets in extremis leaders apart from other leaders is their willingness to share the same, or more, risk as their followers. This is, of course, partly true because they join their followers in challenging and dangerous circumstances. We found, however, such profound and consistent sharing of risk that it clearly stands out as a defining characteristic of in extremis leaders.

Leaders themselves expressed powerful feelings about shared risk; for example, consider the following comments made from a SWAT team leader and a tiger hunter:

> If you put the plan together and you're not comfortable being up there with a foot through the door, what the hell is up?
>
> *Special Agent James Gagliano, SWAT team leader,*
> *New York City Office of the Federal Bureau of Investigation*

> I assume twenty times the risk [of my team, although] . . . there is some equal risk in the field. Any of us could fall off the elephant, and any of us could be thrown from the jeep, and we did get injured,

all of us, and hurt on a daily basis. There wasn't anybody that didn't come back bloodied or badly bruised or hurt. We have a seventy-pound tripod on top of an elephant, it sometimes got hinged against a tree and the tripod will fall. . . . Every day we got hurt. So I went through like ten bottles of Advil, which I gave to my team to help them get through that.

Carole Amore, professional videographer, expedition leader, and author of Twenty Ways to Track a Tiger

These interviews also made it clear that this shared risk was not merely a form of leader hubris, showboating, or simple impression management. Rather, it's part of the in extremis leader's style or technique. It profoundly affected the followers; followers recognized it, knew what it represented in the heart and character of their leader, and deeply respected their leader as a result. This phenomenon was acute on the battlefields of Iraq, as these American soldiers described the importance of their leaders' sharing the risk the soldiers faced:

You have to learn confidence in your leaders and trust in their judgment. They are not going to throw you out into something that they wouldn't put themselves in as well.

U.S. soldier, Third Infantry Division, Baghdad, Iraq

I think that the only difference in their roles was that they got a little more information a little sooner than the rest of us. Other than that, they weren't really that much different than anybody else. . . . Other than seeing what was on the collar [their rank insignia], it's hard to decipher who was who. . . . The officers here, they showed leadership and they get out there and do the same things that me or him were doing.

U.S. soldier, Third Infantry Division, Baghdad, Iraq

Conversely, soldiers who found their leaders unwilling to share the risk had little will, and lost motivation, as in the case of this captured Iraqi soldier:

The leader . . . was a lieutenant colonel. An older man, forty-five, forty-six, forty-eight years of age. He was a simple person, but the instruction come from the command in Baghdad. Like, "do this," but he doesn't do that, and he ran away. . . . He told us if you see the American or the British forces, do not resist.

Captured Iraqi soldier, Um Qasr, Iraq

The common practice of providing business leaders with buyout plans, generous rollover contracts, or golden parachutes does little to inspire follower confidence. Certainly it puts business risk, compared to risk of life, in perspective. When performance means life or death, the best leaders don't wear parachutes unless their followers do too.

In Extremis Leaders Have a Common Lifestyle with Their Followers: There's No Elitism

A fourth unique characteristic of the in extremis pattern emerged when we asked interviewees about their remuneration and lifestyle. In an era where there are entire conferences devoted to executive compensation, it was refreshing to focus on authentic leaders who lacked materialism and instead focused on values.

When I asked public sector employees such as police officers and soldiers about the nature of their pay structure, the leader's pay and the follower's pay were unequal but uniformly modest. I found consistently that most in extremis leaders earn at most an average wage but that they felt it was sufficient for their needs. This made sense to me and my colleagues who also interviewed these people. In contexts that routinely threaten the lives of the leader and the led, value attached to life is morally superior to value attached to material wealth. Pay should take a backseat to other concerns. Economists might deconstruct this phenomenon differently with respect to public service jobs, arguing that the availability and skill sets of such work drive wages down. Perhaps. But the often overlooked mechanism is the irrelevance of symbolic value in the face of danger.

Money has no meaning. Even future rewards or punishments have little meaning when the promise of a future is uncertain.

Current leadership theory recognizes that symbolic value is only applicable in limited circumstances. James MacGregor Burns initially developed the notion of transformational leadership, based largely on a charismatic leader establishing vision, a way ahead.[5] This contrasted with other theories that together were characterized as transactional, based on leader-follower transactions such as giving pay and rewards and establishing perceptions of equity and fairness. The idea that organizations could be changed by a transformational leader took root, was elaborated by Bernard Bass and others, and is a dominant theory in the art and science of leadership today.[6]

Earlier writers, however, presumed that a transformational approach was due to either a leader characteristic such as charisma or a leader approach such as visioning. For those who understand the dynamics of dangerous settings, it's clear that the immediate threat places value on human life and strips away the value inherent in transactional leadership. In fear of their life, people don't care about fairness, equity, future rewards, or anything else except being led out of the circumstances that threaten their existence. In extremis settings are the perfect incubator for transformational leadership. Due largely to the irrelevance of symbolic value, transactional leadership is almost completely ineffective in in extremis settings. The nature of the context is developmental. Over time, a values-based form of transformational leadership emerges and becomes part of the operating style of in extremis leaders. Consider what one FBI agent said that reflects the values-based conditions under which he serves:

> I think it's the respect for the guys that I work with [that is] more important than anything. I don't need this job; I mean, I love my job, I love my country, I love the Bureau. But more important than any of those things, I think it's like that philosophy that you've probably heard a million times before about why does the individual

infantry soldier fight. He doesn't give a shit about his commander, he doesn't care about red, white, and blue. He doesn't care about anything else except for the guy that is on either side of him. To a man, the people I work with feel the same way, and I do too. It's their respect that they go home at night and say, "The guy who put this plan together, the guy that led us on this mission, [he's a] squared-away guy, and he's got our best interest at heart. That's more important to me than anything else.

Special Agent James Gagliano,
FBI SWAT team leader, New York City Office

Outside the contexts of military, police, and firefighting, the pattern of common lifestyle continues. People who live and work in dangerous environments learn to love life. They seem to live in a world where value is only loosely attached to material wealth, as one mountain climbing guide confirmed when asked to characterize his financial and material well-being:

Well, you can look at it a couple of ways. There is an old Yosemite climber that said at either end of the social spectrum, there is a leisure class. So in many ways, I am part of a leisure class in that I get a lot of free time to go and do the things I want to do. I don't have, financially, a lot, and so to answer that question, I think there are a couple ways to look at it. Financially, we aren't as well off as most of my clients. Most of my clients have corporate jobs, making good money. But they are also living in the city, places I would not want to live. [They] work nine-to-five jobs. So in that regard, I think I am better off than they are, because I think I am healthier, probably less stressed. Financially? No, but lifestyle wise, yes, and better off than most folks.

Christian Santilices, professional mountain guide,
Exum Climbing School, Jackson Hole, Wyoming

We believe that in extremis leaders accept, even embrace, a lifestyle that is common to their followers as an expression of values and that such values become part of their presence and credibility as leaders. There is an inspirational Quaker saying that underscores the value of a transparent lifestyle: "Let your life speak." The idea is that followers come to understand values by watching the leader.

In Extremis Leaders Have and Inspire High Competence, Trust, and Loyalty

Although many characteristics of in extremis leaders tend to set them apart from other organizational leaders, they also hold several characteristics that are widely exhibited by successful leaders across a range of contexts. In extremis leaders, like most other leaders, are highly competent, and they engender loyalty and trust. The following quotations, both taken within a seventy-two-hour window during the fall of Baghdad, illustrate the stark difference between success and failure at establishing loyalty in dangerous times:

> We got our boy back here that we are trying to fix up, and he had a good chunk taken out of his forearm. He was definitely in some pain and he definitely had some tears, but he hung on. He was apologizing for getting blood on our boots. He was apologetic. "Sorry for bleeding on your boots." I said, "You want to apologize for bleeding on my boots?" I got a lot of respect for him.
>
> *U.S. soldier, Third Infantry Division, Baghdad, Iraq*

And then, in contrast:

> Not the officers. We couldn't talk to them. They put us in jail, they kill us. We cannot talk to them.
>
> *Captured Iraqi soldier, Um Qasr, Iraq*

Competence Is Critical in High-Risk Environments

Followers demand leader competence, and nowhere is that more critical than in dangerous contexts. No amount of legitimate or legal authority is likely to command respect or obedience in a setting where life is at risk, whether in a war zone or on the side of a mountain. This is the ironic contradiction of the common stereotype of the military leader: an authoritarian martinet who commands subordinates who must robotically obey. That's not how leadership in the military works, at least not the Army and the Marine Corps units we visited, and certainly not in combat. The average troop is likely to find court-martial to be a more attractive option compared to following the orders of an incompetent leader in a war zone. Only competence commands respect, and respect is the coin of the realm in in extremis settings. For example, witness the respect that this American soldier fighting in Iraq had for the leader of his unit:

> He took charge every time that he needed to take charge. He was doing a hundred things, while I am down there doing one thing. At times, I knew he was overwhelmed, so I would hop up and say, "Hey, sir, I got the con [meaning "I can lead": originally, a reference to manning a conning tower], I can battle track [keep track of where everybody is in order to focus on fighting the battle], I got a lot to do with this, we have been together for a while, you need some rest." He was overwhelmed, but he handled it very well. He did everything that he had to do. He maneuvered the troop or parts of the troop when nobody else was around to do it. He did more than you could ask of him.
>
> U.S. soldier, Third Squadron, Seventh Cavalry, Baghdad, Iraq

Respect accrued from competence does not imply that in extremis leadership is merely technical or somehow emotionless or soft. Much to the contrary, dangerous settings often demand leadership styles that are unambiguous, pointed, and aggressive to the point of grating on followers. For example, consider how another American Marine described the leader of his unit:

> I don't like the guy. I don't know how to deal with him when we get off work, but as far as being a professional and being out there in the

trenches, he is a great squad leader. He [will do] the right thing, but sometimes it's a very unpopular thing, because he's the squad leader. I admire him. He definitely deserves the Marine Corps Achievement Medal for Valor. We put him in for that.

U.S. Marine, First Marine Division, al Hillah, Iraq

Leadership in dangerous contexts places incredible demands on leaders, who view virtually all outcomes as related to their personal competence and ability. These leaders work hard to achieve situational awareness and control. Yet the truth about in extremis settings is that awful things happen, often without warning and without leader competence casting a deciding vote. Nonetheless, the perception of control and personal efficacy is critical to the functioning of an in extremis leader. Imagine trying to accommodate feelings of inefficacy in a setting where effectiveness is the only link to life itself. In contrast to those who lead in settings that are benign enough to allow finger-pointing and denial of responsibility, in extremis leaders tend to assume responsibility for outcomes, even when any objective observer would let them off the hook for circumstances obviously outside their control. Here's how one leader described the disastrous outcome of a situation he was in charge of:

My worst day, well, back in 1980 something . . . , I forget when, it's been so long and I try not to think about it, . . . I was instructing some students, and got invited onto a jump, onto a larger skydive, . . . there was a [high-speed, midair] collision, a friend of mine was tumbling through the sky, and I went down and missed him, and he went in [slang for hitting the ground at penetration speed and dying on impact]. . . . That's a performance failure.

Guy Wright, professional skydiver, leader of
large-formation and world-record skydiving events

Competence is the building block for leader-follower trust relationships in in extremis settings. As one might expect, then, the competence in extremis leaders exhibit must be authentic, like their leadership style. Organizations run by appointed leaders without legitimate competence can muddle through mundane events, but they will predictably crumble when pushed in a crisis that poses genuine threat. People in fear of their lives will not trust or follow leaders if they question their competence. The incompetence of bureaucratically appointed leaders exudes from this comment from a captured Iraqi soldier about officer appointments:

> There is some kind of government decree that simple soldiers can go to the [Baghdad Military] Academy for six months, end up graduating as an officer. So you can see soldiers becoming officers. [Others] become officers without ever entering the military academy. Some of these are part of the Army of Amquds [Jerusalem]. And some of them are members of the [Baath] Party, and being members of the Party they become officers. They become officers without even special training or the like. All you have is the government decision and they become promoted to officers. So you find intelligence Muqaddim [sergeant], Amid [higher officers], their expertise is very weak because their schooling is limited and they have too wide experience [that is, no experience specific to the role], very limited throughout the years. It used to be before the [First] Gulf War, the officer who graduated first in their class at the military academy, they would go to like Sandhurst [the British military academy] or to India. So we are talking about a total of one or two or three officers from eight hundred graduating. The study at the military academy is a far cry or does not correspond to the reality of the battlefield. All of the studies are theoretical. The practical side or the practicum is not taken seriously.
>
> *Captured Iraqi soldier, Um Qasr, Iraq*

High-Risk Situations Demand
Mutual Trust Between Leaders and Followers

If competence is the building block of in extremis leadership, trust is the house. The leaders we interviewed often spoke of competence leading to trust relationships in dangerous contexts:

It's taken a year and a half to get to the point where I think we are still six months away from being where I fully want them to be, but I think we are now at the point where to make an entry, if I'm the third guy in the door and the first guy goes left and the second guy is going right and he is driving his corner, he's not worrying about the guy on his left, he knows that that guy is taking care of any threat in that corner. And that's a good place to be.

Special Agent James Gagliano,
FBI SWAT team leader, New York City Office

In addition, it was made clear that such relationships were not incidental but were built quite deliberately:

I mean, really, I established a relationship with all my subordinate leaders and the soldiers. They weren't just a name on a battle roster, a voice uttered into the radio to me, and I wasn't just a voice uttered on the radio to them. Everything I was saying, basing on where I wanted to go on, was building a team, a group that completely trusted each other. You aren't going to establish that if you can't talk with each other, if you can't interact with each other. It wasn't just my XO [executive officer] or one or two platoon leaders, it was all my platoon leaders, all my platoon sergeants, my first sergeant, all the leadership of the troop. You know, I didn't do anything without that cast of ten or twelve buying off on it. We went to lunch every day together, you name it. I mean, I had high standards, but I communicated those standards and they knew why I had high standards, but to be some dictatorial commander with blinders on that just says "This is the path we are going to follow," I don't think that kind of leadership style and mentality could succeed with today's soldiers and NCOs [noncommissioned officers].

Captain Clay Lyle, Commander,
A Troop, Third Squadron, Seventh Cavalry

And, predictably, when such trust-based relationships were never built, organizational cohesion was nearly nonexistent in in extremis conditions, as indicated by this Iraqi soldier describing how his own leader failed in this regard:

> The Mair Liwa [brigadier] left and went to his family. He was an authoritarian, and left everyone afraid of the other. Saddam [Hussein] made a situation where even a brother cannot trust his own brother. We don't trust anyone.
>
> *Captured Iraqi soldier, Um Qasr, Iraq*

Interestingly, at the same time I was conducting interviews in Iraq and back at West Point, someone else was in Iraq collecting information on trust in in extremis conditions. Lieutenant Colonel Pat Sweeney had left the safety of graduate school at the University of North Carolina, Chapel Hill, to accompany the 101st Airborne Division into combat. He had formerly commanded in the division and was in graduate school to finish his doctorate in social psychology, en route to West Point and a teaching assignment.

Sweeney has boundless energy, and he decided to gather some data from his vantage point in the division's headquarters. The two main purposes of his interviews were to map the attributes of a leader who can be trusted in combat and explore the relationship between trust and influence in combat as scientifically as possible in an in extremis environment. Pat interviewed dozens of soldiers, and seventy-two of them completed an open-ended questionnaire that was designed to explore trust and leadership in combat. The soldiers were conducting combat and civil military operations in northern Iraq, and Pat visited them at their respective base camps in Mosul, Tal Afar, and Qayyarah West Airbase.

Sweeney's questionnaire asked soldiers to describe in their own words the attributes they look for in leaders they can trust in combat. They then were asked to discuss why each attribute influenced trust, rate the relative importance of each attribute to the establishment of trust, and share their perceptions of how trust and leadership were related.

The soldiers Sweeney interviewed cited leader competence as the most important attribute for influencing trust in combat. In in extremis conditions, followers depend on their leaders' technical expertise, judgment, and intelligence to plan and execute operations that successfully complete the mission with the least possible risk to their lives. After organizing the followers' responses into categories of attributes, Sweeney quantitatively determined the top ten attributes soldiers look for in leaders who can be trusted in combat. They are listed in order of importance in Exhibit 1.2.

I consider Sweeney's work to be the fullest explication of trust and competence in in extremis conditions to date,[7] and his findings reinforce and underscore the in extremis pattern:

- Trust and loyalty follow after competence in terms of relative importance.

- Leading by example in dangerous conditions means sharing risk and requires confidence and courage.

- Self-control is necessary to be a level-headed, low motivator focused outwardly on the environment.

Exhibit 1.2. Attributes of Leaders Who Can Be Trusted in Combat

1. Competent
2. Loyal
3. Honest/good integrity
4. Leads by example
5. Self-control (stress management)
6. Confident
7. Courageous (physical and moral)
8. Shares information
9. Personal connection with subordinates
10. Strong sense of duty

Note: The attributes are shown in rank-order of importance as rated by their followers.

- Integrity, sense of duty, and personal connection bind leaders and followers through a common lifestyle that reinforces trust.

The in extremis pattern emerges consistently when danger is present.

Dangerous Work Demands Mutual Loyalty Between Leaders and the Team

In extremis leaders sometimes have short-term relationships with their followers. Climbing guides, skydiving organizers, expedition leaders, and even astronauts can rapidly inspire trust and confidence among followers. In police, military, and fire departments, however, leaders have long-term associations with followers that can grow into deep loyalties. These loyalties are both personal and professional in nature, and the value of loyalty between leaders and followers is abundantly clear when the followers speak:

> I think what makes him [his leader] better is that he is there for what he can do for us, not what the soldiers can do for him. He has proved that many times, to the whole platoon, that it's about what he can do for us, not about what we can do for him. The whole platoon will do anything for him, anything he ever asks.
>
> *U.S. soldier, Third Squadron, Seventh Cavalry, Baghdad, Iraq*

> What did I learn about him as a leader? I think he likes his job. He likes doing what he's doing. He likes to be in control. He doesn't like to sleep very much. He needed to be out with Marines. He always puts his Marines first. That is an awesome [trait] of a leader. No matter what, if something wasn't going right, he would get up, do whatever was needed, and he would say, "get it done." He is always there for everybody.
>
> *U.S. Marine, First Marine Division, al Hillah, Iraq*

Such loyalty from followers is usually engendered by loyalty on the part of leaders. It has been well established in the leader development literature that loyalty is a two-way street. We found this point to be especially striking among in extremis leaders:

> I told them to go [flee from the fight]. Because there is an expression in Arabic, "somebody is in my neck," meaning I am totally responsible morally and especially morally for that person. These soldiers were in my neck; in other words, I was responsible for them. I am responsible for those people in front of guard, and I am not going to let them perish if I don't have to. I am not going to let them die for something that's not worthwhile.
>
> *Captured Iraqi lieutenant who had graduated from*
> *the Baghdad Military Academy only twenty-one*
> *days prior to this comment, Um Qasr, Iraq*

> My personal heroes are the people I work with, many of the people I work with. Many of the people I have the privilege of working with, even many of them who are younger than I am, are sincere, genuine, trustworthy, competent, caring people, that were really working hard, in many cases against the odds, to do what they really feel is the right thing. And they are motivated not by money and not by anything but the ultimate objective of doing something good for somebody else. And that's difficult to do, day after day.
>
> *Special Agent Steve Carter, senior team leader,*
> *FBI SWAT, San Francisco Office*

> It was always for them. It was for my soldiers. . . . By the time I took command, [I felt] that I loved them. That it was more than just a job or some people I worked with, and certainly by the one year point, [they] were as close as any family member. I felt they needed me.
>
> *Captain Clay Lyle, Commander,*
> *A Troop, Third Squadron, Seventh Cavalry*

Final Thoughts: Consider Your Own Leadership Competence

Obviously, and as we've seen in this chapter, followers are profoundly influenced by their leaders in combat and other dangerous settings. The interviews I (and Pat Sweeney) conducted with people working in in extremis situations give testament to that, and those who lead in dangerous circumstances should take careful note of the unique pattern.

It does not follow, however, that the positive effects of in extremis leadership are necessarily limited to dangerous contexts. Proper levels of motivation, a learning orientation, sharing risk, living a common lifestyle, competence, trust, and loyalty can help build a leadership legacy among followers in many walks of life.

Leaders' most enduring legacy exists in the people they have led. They can build corporations, make loads of money, write books, name buildings after themselves. In the end, however, for leaders, the only lasting effect is in the people they develop by giving them motivation, direction, and purpose. It may be insightful for those building a leadership legacy in their own organization to contemplate how an expert in extremis leader might behave if the stakes were just a bit higher regardless of the nature of the work. Leadership principles from routine settings don't necessarily transfer well to in extremis settings like combat, but in extremis leadership may have a lot to contribute to leadership in everyday organizations.

Those who lead in more ordinary contexts might do well to decide the relative importance of their own competencies. Work through the list of nine leadership competencies shown in Exhibit 1.1, and identify your top five or six personal strengths. Does the pattern suggest that you are ready to lead in dangerous settings or in organizational crisis or that you will need to adapt? In either case, it may be worthwhile to consider the need for both steady leadership and an outward focus the next time you find yourself in a sticky situation.

The in extremis project is essential to understand leadership under conditions of exceptionally grave risk. If you lead in other circumstances, you have the opportunity to take the in extremis pattern to an equally relevant level of application. It takes some attentiveness and effort to peer into the soul of people led in times that are often best forgotten and to understand fully what their leaders gave to them. For those of you who lead professionally, a look at in extremis leadership can be a magnifier, adding clarity and detail to what you already sense: that leaders can make anything possible, and without leadership, even basic tasks can seem insurmountable.

Summing Up

1. In extremis leaders are inherently motivated because of the danger of the situations in which they're working; therefore, leaders don't need to use conventional motivational methods or cheerleading. If you're leading in a more conventional situation, consider how you need to motivate the people on your team.

2. In extremis leaders embrace continuous learning, typically because they and their followers need to rapidly scan their environments to determine the level of threat and danger they're facing. Leaders in other environments are fortunate in not facing physical threats; nevertheless, they should continually scan their environment for competitive or market threats and embrace learning so they can stay ahead of the pack—or at least on top of solving problems.

3. In extremis leaders share the risk their followers face. This isn't just grandstanding; leaders truly share—and even take on greater—risks in in extremis situations. Leaders in other environments should keep this in mind: don't ask your followers to do anything you wouldn't do yourself.

4. In extremis leaders share a common lifestyle with their followers. Leaders and followers in high-risk situations don't earn the same amount of money, but the pay is uniformly modest. In recent years, there has been much attention paid to executive compensation, and all leaders should consider how much they truly have in common with the rest of their organization.

5. In extremis leaders are highly competent, which inspires their followers to emulate that level of competence. Whatever type of organization you're leading, you'll obviously gain more respect if you show that you know what you're doing.

6. Dangerous situations demand a high level of mutual trust. In extremis leaders trust their team, and they themselves can be trusted. And even if someone's life isn't at stake in an organization, his or her livelihood may be, so do everything you can to be trustworthy and to trust your team to do what you've hired them to do.

7. High-risk environments demand mutual loyalty between leader and followers. And although corporate America has changed from the era when workers stayed with a single company for fifty years and retired with a gold watch, leaders should do everything they can to foster a culture of mutual loyalty.

2

In Extremis Lessons for Business and Life
Strengthening Your Own Leadership by Example

It is my fervent hope that in extremis leaders—police, firefighters, soldiers, Marines, extreme sport coaches, and guides—may use this book to be introspective and thoughtful about their own leadership at the point of death. It is also my wish that every leader or follower gain insights from the principles found in leadership at the point of death. This chapter is focused on the latter aim.

Throughout the twenty-five years I've led people and studied and taught leadership, I have always thought that discovery learning was the best way for people to develop their own abilities as a leader. Leadership concepts have to be tailored to individual circumstances, and in this chapter, I invite you to do that. This chapter describes nine observations about in extremis leadership that have broad applicability across circumstances, and it offers examples from my own experience and that of others. Use these observations as keys to unlock the links between your own circumstances and that of life-or-death leaders. The parallels and commonalities may surprise you.

Moving from Transactional to Transformational Leadership

When the search to understand in extremis leadership began, I made the assumption that this was a unique form of leadership suited primarily to the rigors of extreme sports, combat settings, and actions in the face of disaster. It is, after all, the conscious recognition of the threat of death, the salience of an individual's mortality, that gives rise to the changes in leader and follower behavior typified by the in extremis pattern. In contrast, business risk is about the loss of money, not the loss of life. In the special case of businesses that do involve some physical risk, the mitigation is procedural and actuarial. Therefore, there was no intention of—and even some contempt for—a business interpretation of in extremis leadership. But I've come full circle. The more I study leadership, the more it is apparent that thinking like a life-or-death leader can be a useful form of introspection for almost any leader.

But isn't it interesting that most people would call a threat to their pension arrangements "a threat to life savings" rather than "a threat to career earnings"? For individuals, "life savings" and "saving lives" both connote grave interests (pun intended). There are compelling parallels between leadership in in extremis settings and leadership in elite business organizations that engage in high-risk enterprises with large amounts of capital.

This fact became apparent during a presentation on in extremis leadership to a managing director from the financial firm of Goldman Sachs. The director was a former Army officer and seemed fascinated by the concept of in extremis leadership. I assumed he was interested because his prior military service was distinguished and had involved some personal risk. It soon became apparent, however, that he was focused on in extremis leadership as a way of informing his own leadership in the world of finance. This was exciting. In extremis leadership might have value outside the world of extreme sports and military training.

In fact, understanding authentic leaders in in extremis settings has significant value when applied to business practice. Authentic leadership, with its emphasis on the development of hope, resilience, and optimism, gets at the heart of what is important to followers, whether their aspirations are physical, social, or material. Authentic leaders, whose behavior often reveals a heightened moral and ethical perspective, earn the trust of followers who interpret their motives in a positive way.

In business management circles, leadership is sometimes inappropriately treated as merely a skill or ability, a mechanical array of actions to increase the effectiveness of individuals and consequently improve the performance of the organization. Such an approach is inherently transactional because the primary motivation is known to be profit based, and as a result it doesn't work very well. In contrast, leadership in in extremis settings exemplifies how people in organizations can move beyond purely transactional relationships. By comparison, coercive leaders or policy-oriented managers are eventually rendered ineffective by the seriousness of the circumstances. Bonuses or promises of other tangible rewards are less relevant when it comes to putting one's life in the hands of a leader. Why should people tolerate lesser leadership in matters outside dangerous environments?

The primary focus of both the leader and the led in in extremis settings is on the preservation of life and success at the task or mission. Business leaders who find it difficult to make the transition from transactional to a more authentic, transformational leadership approach may gain both understanding and inspiration from in extremis leader role models. Learning how such leaders have operated in in extremis environments can provide some important lessons that can be applied in parallel to some of the stressful challenges facing leaders today, even if the risks are not of a physical or life-threatening nature.

What Leaders in Business Can Learn from In Extremis Leaders

Some of the parallels between in extremis leaders and leaders of businesses or other organizations are obvious. First, competence is as much the coin of the realm in business as in in extremis settings. For example, one of my favorite, most accomplished and successful acquaintances made millions in merchant banking, but virtually all his gains were the result of his own competence and ability in a job where there was not much in the way of guaranteed salary (he referred to his circumstances as "eat what you kill"). It is an in extremis metaphor to be sure, but the point is that elite business has an unforgiving character, much like a physically dangerous environment. Competence is the price of entry for anyone hoping to take a leadership role.

Another parallel involves trust: elite businesspeople live in a world where trust is a precious commodity, and it can be an advantage worth millions of dollars in predicting business outcomes. Lack of trust is organizational poison in business. For example, the recent congressional investigation of Hewlett Packard for alleged spying on journalists has at its root the lack of trust in the HP boardroom. As early as January 2005, Carly Fiorina, CEO at the time, had determined that someone on the board was leaking information to the press and others about HP deliberations and positions. Furious, she began a secret investigation, using a team of lawyers, to determine who was violating her trust. The next month, she was ousted by the board and replaced, first by Patricia Dunn and then by Mark Hurd, the current CEO.

In January 2006, a reporter named Dawn Kawamoto, working for CNet, a technology news organization, released details of an HP offsite meeting for senior leaders. In response, Hurd allegedly approved a number of investigative approaches, including staking out board member George Keyworth and phishing Kawamoto's e-mail account with fictitious e-mails with attached tracing software. Director Tom Perkins, who found out about the tactics in a board meeting where Keyworth was accused of being the leaker, resigned in protest. Subsequently Perkins discovered that his own telephone records had been compromised; under pressure from Perkins, HP notified the Securities and Exchange Commission of the questionable investigative practices. The issue resulted in a probe by the House Energy and Commerce Committee. Investigations subsequently absolved Hurd of criminal wrongdoing in the matter.[1]

Under conditions where deals may involve profits and losses of such magnitude that lives are changed forever, it makes sense that in extremis principles apply. The unique in extremis pattern of inherent motivation, learning orientation, shared risk, and common lifestyle described in detail in Chapter One may never be as universal as competence, trust, and loyalty among most organizational leaders. The unique pattern emerges from a context that most of us either don't care to inhabit or visit only on rare occasion. Yet there are lessons with broad applicability that can be learned from in extremis leaders. Following are nine important leadership lessons for leaders in all walks of life that I uncovered, or underscored, by studying in extremis leadership.

Lesson One: Motivation Is Most Powerful When Paired with an Emphasis on Learning

Recall from Chapter One that parachute team leaders focused on learning rather than motivation in their inherently motivating in extremis circumstances. When leaders find themselves among followers who are highly motivated for any reason (dire threat, tremendous opportunity, or earnest obligation, for example), those leaders should not rest in the comfort caused by their followers' excitement and dedication. Instead, the leader should pay extra attention to precursors to learning, such as awareness of the environment, creativity, critical thinking, and outcome analysis. They should focus the motivated crew on new solutions, problems that might seem impossible to solve, or unresolved issues. For an average leader, motivation is a way to make people work harder, but for an outstanding leader, motivation is a way to help people work smarter. This is when innovations and breakthrough management techniques usually occur. Most people wake up in the morning wanting to work hard enough to earn their pay, but without a clear external focus, the way ahead is sometimes not clear. Let's look at an example.

Learning a New Approach to Helping the Homeless

Rebecca (Becky) Kanis, a former Army special operations communications specialist turned social sector professional, used planning techniques developed for in extremis settings to motivate volunteers. For her, "smarter, not harder" meant she and her colleagues had to reframe the problem of homelessness in New York City in order to make a difference. She is the director of innovation for Common Ground, which seeks to eliminate homelessness in the city by purchasing real estate to use for sheltering people who are chronically homeless.

When she began her efforts, the problem was not that volunteers weren't willing to work hard to help the homeless. The problem was that there was no workable strategy, and the nature of homelessness was ill defined. In police and military operations, this phase would involve a formal (or if conditions dictate, hasty) mission analysis and intelligence estimate. No in extremis leader would consider undertaking a mission or dangerous event without having some sense of the nature of the environment: enemy and friendly forces, locations, weather, terrain, or other conditions. Yet people were trying to help the homeless, some of whom were in fact dying, without sufficiently considering problem definition.

Kanis started by insisting that Common Ground and other volunteers accurately count the number of people sleeping outside to know how many homeless people there were. She described her challenge to me: "You can't solve any problem unless you know how big it is and what it looks like. When my boss started working to solve chronic street homelessness in New York City in 2000, she convened the service providers who worked in west midtown to discuss this problem. She pressed them to do a midnight street count like London had done in 1997. The conventional wisdom at the time was that since in New York you have a legal right to shelter, there wouldn't be more than a dozen people sleeping outside in the middle of winter. She continued to press, and they reluctantly agreed to canvass the neighborhood to count homeless sleeping outside in the middle of winter. Much to their surprise, they found 479 people in one neighborhood alone. That was the beginning of what would become the Street-to-Home Initiative at Common Ground."

Kanis continues, "Since then, our work has taken even more cues from military training and techniques. I convinced my team to create a huge map of west midtown. We laminated it just like the ones we used to take to the field in the military. Then we went out night after night after night to not only count those sleeping outside, but get their name, date of birth, and take their picture. We then created a by-name registry of people sleeping on the streets and plotted the pictures on the map so that we could have an accurate representation of clusters and patterns. We then aligned our teams to go help them get housed based on a better understanding of who was sleeping outside and where they were.

"Some other service providers and city government workers were concerned about our practice of taking their pictures. They were more concerned with the homeless person's civil liberties and right to be left alone than they were with accurately dimensioning and defining the problem. We persisted despite the criticism, and slowly people recognized this wisdom of our approach. Now at meetings, other service providers insist that the first thing you have to do is get everyone's name and picture in your catchment area."

Kanis's approach cannot be written off simply as police or military planning techniques. I know many military people who would never have delivered the intensity and environmental focus that she used to dimensionalize the life-and-death problem of homelessness in New York City. Her actions were typical of a leader who has lived and worked in truly dangerous contexts. Kanis is an experienced military parachutist, earning the coveted jumpmaster star for her parachutist wings, and she has worked in special operations that were so sensitive that portions of her formal evaluation reports are blacked out (and the portions that are not blacked out are ringing endorsements of her leadership ability). The underlying secret to her success was developed because her background in the special operations community included a large dose of dangerous work where she was responsible for other people's lives. Experience with personal responsibility in high-risk settings should be a red tag for every human resources manager and headhunter.

Lesson Two: Sharing Risk Strengthens Credibility and Can Improve a Leader's Effectiveness in Situations Involving Risk

In extremis leaders place more value on taking care of their clients, followers, soldiers, and citizens than they place on their own comfort, personal safety, or ability to accumulate wealth. These are the leaders people seek when the stakes are at their highest. To be the best leader you can be, especially in a high-stakes situation, you'll gain the most trust and loyalty by demonstrating in tangible ways that both risk and reward are distributed fairly in the organization and that much of the risk is your own.

People often make sense of their environment by comparison to the reactions of others. That includes reading both the expressions and the actions of others, especially leaders. In in extremis settings, the principle is taken to an extreme: for example, both SWAT teams and parachute teams frown on tinted eyewear or tinted goggles for this reason. When noise or other circumstances limit oral communication, team members need to read the gravity of a situation by focusing on the eyes of their peers, superiors, and subordinates.

In the same way, the willingness to assume personal risk is an unmistakable nonverbal cue that the leader has confidence in a given course of action and is willing to put as much on the line as the people he or she is leading. The following example is about an in extremis leader expertly managing nonverbal cues and accepting personal risk in a dangerous setting.

Leading Successfully in Hostile Territory: Cultural Awareness Saves the Day

In April 2003, sixteen days before my interview team launched into Iraq, the Second Battalion, 327th Infantry, was fighting its way north, part of a major Army undertaking to secure the city of Najaf. Najaf, considered a particularly holy place by the dominant Shi'ite population, straddled an important route to Baghdad. Standing representative of the religious importance of Najaf was the grand Ali Mosque, a holy shrine and focal place of worship for the displaced and desperately concerned Iraqi citizenry. Ayatollah Ali Sistani, a major religious leader who had endured years of imprisonment under Saddam Hussein, personally led worship at the Ali Mosque.

Lieutenant Colonel Chris Hughes commanded the battalion and was with his soldiers as they approached the mosque. Part of Hughes's mission was to work with the religious leadership at the mosque to obtain a religious decree (a *fatwah*), allowing the American troops to continue to advance to Baghdad without resistance. But a crowd of several hundred Shi'ites had gathered at the front of the mosque as a means of protection. Seeing U.S. soldiers advancing on their beloved holy place, the crowd became angry, thinking perhaps the soldiers intended to destroy the site. Hughes had a translator, but the animation of the crowd made communication through translation almost impossible. They were chanting loudly and posturing to protect the mosque. If the situation worsened and devolved into shooting, the outcome would be disastrous. Not only would many innocent Iraqis be killed, but without the fatwah, resistance on the road to Baghdad would be stiff, and many coalition lives could be lost as well.

Hughes immediately pointed his weapon down at the ground as a signal to both his soldiers and the Iraqis that the situation was peaceful and that he had no intention of harming them or the mosque. Recognizing that his gesture was too subtle, he then kneeled, and he commanded his soldiers to "take a knee," which is the temporary resting posture of the American soldier during peaceful lulls in combat. Remarkably, as they saw the U.S. soldiers kneel, the Iraqis began to kneel as well. Hughes also commanded his troops to smile, a universal gesture of goodwill and well-being. The crowd calmed down, and after a few minutes, Hughes was able to lead his soldiers away from the crowd. The Ayatollah Ali Sistani issued the fatwah, no one was shot, and the mission continued to Baghdad.

Hughes's actions in Najaf that day were brilliant, informed by years of experience as an infantry leader and cross-cultural experience on a joint antiterrorism task force and as part of the team of investigators that investigated the bombing of the USS *Cole.* His leadership was pure in extremis:

- He was tactically competent and culturally aware.

- He shared risk with his soldiers by being at the front of the formation and leading the critically important endeavor from the ground rather than controlling his men by radio from a helicopter or Humvee.

- His focus was on communicating externally to the threatening crowd rather than developing some tactic internal to his surrounded men.

- He focused outward rather than internally on his emotions, which could have elicited anger, concern, or frustration.

- His competence had engendered levels of trust among his men that enabled them to immediately obey his command to kneel in front of an enormous crowd of angry Iraqis.

Chris's actions in Najaf are a showcase of in extremis leader behavior.

★ **Why This Is Important for All Leaders**

Among the many important lessons in this example, the value of nonverbal communication in cross-cultural settings stands out. Dangerous settings often occur in mixed-cultural contexts. Police officers and other public servants routinely interface with non-English-speaking segments of their communities. Cross-cultural communication is also extremely common in top-tier extreme sports. For example, on February 8, 2006, large-formation-skydiving organizer B. J. Worth and a group of international skydivers set a world record for the number of participants linked in a free-fall formation—four hundred skydivers held for more than four seconds (just under a thousand feet of free-fall distance). The formation, built in the skies over Thailand, included the pinnacle skydiving talent from thirty-one different countries. Although English was the dominant language, the ability to communicate in nonverbal ways was also essential in the preparation and execution of both the practice jumps and the eventual record skydive.

Lesson Three: Your Lifestyle Reveals What You Value to Followers

The common lifestyles led by in extremis leaders broadcast an important and unmistakable message to followers: "I'm not in this role for my personal gain." But the issue is not how much money the leader makes. A leader's expressions of humility influence followers in much the same way. Such messages are enormously powerful because they reflect the leader's lack of ego investment and willing commitment to followers and the organization, which establishes a basis for trust and loyalty.

For some leaders, selflessness and concern for others is so unmistakably internalized that one can carry their example in memory like a personal talisman. For me, the leader who burned "selflessness" into my memory is a retired Army general named Richard Cavazos.

Proving What Matters: Declining
a Promotion to Stay with the Unit

Dick Cavazos made military history in 1976 by becoming the first Hispanic to attain the rank of brigadier general in the U.S. Army, but when I met him he was a retired four-star general—also a first for a Hispanic officer. He had come to Fort Leavenworth, Kansas, and was spending the morning with a group of officers, including me, who were in a professional master's degree program. The year-long program was under the Army's School of Advanced Military Studies and was competitive and expensive to administer. The purpose of the program was to create a small core of operational planners who would be capable of writing coherent, successful war plans from presidential intent through execution by Army Corps and Divisions— organizations of more than 100,000 men and women. The Army was investing a lot in us intellectually and financially.

We were mesmerized by Cavazos, a native of Kingsville, Texas, who was raised on a ranch; he was a dyed-in-the-wool Texan. He attended Texas Technological University, earned his bachelor's degree in geology in 1951, and was commissioned as an infantry officer through the Reserve Officers Training Corps program there. He topped off his degree with officer basic training at Fort Benning in Georgia and then completed Airborne School before heading off to Korea with the Sixty-Fifth Infantry. He joined Company E as a platoon leader and eventually became a company commander, with all of his early service in combat in Korea.

The Sixty-Fifth Infantry was composed mostly of Puerto Rican soldiers; it was a minority unit where Hispanics were segregated. Prior to the desegregation of the military, such race-cast units were common; the best-known example is the African American Tuskegee Airmen of World War II. The soldiers of the Sixty-Fifth Infantry were called "The

Borinqueneers" after an indigenous Puerto Rican Indian tribe, and they had tremendous esprit and cohesion—but they also suffered racism and segregation away from the front lines and could be a challenge to lead. Cavazos led the unit in combat in Korea, winning a Silver Star and later the Distinguished Service Cross, two awards for valor ranked just under the Congressional Medal of Honor in precedence.

As we closed the seminar with General Cavazos, he took the discussion and framed the future of the Army as somewhat dismal. It was late 1991, and the United States had recently defeated the Iraqis in the first Gulf War with only a hundred hours of ground combat. Our Army was effective, but it was perceived as inefficient. Therefore, the strategic plan was to radically downsize the Army from approximately 800,000 soldiers to its current size of about 480,000. Cavazos knew that many good officers would become discouraged in the downsizing and would leave the Army. He decided to tell us a personal story of how loyalty can be expressed only in terms of self-sacrifice and personal risk.

His story was that things had gone quite well for him as a lieutenant in combat with the Sixty-Fifth Infantry in Korea. His men respected his competence and ability in combat, and they fought successfully together for more than a year under some of the worst conditions imaginable, especially the record cold winter of 1952. Word came down from higher headquarters that Cavazos had been selected to be the regimental operations officer, a job usually held by an officer two grades senior to Cavazos. It was an incredible honor, especially in combat, and would be an unmistakable feather in Cavazos's cap. Many career opportunities in the Army would develop because of this stroke of good fortune. The Borinqueneers would be justly proud of their favored son.

During a lull in combat, Cavazos's men formed on a frozen hillside to say good-bye to their commander. It was an emotional moment for them all. Cavazos went to every man in the unit, one by one, shaking their hands. They gave him mementos, Christmas ornaments made from C-ration cans, small Korean artifacts, and one soldier gave him a pistol taken from a dead Chinese officer. Cavazos had bid farewell to about half the soldiers when he came to a tough gunner who stood at parade rest when Cavazos approached. Cavazos offered a handshake, but the soldier refused. Puzzled, Cavazos asked him why he wouldn't shake his hand.

The soldier replied, "Sir, you're leaving us out here. You're going back to where it's safe and warm, where there is always food, and you'll have a dry place to sleep. And we'll be out here in the cold, getting shot at. I know headquarters is a good job and you have to go, but I don't have to like it, and I'm not going to shake your hand."

The first sergeant started to discipline the soldier, now standing eye to eye with Cavazos, but the officer wouldn't allow it. He paused a moment, walked back to his jeep, picked up the radio, and told his higher headquarters that he wasn't coming, that he was staying with his unit. Just like that. And he fought with that unit in combat for more than nine months, to the establishment of the cease-fire and the Demilitarized Zone that separates North and South Korea to this day.

Cavazos was passionate but composed as he told us the story. He then said to us, "Ladies and gentlemen, I'm not going to lie to you. It's going to be difficult in the Army for a very long time." At this point, the four-star general's eyes welled with tears. "You're all smart, and you have a lot of options, but please, for the love of your country, stay committed to the profession and follow your careers through to the end. And when this is all over, you can retire, and then I'll shake your hand." The group of forty Army majors was stunned speechless in the grip of this American hero crying before them. I don't know how many of those officers remember the day, but I do know that most of them remain on active duty fifteen years later, that nine have been selected for service as general officers, and that several others remain in senior executive service in government. Cavazos, an authentic, humble leader, left a leadership legacy having talked to mid-career Army officers for only twenty minutes.

Leaders who are mediocre but nonetheless seek organizational effectiveness sometimes develop a variety of impression management strategies so they will appear selfless, concerned, and humble.

One of my past bosses had his secretary prepare birthday and anniversary greetings for the people who worked for him, and they were exceptionally personal in tone. The problem was that the secretary used the first names from the official social roster, and most of us went by nicknames that didn't match the more formal document. Therefore, the notes, although well intentioned, highlighted the fact that this leader hadn't taken the time to learn our names or our spouses' and children's names. His impression management efforts instead called attention to the fact that he was out of touch.

Among outstanding leaders, however, selflessness and humility are internalized and part of their character; they are characteristics, not techniques. Such characteristics are not merely things a leader should do. They represent instead what a leader must be. This is one of the major vulnerabilities of leader development training that focuses solely on knowledge, skills, and abilities (producing the widely used training acronym, KSAs). Skills such as decision making, communicating, or planning may simply manifest (albeit in more effective ways) the character one already has.

Whether in routine or dangerous settings, it is disconcerting for the rank-and-file to believe that their leaders are out of touch. It's important that all leaders take the time to connect with the life experiences of the people they are leading. If lifestyle reflects values, then a common lifestyle reflects common values. And common values are the key to resilient, high-functioning organizations, as illustrated in the following example.

Taking Care of a Team at the Most Basic Level: Going Hungry So Others Can Eat

On April 30, 2003, I was camped out with a division of Marines in what had been Saddam Hussein's palace at Al Hillah, Iraq. The palace rose out of the forest floor on an artificial mountain some ten stories high, the slopes covered with flowers that were now dead or dying from lack of irrigation. Sparkling here and there in the dry land-scape were round pieces of glass chandelier crystals lost as looters had bounded downhill with their palace booty.

I rolled off my air mattress from six hours of sleep in what must have been a receiving area near the front of the palace, with forty-foot ceilings and several intact chandeliers the size of Volkswagens that were too high and too large to loot. The remainder of the palace had been stripped of anything removable: electrical sockets, sinks, toilets, doors, hinges, everything. I grabbed my plastic canteen, a dis-posable plastic razor, and toothbrush and headed outside.

As I began my field hygiene, I looked to my right and saw a Marine peering through the infrared sight of a wire-guided missile launcher atop a Humvee parked just above a gaping concrete hole that was once the palace swimming pool. I noticed some ruins to our front and asked him if he'd been down there. He replied, "No, sir, but a lot of people have. Them's Babylon." Saddam had chosen to locate his palace aside the historic biblical town.

For me, the palace was where I conducted two days of interviews with these Marines, who were infantry fresh from heavy fighting a few days before. Their stories were compelling: the Marines I spoke to had seen heavy fighting in the area, and it had cost them a few friends and comrades. One squad in particular had lost a beloved fellow Marine, shot straight through the back with a bullet from an AK-47, his last words the echo of countless soldiers and Marines through history: "I'm hit." His body armor had been insufficient to stop a rifle bullet, and he bled out in a minute or so. His body was evacuated, and the nine-man squad was left with a gaping emotional hole.

But this squad had continued to fight, and by all accounts, it was as resilient as a fresh squad. They came into the palace for the inter-views I had arranged, and they sprawled out where they could, sleep-ing instantly in the short-term, instantaneous way that only soldiers and Marines understand. They were filthy, and their weapons were covered with dust—except the moving parts, which appeared spotless.

When I asked them to describe what kept them going and made them do the best they could, they kept referring to their squad leader, a mere two-stripe Marine corporal. The average age in the squad was about twenty; the corporal was about twenty-four years old, Hispanic, and maybe five feet six inches, and 145 pounds at most.

The tales they told of their corporal included a few references to their leader's personal ability in combat. It was clear they respected him as a rifleman because he had personally dispatched a number of unfortunate Iraqi soldiers. "Every Marine a rifleman"—a slogan that means that every Marine, regardless of rank, is expected to shoot well—certainly applied to this corporal. They made clear that he never volunteered for a fight, but when they were assigned a mission, it got done. Their most passionate description of their corporal had to do with his taking care of them, making sure they were okay. He insisted they do their job, but he also endured every hardship they endured— and with less sleep, less water, less food, and every bit of danger.

The two weeks leading up to our interview had been tough for the First Marine Division. The movement across Iraq to Baghdad had been rapid and relentless, and the supply trains could not keep up with combat troops. Although the pause in late April had permitted resupply and we were all eating well and drinking our fill, life had been difficult during the heavy fighting. For thirty days, there had been no mail, no hot food, and little sleep. It was during this time that the corporal won his squad's commitment, trust, and loyalty. They spoke of a particularly tough four-day period where circumstances made resupply impossible, and the squad had to share among all of them little more than one prepackaged MRE (meal, ready to eat) per day. An MRE ration is ordinarily a single meal for one person, but in this case, it was shared among nine people every day for four days. An MRE contains about two thousand calories. Typically it has a main meal such as beef stew, a packet of crackers, a tube of cheese or peanut butter, a dessert cake, sometimes shelf-stabilized bread, some candy, salt and pepper, coffee, sugar, nondairy creamer,

Tabasco, and toilet paper. After the corporal had ensured that each of the other Marines got a fair portion of the MRE, they noticed that he consistently took only one part for himself: the single-serving package of coffee creamer. One a day, for four days, in combat, that was all he ate.

Contrast this corporal's decision to leadership dynamics, where the higher someone climbs on the leadership ladder, the more perquisites he or she enjoys. There are no executive dining rooms in in extremis settings. It would have been easy for this corporal to justify taking a more substantial portion because his mind needed to be clear for decision making, or because he had been on active duty longer, was older, had a higher rank, and therefore deserved more. But he didn't, because his Marines came first.

The eight Marine infantrymen, some of the toughest people on this planet, would have walked through fire for their leader. As we did in many of our interviews, we protected the identity of this corporal, but we began to refer to him among ourselves as "Corporal Creamer." I had the honor of interviewing Corporal Creamer, who turned out to be a husband and father who loved the Marines but thought he'd probably get out after his enlistment and do something else that required less travel. And I consider my chat with him in the looted palace to be one of the most inspirational experiences of my career thus far.

As we concluded our discussion, I asked him if I could do anything for him. After passing me some carefully considered strategic recommendations for "the Pentagon" (every colonel from outside your unit is from "the Pentagon"), he said that it had been a long time since his men had seen a laundry, and he asked if I had any clean socks. Clean socks are the equivalent of gold in a combat zone. I gave him every pair of clean socks I had, and I considered it a fair exchange for an incredible leadership lesson of selflessness and the value of living a common lifestyle with subordinates.

During the course of the battle for Baghdad, the Marine and Navy aircraft that flew from aircraft carriers in the Persian Gulf may have saved Corporal Creamer's life and perhaps the lives of his men. But it was Creamer, and other leaders like him, who saved their souls.

Lesson Four: When You Develop Competence, You're Also Developing Trust and Loyalty

The seriousness of in extremis circumstances reveals the importance of competence in the establishment of trust and loyalty. Competence has always been recognized as a valued leader attribute, and trust and loyalty are obviously important in leader-follower relationships. The real lesson, however, is that the three are inextricably intertwined.

Leaders who find that their followers don't trust them or are not loyal usually take it personally, almost like a social rebuff. And leaders who wish to build trust and loyalty often turn to social events like golf, off-site meetings, or other team-building activities. Leader competence is often at the root of loyalty and trust problems, and it can't be fixed with a trip to a rock-climbing school. Use care to identify the root cause of trust and loyalty issues, and never forget that competence may be the essential, if not sufficient, characteristic of a great leader.

A corollary to this principle is that when leaders demonstrate competence, they are developing trust and loyalty. Most leaders have gotten to their station in life through their own competence, but that becomes lost on followers unless the leader's competence is occasionally revealed by action. Leaders need to take the time and effort to show followers what they're good at and why followers should be confident in the leader's ability. Use care, however, never to upstage or embarrass someone else as you demonstrate competence. In the end, leadership is about the success of your people, not about you.

Lesson Five: Extreme Threat, Whether to Corporate or Living Bodies, Reveals the True Character of Leaders and Followers

How people act when things look bad is an indication of their fundamental relationship with their organization and their leadership. Adversity unifies a strong team and destroys a weak one. Leaders must become adept at reading individuals when the stakes are high, especially when the future appears dim. Two examples illustrate these opposing ways groups respond to threats.

Facing a Threat Without Strong Leadership: Why Iraqi Soldiers Routinely Surrendered

The disintegration of the Iraqi Army provides an excellent example of how the ability to lead successfully can change in an instant when the stakes go up. This became clear to me in a series of interviews off the tailgate of a gray sport utility vehicle in the prison encampment of Um Qasr, just forty-five miles north of the Kuwaiti border (not far from the "Highway of Death" that became infamous when thousands of fleeing Iraqi soldiers were slaughtered by U.S. airpower there during Desert Storm, ten years earlier).

Of the thirty-six Iraqi prisoners fresh from battle, whom my team and I interviewed, all but two reported that the decisions to surrender were usually made at very low levels, and usually in response to an immediate threat—a bomb dropping, an artillery strike, or a tank appearing on the horizon. Such an immediate threat is a classic representation of the in extremis context: the promise of violent death. Surrender plans were usually composed among small groups of soldiers and were seldom attributed to the capitulation of a higher headquarters. Officers permitted their organizations to surrender— sometimes by their own desertion, sometimes by benign neglect. The ability of Iraqi small-unit leadership to invoke loyalty and influence up and down the command chain was almost completely lacking and unquestionably contributed to their disintegration in the face of advancing U.S. forces. In other words, the leaders did not surrender their Army; the Army surrendered out from under their leaders. It disintegrated. The corporate equivalent would be a walkout in the face of a buyout.

It should come as no surprise that further conversation revealed that if Iraqi soldiers had emotional ties, they were almost always with soldiers from their tribe or region, not with their military organization. Squads and platoons had little or no cohesion. Iraq's approximately 150 major tribes comprise more than two thousand smaller clans with a wide range of religions and ethnic groups. Soldiers spoke of units divided by tribal or regional differences. When asked about group relationships in his unit, one Iraqi prisoner of war told me: "Usually the relationship is according to the place of origin: if we have soldiers from Basra, they tend to be close to each other. Soldiers from Baghdad will do the same. Or soldiers from Nasiriya will also do the same. A soldier from Basra doesn't like to cooperate with a soldier from Nasiriya." When I pressed him about whether deserters left in groups or alone, he volunteered that they also deserted in groups, "Again, usually according to our place of origin. Because all done by themselves, they were the ones who organized themselves."

Facing a Threat with Strong Leadership: Why One New Orleans Hospital Evacuated Safely During Hurricane Katrina

One of the best examples of adversity uniting a strong, well-led business team is the Hospital Corporation of America (HCA) response to the devastation of Hurricane Katrina. Although Katrina is often considered an exemplar of failed organizational response, the HCA successfully coalesced its organization, developed a plan, and evacuated patients from Tulane Hospital.

HCA comprises 170 hospitals, mostly in the Southeast and Southwest United States and in London and Geneva. It manages approximately 5 percent of all hospital care in the United States, including deliveries, surgeries, and transplants. More than $23 billion of revenues flow through it each year. The CEO is Jack D. Bovender, a humble, soft-spoken Nashvillian. He dissected HCA's recognition and response to Katrina at an October 2006 meeting of leader developers at the Center of Ethical Leadership (COLE Center) at Duke University, where he sits as a member of the board of visitors.

Bovender explained that an entity of the size and complexity of HCA was well prepared in terms of planning for hurricanes. Its hospitals had successfully weathered many such storms, sometimes with near-catastrophic damage, but their plans and preparations led to rapid recovery of routine operations. The problem with Katrina (as we all know) was the extensive flooding and attendant lack of communication and transportation infrastructure. The aftermath of Katrina presented Bovender and the leader teams at HCA and at Tulane hospital with, in Bovender's words, "a whole new paradigm."

From the leadership perspective, the paradigm shift had to occur throughout HCA, it had to be flexible in order to be effective, and the senior leadership had to make it happen with their own people, with a dependency on outsiders only where absolutely necessary. Jack said two things that reflect leadership when lives are on the line: "One of my favorite quotes is from von Moltke [a nineteenth-century Prussian military strategist]: 'Strategy changes when the first shot is fired.'" Jack's second comment, which seems to inform HCA's eventual approach to unify its team through the Katrina disaster, was, "You can't change yourself in thirty minutes into something you haven't been for thirty years."

Bovender characterized the unification of the HCA team under the incredibly adverse conditions of Katrina as the result of four elements:

1. Commitment. The HCA approach during Katrina built on a characteristic value that had been grown in the business over many

years: hospitals' first commitment was to their patients. With that as the guiding value, the right decisions were made at the personal, team, and organizational levels.

2. Empowerment. The HCA response was, in Bovender's words, "incredibly decentralized and empowered locally." People understood that they could take action because, he said, it was "easier to beg forgiveness than to ask permission." Importantly, this extended to actions or communications that may have exposed HCA to lawsuits, especially when it came to telling the truth about problems with the evacuation. Bovender helped set the tone of truthfulness and can- dor: "I'd rather lose the lawsuit and come out with people respecting me or the institution." It's easy to see why HCA found itself on the moral high ground.

3. Responsibility. Bovender and the rest of the leadership at HCA did not wait for governmental assistance or depend on it beyond what was absolutely necessary. They did coordinate with state government for the use of some helicopters and for the use of the Alexandria and New Orleans airports. They not only marshaled an air fleet of more than twenty-four helicopters from various sources, but they heavily augmented the airlift with ground convoys of ambulances and buses, including armed security, some of it rather hastily composed.

4. Communication. Bovender and the leader team communi- cated as best they could throughout the operation. Because e-mail remained one of the most reliable means of communication, they used the "HCA Everybody List" on a daily basis to keep everyone tied together, communicating, and informed.

The *Wall Street Journal* would later characterize the operation in the following way: "HCA's evacuation of critically ill patients in the midst of poor flying conditions, no electricity, weak phone links, and frequent sniper fire stands out among rescue operations in New Orleans."[2] Clearly, adversity can unify a strong, well-led team.

Lesson Six: Your Résumé and Pedigree Are Irrelevant

In extremis demands are always in the here-and-now. Dangerous circumstances tend to be equally threatening to the rich and the poor. Put a driver in a Ferrari or an Apache helicopter, and at 150 miles per hour, both vehicles represent an opportunity to die; neither vehicle cares where the driver went to school or how well he or she had driven in the past. The driver has to perform to the demands of an in extremis situation at that moment. There is no entitlement. The best business leaders behave the same way. Here are three examples.

England's Prince Andrew Fought in the Falklands

Because people tend to be fascinated by the egalitarian quality of dangerous contexts, the British press covers the progress of the military training inevitably undertaken by the royal princes, who have traditionally been educated and then passed through Sandhurst (the British finishing school for officers). Prince Andrew, the duke of York, not only made a career of the military, but in 1982 when the British colony of the Falkland Islands was invaded by Argentina, igniting the Falklands War, Prince Andrew operated in extremis. His ship, HMS *Invincible,* was an operational aircraft carrier in the Royal Navy, and it therefore assumed a major role in the navy task force that sailed south to retake the Falklands.

Despite the possibility of his being killed in action, the queen insisted that Prince Andrew be allowed to remain with his ship, serving as a helicopter copilot. Throughout the war, Prince Andrew flew a multitude of missions, including antisubmarine warfare and antisurface warfare search, and, remarkably, as decoy for Argentine antiship missiles. I could not find evidence that anyone ever asked the queen of England why she permitted her son to go to war, but it seems that such service validates the authentic values and abilities of a leader. In addition, Prince Harry's recent commitment to the war in Iraq defines the next chapter of service by royalty in an in extremis context.

U.S. Football Star Pat Tillman Fought— and Died—in Afghanistan

Because professional sports figures are about as close to royalty as we get in the United States, the country was stunned when Arizona Cardinals National Football League player Pat Tillman walked away from a $3.6 million contract to join the Army. He made the move without fanfare or publicity, and numerous sports writers later recognized his authenticity and humility. When Tillman was shot and killed in action while on a patrol in Afghanistan, sports fans had to come to grips with the unforgiving, indiscriminate brutality of war—ironically in Tillman's case an unimaginably tragic case of "friendly fire." Sportswriter Tim Layden observed in an April 2004 memorial, "There was a rare purity about him. I've not seen it since. I don't expect to soon see it again."[3]

Ford CEO Bill Ford Stepped Aside for a Stronger Company Leader

The advantage to a leader in serving in an unforgiving, in extremis environment is respect for the authentic nature of his or her sacrifice. But the price for such authenticity is that an individual's background means nothing when the stakes are high. The reality of such a dynamic really hits home when family-owned businesses are in crisis. In a recent example, Bill Ford, the CEO of Ford, resigned to name his replacement, a highly successful executive from Boeing. It would have been understandable if Ford had fought to remain at the helm of his family's company, but the nature of the crisis of leadership at Ford dictated a change. Bill Ford had the courage to replace himself, though he remains as executive chairman. In a press release on September 5, 2005, he stated, "As executive chairman, I intend to remain extremely active in the direction of this Company. I'll be here every day and I will not rest until a prosperous future for this Company is secured."

Bill Ford had the wisdom and courage to deal with the here and now. Whether in a life-threatening circumstance or an elite business, the greater the threat, the less the relevance of what has gone before.

Lesson Seven: Use the Life-Altering Quality of Your Business or Your Actions to Inspire

You're not a leader unless people depend on you for purpose, motivation, and direction. Under no circumstances is that dependence more apparent than in dangerous conditions. In my interviews, I asked in extremis leaders, "Can you describe a time when your leadership had a profound impact on the lives of those you led?" I was hoping to uncover a rare story or two. Imagine my shock when one of the first interviewees, a mountain climbing guide, said, "People tell me that almost every week." He was inspired, and so were the people who climbed mountains with him.

To use in extremis lessons in business, "Other People's Money" has to become a proxy for "Other People's Lives." Almost any large business or enterprise has an impact on people's lives, even if the people are simply shareholders, and calling attention to the life-altering impact of a business is an effective way to inspire an otherwise jaded work force. Following are a few examples.

How Insurance Underwriters Help Prevent
Financial Disasters in Their Clients' Lives

In February 2004, I was delivering a keynote to a group of actuaries, a state insurance regulatory group. We were having lunch prior to the speech, and I was quizzing a woman about what she did in the organization. She was humble and felt her job was uninteresting, so I pressed her about what would happen if state insurance regulators didn't exist.

She was able to describe to me, in great detail, the corruption and unfairness in completely unregulated insurance underwriting. She described lost fortunes, ruined lives, despicable treatment of consumers, and lost jobs due to failed businesses. After listening to this litany of disaster, I asked her, "How does it make you feel to be a person who helps prevent all that from occurring?"

She seemed stunned. She paused and then said, "No one has ever asked me that before. I suppose I feel pretty good about that." It was one of those magic moments that causes a keynote speaker to place his prepared remarks under the salad plate. I used her depiction of life without insurance regulation to tie the lifesaving character of in extremis leadership to the organization's purpose and mission. There are few epiphanies more satisfying than the knowledge that you've saved a life. These insurance regulators left their lunch satisfied in the inspiration that even dry actuarial analysts are lifesavers.

How a Hospital Learned from Its Loss-of-Life Mistake

In other businesses, the connection to the point of death is more apparent. At a conference in October 2006, I met the CEO of a major university hospital. A physician with an M.B.A., he had a lot on his hands: forty thousand surgeries per year, 1.2 million outpatient surgeries, and a billion-dollar revenue base forming a platform for a thousand physicians working in the hospital and serving as faculty in the university medical school. He related a tragic, fascinating story about an organ transplant that had failed due to significant malpractice on the part of his staff: incompatible organs were transplanted into a patient, who subsequently died.

The immediate aftermath was grim. Doctors informed the family, and guarded optimism turned into near hopelessness. Various regulatory agencies were immediately notified, including Medicare and the United Network for Organ Sharing. The CEO said that he met with the surgical team the next morning, a group of ten, and asked them to walk him through the steps that ended with the wrong organs placed into the patient. He recalled being shocked at the informality of organ allocation, distribution, and transplantation. The system was, in his view, rife with the potential for error.

During the intense media coverage in the thirty-six hours subsequent to the surgery, he gave more than thirty interviews. The message was about people: sympathy for the family of the dying patient and an emphasis that the error was the result of bad systems and processes, not bad people.

What struck me most about his story was the nature of the lessons that he said he derived from the crisis. He had used the life-altering aspects of the situation to drive constructive behavior in his organization. The threat to life caused this organization, in the wake of crisis, to work hard in four specific directions to avert future disasters:

I. Identify. Look for weaknesses throughout the organization. The life-altering circumstances, including the tragedy itself, caused the team to identify areas of weakness and risk in their procedures and fix them with checks and balances to eliminate the potential for error. Although this is somewhat akin to closing the barn door after the horses have run away, it was a necessary first step in moving forward.

2. Diversify. Solve the problem throughout the organization, not just in the area initially afflicted. The sadness and tragic inspiration from the crisis caused the staff to look into otherwise unrelated areas and attack solutions to procedural problems with a new aggressiveness. This caused the incident to contribute to fixes throughout the organization, not merely in transplant procedures. This is important, because similar to other in extremis environments, hospitals have great potential for accidents and incidents. The life-altering nature of their business—an in extremis condition—drove them to ferret out and fix the next problem before it manifested itself in disease, injury, or death.

3. Acculturate. Change the organizational culture. The staff developed, in the CEO's words, a "culture of accountability." People developed a willingness to question what they were doing procedurally and talk among themselves with an openness and candor not common before the tragedy.

4. Expand. Analyze other practices and procedures. Once the hospital staff had uncovered risk and weaknesses in the new willingness of the culture to self-examine, it expanded its risk management analysis beyond the specific, micro-issues into the processes and practices that allowed the risk or weakness to develop in the first place.

In a hospital only marginally familiar with preventable tragedy, it took a crisis to shake loose what was already, at some level, apparent to the staff: their actions had a life-altering quality that demanded different leadership and management habits. The lesson of in extremis leadership is that some people (like the mountain-climbing guide mentioned at the beginning of this section) are reminders of the inspirational power of the perception of life-altering influence. It makes sense for most people to take stock of how they and their organizations add value to the lives of others.

Lesson Eight: Leadership Effectiveness May Be Contextual

Organizations that are not under stress can be headed by a relatively poor leader, and neither the organization nor the leader may realize it until a crisis occurs. In extremis conditions, due to their unforgiving character, prevent leaders and followers from fooling themselves. For example, a former Army division commander and three-star general recently related a story to cadets in our Black and Gold Leadership Forum. This forum is an invited lecture series that brings high-profile leaders into personal contact with small groups of students. The general related that while en route to Afghanistan, he relieved three platoon leaders of their commands: their leadership had been okay in peacetime, but with war imminent, the followers required better leaders, and the necessity to fire the willing but weak leaders became apparent. What is the break point for your organization to decide that things are so bad, that you need to go?

How the Iraq Army Proved That Coercion Is Not an Effective Leadership Strategy

In February 2003, before the U.S. Army left Kuwait in March and headed north across the sands of Iraq toward Baghdad, the Iraqi leadership was, by its own assessment, fully in charge of its own army. Yet my April 2003 field interviews of captured Iraqi soldiers uncovered no evidence of higher-order concepts, such as nationalism or the obligation to withstand an invasion. Instead, the near-universal theme was that Iraqi Regular Army soldiers were motivated by coercion. One prisoner related that he had been called to the Baath Party office and pressured to go into the Army. I wondered what recruiting tricks were being used, so I asked him to describe the pressure. He said, "By cutting off our food, by destruction of the house, of the home, and they jailed me for a year for knowing I didn't accept, that I didn't join the Army. And they tortured me. Why? Because I didn't go into the Army."

The Arabic term *sumoud* means "withstanding" or "steadfastness" and is a common value in Arab culture, yet this value was not demonstrated by the Iraqi soldiers I spoke to. Their behavior was driven by fear of retribution by party loyalists if they did not complete their soldier duties and punishment by Baath Party or Fedayeen Saddam (the death squads, who killed deserters) if they avoided combat. Iraqi soldiers related stories of being jailed or executed by Baath Party representatives if they were suspected of leaving their units. When I asked about physical abuse, one prisoner responded, "No, he doesn't hit me, but the punishment is jail. For instance, I am absent for seven days, they will end up hitting me [with jail time], twenty days or fifteen days." Another prisoner reported entering the Iraqi Army in 1989 and spending the entire time either absent without leave or in jail, often in the now-infamous Abu Ghraib Prison run by the Iraqi government in Baghdad. He had been taken from prison to fight, and I asked him if he preferred his present circumstances in the U.S. prison camp, or his former circumstances in Abu Ghraib. He replied, "Now is much better." The Iraqis universally deserted with their weapons in hand to fight through death squads to their rear—unmistakable evidence of coercion because the weapons also made them targets of U.S. forces, despite their willing desertion.

The in extremis lesson is that leaders must establish crisis-quality credibility and influence on a daily basis, before pressure is brought to bear on the organization. The best way I know to do that is to develop leadership habits similar to those who lead in life-or-death circumstances. Study and emulate in extremis leaders. This gets beyond the limitation of crisis leadership, which is the study of ordinary leaders thrust unwittingly into crisis. In extremis leaders are professionals. Just like the saying, "Practice doesn't make perfect, perfect practice makes perfect," it's important to focus on those who deal with high-threat situations expertly, not as a reaction to poor planning or ill fate.

If you lead a business or an organization, how much of your ability to lead is based on positional authority rather than people's desire to be on your team and to accomplish common goals? If you can't answer that question, it makes sense to assess your influence until you can. I have a friend who has built a successful consulting practice in Manhattan on the principle that people are often trying to lead only by positional authority—authority sometimes granted by senior management for the wrong reasons. It is an ugly fact that in many bureaucracies, it is easier to promote a poor leader away from a key job than it is to fire him or her. My friend added that she found this to be particularly true of women and minority leaders because of an increased risk of litigation if they are let go. Businesses hire her to help such leaders because the senior leadership knows that the advantage of mere positional authority will erode over time, and it will disappear rapidly in the face of a major crisis. The latter phenomenon is crystal clear in dangerous settings.

It is a rare leader who can organize people with minimal dependence on the basic tools of human resource management: remuneration, reward, working conditions, job security, and benefits. But every leader's goal should be to retain a functional organization through circumstances where those advantages are threatened or nullified by tough times. Being easygoing is not the answer. Most of the Iraqi prisoner of war enlisted soldiers described their officers as distant but usually not threatening. In truth, many officers were politically appointed and not regarded as tactically competent by their men. I examined this with a prisoner who told me, "The officers have little experience. There is some kind of a government decree that simple soldiers can go to the academy for six months, end up graduating as an officer. . . and some of them are members of the [Baath] party and being members of the party, they become officers without even special training or the like."

Iraqi soldiers reported the common practice of constantly asking (and sometimes bribing) their officers for permission to go home to their families for ten days every month. Such circumstances led to little mutual respect between officers and the enlisted soldiers, even though their relationship was far from intimidating and sometimes even friendly or pleasant. Surprisingly, fear of retribution was usually not attached to leaders serving in Iraqi units. Several prisoners reported that if their officers had tried to force them to fight, they would have simply killed the officers and surrendered anyway.

This is certainly not a phenomenon limited to the Iraqi Army; in fact, the U.S. Army at the end of the Vietnam War reflected similar symptoms of coercive first-line leadership and unwilling followers. In an article titled "Cohesion and Disintegration in the American Army," authors Paul Savage and Richard Gabriel formally dissected the decay of indiscipline into violence.[4] Using Department of Defense sources, they found that there were 788 "assaults with explosive devices"—grenade attacks known colloquially as fraggings—on U.S. Army leaders not related to enemy action, in the last four years of the war (1969–1972). These incidents resulted in 714 injuries and 86 deaths, most U.S. Army officers. Leaders can be coercive in benign circumstances, but under in extremis conditions, coercive orders don't work.

Leaders should endeavor to make organizations work independent of the transactional, managerially imposed motivations for people to come to work. Such strategies collapse once the people in the organization feel threatened.

Lesson Nine: The Best Leaders Want to Be Leaders with Passion

Consider the challenge and depth of commitment assumed by people who serve as in extremis leaders, particularly those in public service. Most of us would agree readily that police officers, firefighters, and military leaders are worthy of respect. It takes some intellectual work, however, to probe the depths of their commitment and understand how it influences followers. For example, no mountain climbing client ever wondered if his or her guide was drafted into the sport. Therefore, if you play a role in choosing leaders for your organization, choose people who want to lead, not just those who wish to advance.

All too often, individuals in government or business, in stark contrast to in extremis leaders, find themselves in leadership positions when they may not want to lead. Sometimes the allure of the power and rewards associated with being a leader gives rise to people who find themselves in a demanding leadership role without the necessary commitment, experience, skill, or determination. Certainly the Iraqi Army's overreliance on political appointees as commanders and generals added to its woes during both Gulf Wars. A controversial national exemplar for this phenomenon in the United States is Michael Brown, the former director of the Federal Emergency Management Agency (FEMA).

Blown Away by Hurricane Katrina

Michael Brown was appointed by President Bush to head the nation's disaster agency after having cut his leadership teeth as the stewards and judges commissioner of the International Arabian Horse Association. Brown took the reins at FEMA in 2003 with virtually no experience leading in dangerous settings or in emergency management. He first came to FEMA in 2001 as legal counsel to FEMA director Joe Allbaugh, a friend of Brown; Allbaugh had also served as President Bush's 2000 campaign manager. Brown assumed the position of FEMA director as Allbaugh left the job.

Although FEMA's difficulties with the management of the historic Katrina disaster were nationally apparent, a frustrated Louisiana congressman, Charlie Melancon, whose district south of New Orleans was devastated by the hurricane, posted a sampling of e-mails that Brown had written to followers, and these stand as a poignant electronic archive of a leader communicating to subordinates in a life-or-death situation. The e-mails reflect the difficulty Brown had not only in grasping the situation but also in issuing the sort of competent orders expected of a leader responding to danger. For example, one of Brown's people in New Orleans, Marty Bahamonde, wrote to Brown: "Sir, I know that you know the situation is past critical. Here are some things you might not know. Hotels are kicking people out. Thousands gathering in the streets with no food or water. Hundreds still being rescued from homes. The dying patients at the DMAT [Disaster Medical Assistance Team] tent [are] being medivac[ed]. Estimates are many will die within hours. Evacuation in process. Plans developing for some evacuation but hotel situation adding to the problem. We are out of food and running out of water at the dome, plans in works to address the critical need. FEMA staff is OK and holding own. DMAT staff is working in deplorable conditions. The sooner we can get the medical patients out, the sooner we can get them out. Phone connectivity impossible." Brown's response to this desperate missive was, "Thanks for the update. Anything specific I need to do or tweak?"

In extremis leaders have to share risk with subordinates and be part of the event in order to read the event. Brown would have had more credibility and ability to lead had he immediately established an operations center in an area with solid communications to Washington and within a quick helicopter ride of the devastated area and his fully engaged staff. Such a tactic is so painfully basic that virtually any captain or major in the Army would have immediately recommended it.

Other e-mails reflect a chatty, almost flirtatious demeanor with the people who were juggling the fate of tens of thousands of New Orlean residents. Here are some memorable (though admittedly out-of-context) Brown transmissions to subordinates: "I just feel like I'm getting the s—t beat out of me, but hey, we're working our butts off down here." "Last hurrah was supposed to have been Labor Day. I'm trapped now, please rescue me." And in reference to his attire on televised news, "I got it at Nordstrom's, E-mail McBride and make sure she knows. Are you proud of me? Can I quit now? Can I go home?"

On September 12, 2004, the FEMA leader stepped down. He resigned less than two weeks after President Bush had told him, "Brownie, you're doing a heck of a job. " Brown stepped down in response to virulent accusations that FEMA acted too slowly after Katrina smashed the Gulf Coast, killing more than twelve hundred people. He blamed state and local leaders in Louisiana for failing to act decisively as Katrina approached, and he defended FEMA's approach and response to the tragedy.

Although I would stop short of stating that Brown didn't want to lead FEMA through the crisis, the story of his short tenure as an in extremis leader reflects the tremendous sensitivity attached to leader enthusiasm, commitment, and tenacity.

Final Thoughts: Consider How In Extremis Leadership Might Apply to Your Organization

The relationship between in extremis leadership and leadership in everyday life is more than a series of parallels and similes. The leader behaviors demanded in dangerous circumstances are broadly applicable across purposes. Although in extremis leadership is not a panacea or a universally appropriate leadership style, it can inform a leader's approach to problem solving in business, the social sector, and challenging crises.

Once you understand how the concept may relate to your own leadership, the next step is to explore how to develop in extremis leadership in others. Chapter Three shows how to develop a legacy of leaders, using leadership in dangerous contexts as a template. It develops ideas about in extremis values and character, and it shows how to create the next generation of in extremis leaders.

Summing Up

1. Motivation is most powerful when it is paired with an emphasis on learning. Average leaders motivate their followers by trying to make them work harder, but outstanding leaders motivate by helping their people work smarter, which is when innovations usually occur. Outstanding leaders can help their followers learn to become more aware of their environment and increase their creativity, critical thinking, and analysis of potential outcomes. Keep in mind how Becky Kanis embraced a new approach to quantifying the number of homeless in New York City and changed the way organizations addressed the problem. Finally, they should help followers focus on new solutions, problems that appear to be unsolvable, and unresolved issues.

2. Sharing risk enhances credibility and can improve a leader's effectiveness in situations involving risk. Lieutenant Colonel Chris Hughes defused what could have been a hostile and violent situation outside a mosque in Iraq by sharing the risk his troops faced and applying what he had learned about cultural awareness to calm a nervous crowd.

3. Your lifestyle reveals to followers what you value. Great leaders are often humble. Keep in mind what General Dick Cavazos learned from one of his soldiers in Korea as he was saying good-bye to accept a higher position: at least one soldier felt he was abandoning his troop, so he declined the job and stayed on to fight on the front lines. Similarly, "Corporal Creamer" made sure the eight other Marines in his division shared one meal every day, while all he took for sustenance was the coffee creamer. How you live shows your followers what you really value. Ideally, it's them.

4. When you develop competence, you're also developing trust and loyalty. These three qualities are inextricably intertwined. Some leaders try to build trust and loyalty through social events such as

golf or team-building activities, but loyalty and trust problems can't be fixed with a trip to a rock-climbing school. Instead, show your followers what you're good at and why they should be confident in your ability as a leader. Be careful not to upstage or embarrass someone else as you demonstrate competence. In the end, leadership is about the success of your people, not about you.

5. Extreme threat, whether to corporate or living bodies, reveals the true character of leaders and followers. Adversity unifies a strong team, and it destroys a weak one. Keep in mind how many Iraqi soldiers surrendered freely, on their own, because they didn't trust their leaders and had no loyalty to their leaders. They were a weak team, so when they faced the extreme threat of U.S. soldiers, they gave up. In contrast, Tulane Hospital was a strong team united by a strong leader who safely evacuated all of its patients and staff during Hurricane Katrina. In both Iraq and New Orleans, those responses were ingrained long before the crisis occurred; the crisis simply revealed the true character of each organization.

6. Your résumé and your pedigree are irrelevant. Dangerous circumstances are equally threatening to rich and poor alike. As I already noted, if you put a driver in a Ferrari or an Apache helicopter, and it is traveling at 150 miles per hour, both vehicles represent an opportunity to die; neither vehicle cares where the driver went to school or how well he or she had driven in the past. The driver has to perform to the demands of an in extremis situation right then. The best leaders behave the same way: remember the examples of England's Prince Andrew, who fought in the Falkland Islands; football star Pat Tillman, who gave his life fighting in Afghanistan; and Ford CEO Bill Ford, who gallantly stepped aside to turn over the leadership of his family-run business to a nonfamily member who could lead the company more effectively.

7. Use the life-altering quality of your business or your actions to inspire. Try to think in new ways about how your leadership affects the lives of your followers and your organization. Recall how one insurance underwriter thought her job was mundane and unexciting (and therefore perhaps unimportant) until she realized that she was helping her clients prevent financial disasters that could truly ruin their lives. And learn from your mistakes, the way one hospital changed all its procedures after an organ transplant operation failed so that the system would never again cause the loss of a human life.

8. Leadership effectiveness may be conditional. Organizations that are not under stress can be headed up by a relatively poor leader, and neither the organization nor the leader may realize the leader's lack of skills until a crisis occurs. Make sure your leadership isn't simply positional authority. Instead, see that your organization works independent of the transactional, manager-imposed motivations for people to come to work, such as money, bonuses, and perks. These strategies will collapse once the people in your organization feel threatened—which is just when you need your people most.

9. The best leaders passionately want to be leaders. They truly want to lead followers to success; they don't want just to be higher up on the ladder. Make sure you really want the job of leading a team, and leading it well. Keep in mind what can happen when someone is appointed to a position he or she isn't really interested in, as former FEMA director Michael Brown's e-mails seem to reveal during his handling of the aftermath of Hurricane Katrina.

3

The In Extremis Leadership Model
What It Is, Why It Works,
and How to Use It

The idea that dangerous circumstances influence leadership and leader development in unique, specific ways is somewhat novel. At least it has never before been explicated by authors who write about leadership. Intuitively, veterans sometimes comment that as bad as combat was for them, they grew through the process. This chapter directly addresses why people develop as leaders when they are in dangerous settings.

First, I explain how in extremis leadership fits with an existing scholarly leadership theory, authentic leadership theory (ALT): the defining characteristic of dangerous contexts is stark, unforgiving reality, and leadership in such a context must be real, or authentic, as well. Next, the chapter examines the values and character of in extremis leaders. Then I put the theory to work and show how great leaders can be developed through principles derived by observing leaders in in extremis settings. Finally, I explain why conventional leader development approaches often fall short of their goals and how in extremis leadership can improve conventional leader development. Whether you want to develop leaders for business, the social sector, or dangerous public sector work, it's important to recognize that dangerous settings are not only crucibles for the development of superb leaders; they also represent flashes of unflinching reality that both demand and reveal authentic and successful approaches to leader development in general.

Defining Authentic Leadership

ALT is one of the most popular emerging academic theories of leadership. One of its central precepts is that followers are attentive to and able to recognize a lack of sincerity or an erroneous impression of management strategies displayed by someone trying to lead. In contrast, authentic leaders are confident, optimistic people, high in character, and aware of their own thoughts, behaviors, abilities, and values. Many truisms such as "She is the real thing" or "What you see is what you get" are solid representations of authentic leaders, as shown in the following two examples.

Authentic Leaders Are Not Above Joining in the Fray

One of the interviewers on my team who was working in Afghanistan encountered an Army lieutenant colonel, a battalion commander. The lieutenant colonel had sensed that the soldiers in his command were shaken when two comrades were killed by an improvised explosive device on the streets of Afghanistan. He spoke with them before their next mission, but more important, he opted to accompany them on their next mission as a member of the squad, sharing their risks, accepting the burden of their experience, and showing them the way while serving as a common participant—and without usurping the authority of the actual squad leader.

In another situation, Major General Eric Olson, commander of the elite Twenty-Fifth Infantry Division (Light), left the relative comfort of his headquarters in Bagram, Afghanistan, early Christmas morning and flew unannounced to one of his most remote bases. There, he selected two junior soldiers who were getting ready to go out on patrol, and he sent them back to Bagram in his helicopter to relax, eat, and enjoy the holiday. Then Olson, with his aide, took the places of those junior soldiers on patrol that day, riding exposed in the back of a Humvee with the infantrymen instead of receiving special treatment or perks as a general officer, or enjoying the holiday at his headquarters.

The reaction to Olson's selfless action was immediate and positive, as one soldier remarked: "[For him] to sit in a CAV[cavalry] truck
in one of the worst seats and ride with us, to come and pull guard
with us . . . makes lower enlisted soldiers like myself feel good about
him as our leader." Both soldiers recently reenlisted in the Army.

Such leaders have worked to develop leadership skills in the
worst environments imaginable, making them authentic. Authentic leaders are also attentive to the same characteristics in other
people: it's easy for them to spot a phony or a fake or, more important, an inexperienced leader whose heart is in the right place but
who needs direction. Because of this ability, authentic leaders make
superb mentors. Optimism, hopefulness, and resiliency provide the
key to understanding why leaders who are authentic are also effective at commanding follower loyalty, obedience, admiration, and
respect.

It follows, then, that in circumstances where followers especially
value leader optimism, hope, and resilience, authentic leaders assert
a uniquely powerful influence. Specifically, in dangerous situations
where followers sense that their lives are threatened, perceptions
and feelings of optimism, hope, and resilience define the promise of
future life, and they desperately seek those qualities.

Consider this account from philosopher Glenn Gray's experi-
ence under fire during the D-Day landing at Normandy, France, on
June 6, 1944, at the end of World War II, as related in his memoir,
The Warriors:

> I crouched under my jeep on a landing craft that went in a few hours
> after the first waves of infantry. Shells were exploding in the water
> all around, and I felt sure the next one would land squarely on us. It
> was silly to expect the jeep to afford any protection against the Ger-
> man 88s [cannons] but I could not get up. Then through the tangle
> of gear and machines, I saw an American officer, a captain, standing
> by the edge of our boat. He was smoking a cigarette, and I watched

fascinated as he flicked the ashes into the water. His hand trembled not at all; he might have been on the Staten Island Ferry. Then I felt unreasonably grateful to him. It was clear that he was exposing himself no more or less than I; but his reason was in control. I longed to creep through the gear, clasp him around the knees, and look up to him worshipfully. . . . The sight of him gradually calmed me, so that when our craft reached the shore I was able to get into my jeep and drive it hurriedly through the surf and up onto dry land.[1]

Humans are social animals. We watch each other's reactions to construct an understanding of what's happening to us. This is true in life broadly, and especially in the chaotic, uncertain, and dangerous world of in extremis leaders and followers. Real leaders stand out. Therefore, intense in extremis settings are ideal places to seek and find authentic leaders, assess authenticity in leaders, and, especially, develop leaders.

Is the In Extremis Model Values Based?

Since the term *values based* was first used to describe leaders and leadership, there has been much discussion as to which values apply. The definition of values used by famous psychologist Milton Rokeach in his early work to measure American values simply referred to concepts to which people attached the most worth—for example, life, liberty, and the pursuit of happiness.[2] In some circles, values-based leadership has come to mean conservative social values, or even values concordant with religious beliefs.

Interestingly, not a single in extremis leader I interviewed in my work characterized himself or herself as religious (although about one-third regarded themselves as spiritual). I suppose I always believed the truism that "there are no atheists in foxholes" until I conducted the interviews for this book and talked to a few—and it seems that some also jump from airplanes and drive tanks. It's apparent, however, that when they are in extreme danger, people do place an enormous value on their own lives, and often on the lives of others as well, regardless of their religious beliefs concerning God or an afterlife.

It may be that leaders at the point of death feel so responsible for maintaining the lives of others that they hold any religious recognition of an afterlife in abeyance. They maintain a focus on the environment and operate on the world as it exists in the moment, and no matter how dire the circumstances, they can never afford the luxury of handing responsibility over to either circumstances, a deity, or fate. Turning again to *The Warriors*, read how author Glenn Gray grippingly describes the difference between religious and nonreligious soldiers who are at the point of death:

> The difference becomes apparent when the chances of surviving a given engagement are reduced and death becomes as nearly certain as it ever does in combat. Then such an otherworldly [religious] soldier rarely cringes from his fate, does not become despondent. . . . What is coming has been determined by greater and wiser forces than he commands, and he is content to repeat: "Thy will be done" or its equivalent. The destroyers of such soldiers are astounded at how "bravely" they die and are sometimes deeply shaken by it.[3]

Think of suicide bombers, who walk calmly into crowds to detonate their explosives and martyr themselves.

Perhaps similarly, in the unforgiving, lightning-fast world of skydiving, jumpers new to the sport would sometimes "turn rabbit" during a malfunction—that is, they would become so afraid that they would acquiesce to the situation and plummet to earth without any struggle. As a result, technologists have developed reliable, barometrically calibrated automatic activation devices for reserve parachutes. The devices open a reserve for a person who is in free-fall at low altitude but is unable to activate his or her reserve manually. (Interestingly, in the in extremis culture of the sport, an individual who experiences an automatic reserve activation is usually banned from the drop zone.) No one has ever studied the phenomenon of free-fall paralysis to determine if religious belief has any bearing on the fight for life in the sky.

Whatever the reaction to perceived inevitable death, in true in extremis settings, accepting the inevitability of death can be experienced only once. When danger peaks to the point of the perception of inevitable death, an outwardly focused leader can ill afford despondency or fatalism (individual beliefs focused on the future of the self). Instead, the best in extremis leaders maintain optimism, hope, and resilience, denying fate until they are overcome by circumstances. The leader's job is to create the fate that others experience: leaders are not gods themselves, but they are fatemakers in the sense that their purpose and function are to continue to value the lives of others who are at the point of death.

It's difficult to imbue authentic values among a group of individuals. Organizations that profess values-based leadership often seek to find ways to embed such values in their leaders and followers. For example, General Electric uses several techniques, including a laminated values card, to ensure that its employees understand corporate values. The U.S. Army also developed a values card in the late 1990s and paired it with a values dog tag that all soldiers were to wear on a chain around their neck, along with the more familiar stamped metal identification tags.

But there is a fundamental flaw to these approaches: they lack authenticity. I recall watching several military formations—five companies of about a hundred soldiers each in Korea, and groups in the Pentagon (including the human resources directorate that invented the tag)—receive the values. When the plastic dog tags were issued to soldiers in the near-combat environment of Korea, the event was sporadically punctuated with howls of cynical laughter, and the cynicism was most apparent among soldiers with the most combat time and skill. One soldier humorously opined that because he never pays attention to his dog tags, it would have been more effective to hand out a values toothbrush, with the words printed backward so he could see them in the mirror every morning.

In the executive- or strategic-level leader development organizations headed by chief learning officers, the development of values seems to be cast as an issue of communication. The authentic qualities and stark reality inherent in in extremis leadership place a much greater emphasis on experience as the way that values become embedded in character—they are "caught, not taught." And true character always comes out in the worst of circumstances. One could argue, then, that in extremis leadership is the sine qua non of leadership aligned with values.

Recognizing, at All Times, the Inherent Value of Human Life

A wallet-sized black leather notebook sits on the upper left corner of my desk. When I wear my Army camouflage uniform, it rides in the right cargo pocket of my pants. I don't think anyone has ever noticed the small notebook—perhaps because of its size or because it usually rests inconspicuously among the paper, books, and administrative stuff that cover my work space. Until this writing, no one else has been aware of the contents. It's a private source of inspiration and resolve for me in my teaching, research, and leadership development at the Military Academy. The notebook holds the photographs of former cadets who passed through our department and whom I helped graduate, who have been killed since the beginning of the global war on terror. Today, there are twenty-two smiling faces, treasures lost forever, in the black book.

The book is a direct reminder of the connection of my work to the effectiveness of leaders in a combat environment. It is also a direct reminder of both the value and the fragility of their lives—and all human life. It imparts a seriousness of purpose to work at the Academy that I might not otherwise have. It's a grim reminder that "leadership matters," and it matters the most in dangerous circumstances.

Leadership means different things to different people. For some, it is an organizational effectiveness tool, almost like following a simple recipe: "Take an enterprise, add a leader, improve productivity, and increase the bottom line." Good leadership is good business, and successful businesspeople are assumed to also be good leaders. For others, leadership is the enterprise at the center of a multibillion-dollar consulting industry. For those of us charged with developing cadets into Army lieutenants, leadership is both a talent and a skill that qualify our graduates to take the sons and daughters of America into harm's way. That fact, the Army mission, makes the study and teaching of in extremis leadership a sacred public trust. My own relationship with the study of leadership in dangerous settings can be expressed in one word: duty.

In extremis leadership always comes with a tangible moral obligation. When lives are at risk, an undeniable moral responsibility fosters conscientiousness and total commitment. Responsibility for life fosters an intense focus. Leading under such circumstances is less about power over subordinates and more about an obligation toward their well-being and survival. In extremis circumstances provide a crucible for the development of positive leadership habits.

The In Extremis Leader's Character: Giving Purpose, Motivation, and Direction to Others

In extremis leadership, couched in authentic leadership theory, has nothing to do with techniques. It's about authentic elements of the individual's character and the leader-follower relationship. For example, U.S. Army leadership doctrine uses the "Be, Know, Do" framework to define the characteristics necessary of an Army leader. Recently Frances Hesselbein, president and chairman of the board of the Leader to Leader Institute, and Ric Shinseki, a former Army chief of staff, released these ideas to the general public by capturing Army leadership doctrine in a book titled *Be·Know·Do: Leadership the Army Way*.[4]

Originally the framework was quietly penned into the Army leadership manual by a young infantry major named Boyd M. "Mac" Harris in 1983, a past leadership instructor at West Point.[5] Harris wrote the "Be, Know, Do" concept to ensure that the Academy as an institution and the Army as a whole would recognize that in order for officers to be great leaders, they would need to have not only a set of skills and knowledge but also genuineness of character. In other words, to be a leader is not to hold down a position or perform a job; it is to develop a character that is inextricably linked to giving purpose, motivation, and direction to others. This is authentic leadership. In dangerous settings, it takes on the unique pattern of in extremis leadership.

In leading people, the degree of threat, risk, or danger is an extremely important variable. The threat of death can have a powerful influence on human behavior. In their study of soldiers during World War II, Samuel Stouffer and his colleagues found that when inexperienced soldiers sensed that their lives were threatened, they became desperate for almost any type of leader.[6] In short, they wanted to see a leader as their key to survival. If an individual is uncertain, aware of his or her own mortality, and the environment is hostile, the only real hope is a leader.

Among psychologists, an individual's increased awareness of death is termed *mortality salience*. Mortality salience has been manipulated in experimental studies by asking people to imagine in detail the circumstances of their physical death. Following the mortality salience manipulation, researchers sought to determine the characteristics that followers desire in a leader during these stressful moments. The people they interviewed about in extremis leadership clearly demonstrated a preference for charismatic leaders, followed by task-oriented leaders, and then relationship-oriented leaders (based on ratings of leader communications).[7] In a second replication of the study, the communications included transcripts of political messages delivered by George Bush and John Kerry.[8] The fact that much of Bush's preelection rhetoric centered on danger—winning the war on terror because terrorism threatens our way of life—meshed with the transformational character of the Bush messages as compared to the more rationally based Kerry communications.

A charismatic leader's messages powerfully influence people who have been recently focused on their own mortality. As suggested by the Bush-Kerry comparisons, mortality salience can have enormous impact when large groups of people are being led. When coupled with messages about specific events, it has been shown to directly influence political beliefs, as well as voting behavior. Readers may recall a recent political tagline aimed at the search for a specific reason to invade Iraq: "Don't let the smoking gun be a mushroom cloud." Such statements are not mere attention getters; they are subtle suggestions that conditions are in extremis. Even the most subtle death threats change what people seek in terms of leadership.

Both logically and intuitively, it makes sense that circumstances that cause followers to fear death may encourage the development and exercise of specific models of leadership by leaders who routinely operate in such circumstances. That's in extremis leadership. Active and ongoing research on in extremis leadership will always be dangerous for those who conduct it, but it underscores the value of authentic leadership theory and practice in a unique and valuable way. It reveals the unique leader behaviors required in these situations, as well as the inherent value of in extremis settings as a catalyst to develop these behaviors in future leaders. Now let's explore the idea of developing leaders using in extremis research findings and in extremis principles as a starting point.

What In Extremis Leadership Means for Leader Developers

Recognizing the value of danger in leader development is good news. It articulates and underscores for those who develop leaders professionally or more informally the importance of authenticity and genuineness in leadership, and the vulnerabilities of mere impression management. It points to the key elements of leadership described in Chapter One:

- The motivation inherent in high-risk contexts

- The outward learning orientation of leaders under the gun

- The value of selflessness and shared risk

- The unmistakable impression made by leaders living the same lifestyle as those they lead

- The value of competence in building trust and loyalty

In extremis leadership is an illustration of leadership that is a superb proxy for leader behaviors in conditions of lesser threat. Every leader can learn from the story of in extremis leadership and from the inspirational qualities of those who are willing to put their own lives on the line for their followers, their missions, and their passions.

Putting the Theory to Work: In Extremis Leader Development

For those of us who develop in extremis leaders, the developmental process is simple: coach junior leaders in in extremis settings, teach skills, help impart judgment, and keep people alive. Most extreme sports—and certainly police, military, and fire trainers— establish training standards and protocols to ensure that individuals develop competence and ability in a progressive, sequential fashion. But serious leader developers in high-risk activities, particularly the pinnacle of trainers of trainers, press beyond established doctrine to a higher level of development. Expertise tends to be high, and the experience of the individual leader developer dictates how development progresses.

For example, in the formative years of sport parachuting, usually the person on the drop zone making the decisions and developing other drop zone instructors was the person with the most jumps. Similarly, in the high-stakes merchant banking business, it used to be common for the biggest producer to be placed in charge of running the organization as well. Yet as we learn more and more about organizational dynamics, it's apparent that there are much better ways to develop leaders.

Sometimes a one-size-fits-all education and training approach is applied to in extremis settings. One of the primary reasons the first studies of in extremis leadership were undertaken was the shared perception that the Army was basing many of its leader development policies and doctrines on routine civilian education and training principles. For example, the leadership competencies proposed in a recent draft of the Army's leadership manual were derived by civilian contractors with only minimal military experience, and the competencies read like any list of leader skills and abilities one might find in any large organization or bureaucracy. The one-size-fits-all approach is fine for the significant portion of the Army that is a bureaucracy, but such an approach holds minimal value for combat leaders. In addition, most of the combat leadership approaches were based on either historical anecdotes or expert testimonials. My fellow leadership instructors and I thought that lieutenants headed for the battlefield deserved something more sophisticated and tailored to their needs.

Those who work with people in high-risk contexts—whether in in extremis settings or high-risk businesses—should spend some time thinking about what that means, about how their work is unique, and how their leadership might vary as a result. Direct experience in dangerous contexts shows us, and we have always sensed intuitively, that in extremis settings place unique demands on leaders and followers. Leadership in high-risk settings requires a modified approach, and the in extremis pattern currently represents the best understanding of how to meet the unique demand. Whether you are working with skydivers on the ride to altitude, challenging firefighters with a deliberately torched inferno, or taking SWAT police through a shooting house, make use of what we know about in extremis leadership by thinking through the principles uncovered in the research.

Develop Future Leaders' Competence

Orient on the points that follow as a list—perhaps incomplete—that suggest how you might go about designing training or development of leaders who will face danger or crisis. Whether the examples, when provided, fit your circumstances or whether you must improvise with your own, it is important to be able to articulate how anticipated crisis influences your approach to development.

Confidence, Not Just Functional Ability, Is the Goal of In Extremis Leader Development. Competence is the only authentic basis for trust or loyalty. When a leader has internalized the recognition of his or her own competence, we label the feeling *confidence.* A leader who appears confident sends a tacit message to subordinates: that they should rely on the leader's competence because the leader is convinced it exists. Therefore, confidence is important not only to the individual leader, but it is also an important perception that followers must have in order for the organization to solidify. And the more dangerous the circumstances or threatening crisis, the more important it is for a leader to remain confident.

Always Emphasize That Trust Must Be Justly Earned. People who lead in in extremis settings have to be enormously humble and unassuming. Allow plucky confidence because followers are inspired by it. Crush self-righteousness, cockiness, and arrogance because they will eventually be uncovered as false by followers and by the leader as well, thereby undermining confidence. False pride has been the fatal flaw of many in extremis leaders.

Demand Demonstrated Flawless Performance. Training developers understand this fundamental approach to high-risk training, but the primary principles bear repeating. Because in extremis settings often require perfect execution the first time, teach simple tasks to per-fection, and chain them to complex tasks. Require a minimum of twenty-five repetitions of physical tasks. When possible, teach under safe conditions first, and then transfer the learning to the in ex-tremis setting. The example that follows the next point shows how this can work in real life.

Know When to Pull the Plug. Development often means tolerating minor setbacks and coaching through failure. The same is true for the development of in extremis leaders, but only to a point. It's up to the person in charge of development to sense when failures are an indication of a persistent or dispositional flaw. At that point, the developmental path for that individual ends. And don't apologize for it.

Teaching How to Handle Danger by Simulating a Worst-Case Scenario

Steve Webb, or "Utah Steve" to his friends, is an in extremis leader. A stunt man and professional skydiver, Utah Steve has been around unforgiving environments all his adult life. With salt-and-pepper hair atop a perfect athletic build, at six feet seven inches tall and two hun-dred pounds, and with more than seven thousand professional sky-dives in his jump log, Utah Steve projects bulletproof levels of confidence. His Hollywood credits include the skydiving scenes in the Wesley Snipes movie *Dropzone*. As a leader and trainer, he is re-tained by a company that manufactures tandem parachute assem-blies as its gatekeeper: Webb's responsibility is to train and test those seeking to be tandem parachute instructors.

Over the past fifteen years, tandem parachuting has made free-fall skydiving attainable by the average person. On tandem jumps, the novice is placed in a harness and clipped to the front of a tandem instructor. The instructor wears two enormous parachutes: a main parachute and a reserve (with a barometrically controlled automatic opening device as a mechanical backup in the event of complete instructor failure). Shortly after leaving the aircraft, the instructor places a fifty-four-inch parachute (called a drogue) into the wind stream behind the pair to slow their terminal velocity to a comfy 120 miles per hour. The drogue ensures softer openings, and the modest fall rate allows a freefalling photographer—a skydiver with cameras attached to his or her helmet—to fall even with the heavier, otherwise faster, pair.

Tandem jumps are probably the safest of all skydiving activities when done properly. If done improperly, however, tandems can become dicey. For example, without the drogue placed, tandem terminal velocity can approach 200 miles per hour, which leads to uncontrolled high-speed spins and opening shocks that can damage parachutes and harm passengers. Even with the drogue in place, panic-stricken passengers can present additional problems, from basic instability in the air to unintentionally injuring or disabling the instructor who is skydiving with them. Many tandem instructors have had to deal with their arms held in a death grip—literally—by a passenger paralyzed in fear. Tandem jumps are not an amusement park ride; they are parachute jumps, and they are not without risk.

Therefore, the only way to validate an instructor's ability to handle the worst is to put him or her in the worst-possible position and critique his or her ability to handle it. Part of Utah Steve's job is to serve as an in-air evaluator, riding as a passenger to witness instructor-candidate skills. His mantra was right out of the in extremis notebook: "Validate competence, and require demonstrated flawless performance."

Utah Steve takes his job seriously: he is one of my mentors, and he certified me as a tandem instructor. During my certification process, he was more than willing to add risk to both of us to ensure that I could handle a problem passenger. This is the hallmark of in extremis leadership: embracing and preparing for the worst case rather than hoping to avoid a crisis.

The plan for my final certification jump was simple: the two of us were to leave the aircraft at fourteen thousand feet, with Utah Steve strapped to my front as passenger; we were supposed to achieve stability in free-fall without the drogue; we would then do two con-trolled 360-degree turns while in free-fall; next, we would deploy the drogue for ten seconds to slow us; and finally, we would open the main parachute. It sounded straightforward to me. As a military free-fall parachutist, I had some basic experience jumping with rucksacks, weapons, oxygen bottles, and other gear. I was soon to find out, however, that, compared to Utah Steve, rucksacks and rifles behave themselves.

The ride to altitude was uneventful, although Utah Steve seemed to check our harness attachment points with extra care and deliber-ation. I gave the appropriate commands as we moved to the door of the plane, and I took all of Utah Steve's weight onto my harness so his feet were off the floor. This took some doing: I'm five feet nine inches tall and 185 pounds, and our combined weights, plus the weight of the large dual-parachute assembly, caused us to tip the scales at 440 pounds. Coaching Utah Steve as though he were a student, I had him fix his eyes on the wing tip, grab his harness with his hands, and "READY, SET, ARCH," and we were out the door.

Utah Steve instantly pushed off the door with his left foot and deliberately threw us into an unstable, uncontrolled tumble. To make matters worse, instead of keeping his arms on the harness, he stuck both arms and legs straight out, creating a "badminton birdie" effect that kept us spinning wildly, mostly on our backs. With the drogue out of play, try as I might, I could not control the spin with my body posi-tion alone. Drawing on Utah Steve's earlier coaching about controlling passengers, I swung my arms down as hard as I could, pinning his arms to his abdomen and spreading my own legs wide. This position caused us to begin falling heads to earth, like a spinning 440-pound lawn dart. (Our helmet altimeter computers would later reveal we had reached 210 miles per hour during this phase of the skydive.)

Once stabilized head to earth, I was able to violently throw my arms and legs out into the classic spread-eagle position, putting us belly to earth and stable. The wind was so powerful that it felt as though my clothing would separate at the seams; my bulky cargo pants were flapping so hard, it felt as though a pack of wild dogs were behind us, tugging at them. The flat 360-degree turns at 200 miles per hour were incredibly difficult, but I was able to turn them sufficiently to show Utah Steve that I was controlling our heading.

As seventy-five hundred feet approached, I deployed the drogue, and at fifty-five hundred, I opened the main parachute. As I began to steer the parachute and loosened Utah Steve's harness a bit for comfort, he chuckled and said the words I was hoping to hear: "Dude, I'm glad we don't have to do that one over." I said, "Steve, you laugh when you're nervous, don't you?" He chuckled again and said, "Yep." By the time we landed, I felt supremely confident that I could handle virtually any issue that arose with a tandem passenger. My competence had solidified into confidence.

★ Why This Is Important for All Leaders

The point of my experience with Utah Steve is clear: if you are leading in any enterprise that involves risk, you need to become comfortable close to the edge of disaster and learn personally and organizationally how to handle it. It is worth putting yourself and your people at some risk to build confidence and understanding of what is required when circumstances are grave. Leaders can't afford the actuarial denial game of hoping to avoid crisis: crisis leadership is reactive and weak. High-payoff enterprises routinely take leaders and followers to the edge of disaster. Own the edge.

Teach Future Leaders to Accept Inherent Motivation

The presence of inherent motivation implies that the leader—in any setting—has to gauge and adjust their level of excitement and the excitement of their followers. In developmental activities, set the right tone.

Manage Excitement. Emotions can push an organization into an inappropriate level of excitement and passion. The real problem with emotion in both dangerous and more mundane settings is that it tends to change the way people view the possibilities and probabilities of various outcomes. In other words, emotion influences the judgment of both followers and leaders.

True in extremis settings provide ample motivation by themselves; therefore, don't amplify anyone's excitement when risks are high by spinning up. The best leaders exhibit their calmest and most level-headed demeanors when the circumstances are most dangerous. Hyperenthusiastic or "screaming drill sergeant" types get people killed.

Don't Fire Up the Troops in Dangerous Situations

An Army captain related a story about one of his commanders who put men at risk by inappropriately managing excitement. His company, a subunit of the Fourth Infantry Division, was responsible for a complex civil-military operation that required continuous coordination and contact with Iraqi civilians in order to develop intelligence about terrorist safe houses. The soldiers were nervous about the mission because all missions in Iraq carry risk. The captain's job as a leader was to ensure that his men would not react to perceived threat with lethal force outside the legal rules of engagement, or even in a way that would be detrimental to his civil-military mission. He had trained his men so that when they went out among the Iraqis, they were on guard, but they were not predisposed to shooting or other aggres-

sive acts. Not only did he need the cooperation of local Iraqis to succeed, but he needed to prevent an incident that could turn the local
populace away from supporting coalition forces. A terrorist foothold
in this neighborhood could cost many American lives.

He and his soldiers were making final preparations to execute
their mission when his senior commander came through the barracks
to "fire up the troops." The captain was horrified to hear his commander say to his group of soldiers, "You guys just need to go out
there and kill some of these fuckers."

To the captain's dismay, the buzz among the soldiers instantly
changed from the more technical attitude associated with his mission
to a more aggressive orientation that was changing his soldiers' way
of viewing the people with whom they would soon interact. The men
abandoned the quiet professionalism required for civil-military operations; instead, they appeared to enjoy the tough talk, which fit with
their combat skill background and ethos—but not the mission at
hand. The captain's concern was that if the soldiers looked for reasons to engage the enemy—in this case, mostly civilians—they would
find reasons to shoot. In effect, overexcitement had clouded the judgment of both the leader and the captain's followers. The probability
of conflict had been increased without regard to the mission.

This same commander had also once taken the captain to task
for not opening fire on a nearby crowd when a bomb had struck the
captain's Humvee. It was clear to the captain that his boss was mis-
managing the excitement of his troops, who needed to be calm in
the presence of danger in order to do their job.

Through an additional briefing on the necessary and proper rules
of engagement for the mission, which limited the use of deadly force,
the captain was able to reverse the effect of the senior commander's
"pep talk," and settle down his men and focus them on the task at
hand and at the proper level of excitement and arousal. The patrol
went off without violence, but it also fell flat in terms of the way the
soldiers interacted with the local population. In effect, leader emotion
had changed the followers' worldview.

The lesson to the captain, however, was clear: don't excite the troops when the situation is already exciting, and getting more excited could cause them to do the wrong thing.

Read Other People. Learn to assess when others are in touch with the degree of threat in their environments by watching their excitement level, spirit, and motivation. There should be a match.

"Embrace the Suck." In situations when conditions are difficult or miserable but not necessarily dangerous, it's essential to motivate even the most dedicated individuals. Whether it's heat, rain, cold, filth, or fatigue, deal with the misery intelligently and with some positive energy—in other words, "embrace the suck. " If conditions are bad enough to be life threatening, do not hide that fact. Use the motivating qualities of mortality salience to push others beyond their perceived limits.

How One New Leader Proved He Wasn't Above Doing the Dirty Work—Literally

Former special operations signal officer Becky Kanis recalls that her first platoon was surprised that she would help them put up the tents and the heavy camouflage nets when they set up their fighting positions in the field. The previous lieutenant had stood there with his hands on his hips and watched while the sergeants and enlisted soldiers did the dirty work. Kanis recalled, "I decided I wasn't going to be the kind of leader who watches while other people do manual labor." A corollary is never to ask others to do something you wouldn't do yourself.

Kanis went on to describe how her new first sergeant gave her and her unit a most impressive demonstration of this principle. He spent his entire first day as the first sergeant for Bravo Company,

112th Signal Battalion, 82nd Airborne Division, cleaning the latrine in the company headquarters. Kanis recalls it in living color: "He wore yellow rubber gloves and had those green scratchy things and lots of Simple Green and Ajax. He scrubbed every inch of the latrine. As you can imagine, the NCOs had plenty of business to conduct with the new first sergeant, but he didn't allow that to stop him; he simply had them stand at parade rest outside the latrine door, and they did their business there. I watched this with amusement and wasn't really quite sure what to make of it. When the time came for the last formation of the day, my first sergeant removed the rubber gloves, threw them in the garbage, and said, "That's what the latrine is going to look like from now on, hoo-ah." Then he walked out to formation and dismissed the company.

"I will never forget the example he set," Kanis ended. "He communicated far more than latrine standards that day. In all honesty, the latrine wasn't that bad. He let every single soldier in that company know that he wasn't above doing the dirty work."

★ Why This Is Important for All Leaders

Becky Kanis also told me that in the social sector, there are different ways of rolling up your sleeves to get to work, and they are surprisingly similar to what the first sergeant did in the example. A truly inspirational and effective leader in community psychiatry and housing, Sam Tsemberis, director of Pathways to Housing, asks every prospective employee to his organization whether they are willing to clean toilets. Sometimes this manifests itself as being the last person to go home after staying up all night with the team. Sometimes it is volunteering to work with a client who is especially dirty and ill tempered. Think about how you are willing to embrace the unpleasant work and what you expect of your own followers.

Develop a Learning Orientation in Future Leaders

In all organizations, and particularly in dangerous settings, part of leadership is preventing people from being self-focused. Instead, keep them in the learning mode; orient them on the tasks at hand—the environment.

The Environment Is Trying to Kill You. When people are in touch with environmental threats, they naturally focus outward, inherently motivated toward survival. Therefore, when you are developing leaders, foster and reward continual scanning and analysis of what's happening. Enacted sense making helps keep the leader and the led situationally aware, which equals survival.

The Army, working with technologists at Lockheed Martin, has developed the Combat Leader Environment, a leader development simulation. It's a realistic computer simulation that places leaders in the front seat of a virtual Humvee and takes them into a hostile environment. The leader is forced to make decisions in the absence of enough information to derive a logical decision. The leader is taught the habit of continuously scanning the environment for clues and making instinctive decisions.

Similarly, the best Wall Street performers focus outward to construct reality and get ahead of changes in the market. Charlie Hooker, a former special operations team leader turned investment banker, described to me how the early, sketchy reports of major events—for example, the assassination of President John F. Kennedy, the attempted assassination of President Ronald Reagan, the devastating terrorist attacks of September 11, 2001—form the basis for immediate and instinctive money management decisions by top analysts. Such decisions, usually made by the most experienced traders and institutional investors, can be incredibly lucrative because they occur before everyone else has the details that help form the basis of logical deductions.

Read Other People. Stay alert for signs in others that their attention is turning inward. For example, injuries should be completely ignored unless they are functionally debilitating. Worry or other emotion is an indication that an individual is turning inward rather than maintaining focus outward and continuing to learn and piece together solutions to threats.

Share Language. Sharing a common understanding through language is key. In extremis environments are unique, and every profession, sport, or activity involving high risk has a common terminology. Ensure that definitions are completely shared and commonly understood. Miscommunication kills learning, and it often kills people as well.

Develop a Sense of Shared Risk in Future Leaders

Individuals may perceive selfishness or self-focus as necessary for survival. In groups in danger, however, just the opposite is true: shared risk, particularly among leaders and the led, makes the organization more survivable and the leader more trusted by followers. Leader development needs to foster an appreciation for the effect of shared risk.

Value Selflessness. Often highly competent and ambitious individuals are drawn to the challenge of high-risk activities. Keep in mind, though, the need to recognize, reward, and foster selflessness, self-abrogation, sharing, and looking out for others. Self-absorbed loners and extroverted egomaniacs should not be made responsible for others in in extremis settings.

Dissect Risk Management. No one, leader or follower, can afford to take stupid or unnecessary risks in an in extremis environment. Risk management is a professional tool and a required organizational process. Ensure that everyone understands how risk decisions are made and the difference between a calculated risk and an ill-advised gamble. Immediately sort out and retrain individuals who make poor decisions or take uncalculated actions that threaten their lives, and especially the lives of other people.

Risk management is critical in dangerous contexts and in business settings. My favorite example of taking that to its logical extreme is the story of Alison Levine.

How Mountain Climbers Evaluate Risk and Apply That Skill to Other Life Contexts

Alison Levine was plagued by a heart condition in her early years, but she emerged in her thirties as an extreme athlete, mountain climber, and business consultant. In October 2006, I spoke with her at the Center for Ethical Leadership at Duke University and came to respect and admire her views on risk and leadership.

Among other accomplishments, Levine has climbed the highest peak on each continent and served as captain of the first American Women's Everest Expedition. She founded and is president of her own consulting and speaking firm, and her view of work is pure in extremis. Here's how she expresses it on her Web site: "Every climb requires a unique approach, whether it's up the face of Everest, the corporate ladder or into a position of market leadership. By drawing parallels between staying alive in the mountains and thriving in a fast-paced business world . . . after serving as team captain for the first American Women's Everest Expedition, I realized that many of the strategies employed in the business world are the same strategies used when climbing the world's highest and most challenging peaks. Foresight, focus, and flawless execution are equally important in the jet stream as in corporate America."

When challenged by a question on risk management, she answered as I expected she would: "You have to balance what you're willing to risk. What does failure mean?" Levine explained that risk management in mountain climbing is based on prioritized goals: first to come back alive, then to return with all your fingers and toes, then to come back with the friends you left with, and finally, to conquer the mountain. Much like skydiving and other extreme sports, climbing is virtually all preparation and risk analysis.

On the ground, the leader has to know when the time has come to halt the activity and restore the ability to survive when conditions dictate. Levine put it this way: "You have to be able to walk away from the deal. No matter how much blood, sweat, and tears went into preparing, even if you are this [holding her fingers about an inch apart] close, you have to be able to walk away."

Preparation helps leaders learn when it's time to walk away and when to continue. The U.S. Military Academy sport parachute team plans and executes night parachute jumps as a developmental activity. Prior to the jumps, the cadets and coaches prepare and review a risk management worksheet that identifies the unique risks of the activity. The worksheet is seventeen pages long and includes no fewer than twelve abort criteria for the jumps.

Think back to your last business risk. Were there clear abort criteria? Some strategists would argue that such techniques are constraining, but the lesson from dangerous settings is that without such criteria, the pressure to make the right decision at the right time is almost unbearable. It's easier for some to understand if the decision is simply characterized as telling the truth. One of the biggest challenges with risk management is having the personal discipline to tell the truth. And nowhere is that skill better honed than in physically dangerous contexts.

Managing Risk By Not Being Afraid to Tell the Truth Because the Truth Saves Lives

Becky Kanis, the in extremis leader first introduced in Chapter Two who now does social sector work, related how telling the truth and risk management connected for her in both dangerous settings and in her work with the homeless in New York City. She said, "Speaking the truth, even if the consequences might be negative for you personally, is absolutely fundamental to military culture. It is also essential for solving social problems like homelessness. From the earliest days of basic training, the importance of integrity and telling the truth is stressed. Any hesitation to speak an uncomfortable truth is quickly linked to life-or-death situations, and new recruits quickly learn that it is far better to tell the truth and suffer the consequences than to lie. This became even more important when I was assigned to airborne units and was regularly participating in military airborne operations. One experience sticks out.

"It was 5:00 A.M. in Colorado Springs, Colorado. It was my last day of jumpmaster school, and we were flying over the city before dawn in a C-130 [a large cargo transport aircraft commonly used for Army parachute operations]. We had started with over a hundred jumpmaster candidates in my class, but due to the high attrition rate, we were down to about thirty. The only thing between me and being a qualified jumpmaster was this final test. The Air Force loadmaster opened the door and handed control to me.

"I leaned outside the plane and took in the beauty of the Rocky Mountains as the purple light of dawn started to break. I was also looking on the ground for a cluster of lights that resembled an L. After the pilot turned the lights to green, at the moment when the plane intersected the cluster of lights on the ground, I was supposed to command the jumper in the door to jump out. Failure to time this just right would mean failing the course. I had come so far. I was the only woman in the class. My unit had sent me all the way from Fort Bragg and spent a lot of money for me to do this. I didn't want to fail.

"The pilot light went green, and my mind scanned the ground again and again to recognize the cluster of lights. I knew if I didn't see it and sent my jumper, I would fail. But I refused to send my jumper unless I spotted the lights. Seconds felt like hours as I desperately scanned the ground again and again. I felt myself being pulled back into the plane by the instructor. The pilot had turned the green light off, and we were no longer over the drop zone. My heart sank as I anticipated the bad news: I had failed the actions-in-the-aircraft portion of jumpmaster school.

"The instructor shouted over the engines: 'Did you see the lights?' to which I shouted back 'No!' Then, to my complete surprise, he said, 'Me neither. We're making the pilot circle around and do it again.' Everything went right on the second pass: both my jumper and I made it to the ground safely.

"If I had sent my jumper out without verifying the lights, he might have missed the drop zone and could have gotten hurt or killed. Leaders trained by the military instinctively understand the importance of telling the truth because it can be a matter of life or death."

★ Why This Is Important for All Leaders

Even in safer contexts, telling the truth connects directly to risk. There is always the possibility that the truth may change to something short of falsehood but equally problematic. I am reminded of the title of Gordon Sullivan's classic management book, *Hope Is Not a Method*.[9] Real risk management requires methods. Becky Kanis also explained to me how she connected what she learned in extremis to what her goals were in eliminating homelessness in New York City: "Telling the truth about homelessness is also a matter of life or death. Research indicates that homeless people are more than fifty times more likely to meet an untimely death than the general population. It is essential that we tell their truth for them. The prevalence of mental illness and cognitive impairment among the chronic street homeless population is underreported. It's not popular for me to state that 86 percent of the clients we've served have been diagnosed with a severe and persistent mental illness, because it shatters the dominant myth that homelessness is a rational choice, some kind of urban camping."

Risk management, trust, and the truth all intersect in dangerous environments. They need to intersect in other environments as well.

Teach Future Leaders to Have a Common Lifestyle with Their Followers

People in leadership roles must occupy those roles for the right reasons, and in in extremis settings, those reasons often translate into lifestyles that reflect more passion than practicality. Consider the following comments about leader lifestyle and how it may reflect leader commitment and values.

Build a Culture of Passion and Devotion. We found that among in extremis leaders, working with people in high-risk settings seemed to displace more mundane concerns about material wealth or position. In extremis challenges are great equalizers: fire, gravity, war, and weather place no value on social status or public image. The best in extremis leaders align their values with the challenges they face. Success is defined as excellence, with survival. In the purest sense, lifestyle takes a backseat to the commitment to lead.

Of course, it is impractical to think that all leaders will live a common lifestyle with followers. Nevertheless, the principle of common lifestyle holds true, as we can see in the following example.

How One CEO Rolls Up His Sleeves and Does Every Job in His Company

The CEO of Loews Hotels, Jonathan Tisch, is among the wealthiest men in the United States, yet he wanted to make the point that he was not out of touch with his workforce, and he used a common lifestyle approach to prove the point. Tisch spent two days in Loews hotels performing every job in the hotel. He made beds, cleaned bathrooms, worked the front desk, and cooked meals, all the while being guided by the local experts who ordinarily performed those jobs.

Tisch also hosts a television series, *Open Exchange: Beyond the Boardroom,* where he conducts deeply personal interviews with other CEOs. This permits their lives to be humanized. The program reveals the personality of the leaders and shows that business is about more than numbers; it encompasses guts, passion, hard work, and people as well. Tisch's work, though not exactly a common lifestyle, reveals the leadership value of connecting with followers on a personal and human basis.

Explore Motivations. People who place themselves at risk, whether in a leader or follower role, have personal motivations for doing so. Experts learn to understand and explore these motivations with people. Why does this person want to be a SWAT officer, a special operations soldier, or a tandem parachute instructor? Is it sensation seeking? Ego enhancement? Other rewards? When you get accomplished at deconstructing people's motivations, it's much easier to coach them into the right frame of mind for the challenges they are accepting and the risks they are taking with their lives and the lives of other people.

Training with Physically Challenging Activities

Leader developers should remain undaunted by the obvious challenges to leader development in the concept of in extremis leadership. The most obvious challenge is that it is often impractical to expose rank-and-file nonmilitary leaders to risk of life in order to develop them.

There is nevertheless some value in less threatening activities, including the excitement of taking a team to a rock climbing wall, a pistol range, or a paintball battlefield—techniques that have been requested for corporate team building at West Point. They are en-joyable activities, to be sure, and although they are not physically threatening, the physical element helps participants sense the nature of leadership in in extremis settings.

The Outward Bound organization has recently expanded its developmental experiences into the area of executive team devel-opment. Its approach is to use physically and mentally challenging experiences to teach leadership principles. Some individuals develop personal character through dangerous climbing or risky sports like BASE jumping (that is, leaping with a parachute from Buildings, Antennae, Spans and bridges, and Earthworks or cliffs), extreme sailing adventures, or other extreme sports.

Organizationally, however, only public servants and extreme sport professionals consistently work in settings with sufficient threat to make mortality salience a routine experience and in ex-tremis leadership a way of life. Leadership characteristics developed in such a crucible can't be purchased; they can only be earned through sustained effort, personal commitment, and risk to life. Dif-ficult as the challenge of in extremis settings might be, an under-standing of in extremis leadership shows leader developers the importance of authenticity and the in extremis pattern. There is no easy road map to follow to create these same qualities in ordinary leaders.

Does Conventional Leader Development Fall Short?

Most of the popular leader development activities with which I am familiar fall far short of producing qualities in individuals that are found among in extremis leaders. For example, skill-focused leader training is the most common leader development approach in use today, yet I would argue that it is only minimally compatible with the elements of in extremis leadership. In skill-focused leader train-ing, the assumption is that a leader is the sum of his or her capabil-ity to perform tasks. In order to perform any task, an individual needs to have knowledge of what needs to be done, the skills to perform the task, and the motivation to undertake the task and carry it through to completion.

For many years, training developers and human resource managers have focused on knowledge, skills, and abilities as a basis of employment and for constructing training programs and development programs intended to increase performance. The logic of such an approach is undeniable: knowledge, skills, and abilities can be objectively measured and tested to ensure that an individual has the capacity and the capability of performing work at a given level of performance. Assessments of knowledge, skills, and abilities can then be matched to job requirements to validate the capabilities of employees. Ideally, competence is increased, and the person being developed is therefore a better leader (recall from Chapter One that competence was found to be a fundamental characteristic of in extremis leaders).

Skill-focused training and the use of knowledge, skills, and abilities are popular in organizations. This popularity has a lot to do with the need for leader developers to demonstrate value added to organizational leaders. All leaders in a corporate environment hope for a predictable and measurable return on investment in any training or development. It is often a challenge to assess the value of leadership development in the short term. Knowledge, skills, and abilities can show a connection between measurable outcomes and organizational goals. The assumption, then, is that after they are learned, the organization will perform better.

Interestingly, however, organizations often don't perform better after an increase in individuals' knowledge, skills, and abilities. Although there is a host of causes behind such an outcome, one reason is that even after skill training, an individual's fundamental character is so dominant in his or her leadership style that the person simply reverts to his or her original ways of leading. In other words, skill-based leader development may change what a person knows and what a person is capable of doing, but leadership is also about what one is—the "Be" component (of the Army's "Be, Know, Do" doctrine). It takes time and powerful experience to change the character of an individual. That's one of the advantages enjoyed by service academies: their character-building, leader development immersion is forty-seven months long.

Another problem with the skills-focused approach is that it usually lacks any quality of inspiration. "To inspire" literally means to fill the spirit. There is a spiritual quality to the moral obligation of an in extremis leader who assumes more risk than the person he or she leads. Inspiration is key to embedding qualities in an individual's character: when we are truly passionate and inspired about something, our fundamental character changes to match.

For example, the mission statement of the U.S. Military Academy is "to educate, train, and inspire the Corps of Cadets so that each graduate is a commissioned leader of character committed to the values of Duty, Honor, Country and prepared for a career of professional excellence and service to the Nation as an officer in the United States Army." The three verbs at the beginning of the mission statement—*educate*, *train*, and *inspire*—are commonly shared among many who seek to develop performance in individuals and by organizations. The best leader development—whether military, in extremis, or something else—achieves the best outcome if it capitalizes on all three elements of the mission. That means the need to inspire people.

An Inspirational Leader-Development Approach

Consider the following four techniques that the Department of Behavioral Sciences and Leadership at West Point has used to add to the developmental preparation of budding in extremis leaders.

Inspire by Telling Stories of Real Situations

Perhaps the simplest form of inspiration a leader can provide is a poignant story. One possible way to develop motivation for future in extremis leaders to prepare fully for their combat roles would be to have them study graphs that depict how quickly they might experience combat. But a story is more inspirational, as you can see in the following example.

How One Soldier Inspired Future Soldiers by Vividly Describing His First Wartime Assignment

In 2002, West Point top cadet commander Andy Blickhahn graduated as a leadership major and immediately attended follow-on Army schools at Fort Benning, Georgia. He then reported for his first assignment in the Eighty-Second Airborne Division at Fort Bragg, North Carolina—a historically famous division blooded at Normandy, Sicily, Grenada, and usually the first division to place "boots on the ground" of a foreign war zone. He was at Fort Bragg only seventeen days, with much of his household goods still in boxes, when he boarded an aircraft to Iraq.

The new officer somehow found his platoon in the maze of Baghdad; it was pitch dark by the time he joined the team he was to help lead. The team's mission was to conduct an attack across a bridge in the war-torn city. By midnight, Blickhahn's platoon had been attacked and was experiencing offensive success against organized Iraqi forces. He later wrote how strange it was when the sun came up and he saw the camouflaged faces of his platoon sergeant and his radio operator for the first time, having fought with them all night long. Until that moment, he had only their voices to personalize the relationship.

That inspirational story helps burn "be prepared" into the identities of our emerging in extremis leaders. I know of no skill-focused approach that would have a similar impact.

★ Why This Is Important for All Leaders

If you're developing leaders, build meaningful developmental exchanges into their organization's oral history, and design ways for the stories to be retold over time. Corporate America can do much to capitalize on storytelling, especially stories by the rank and file. Junior associates can be invited to do keynote addresses. Stories can be elaborated in corporate newsletters or online. All organizations have oral histories—some authentic, some merely legends. It's up to the leader to capitalize on them to add inspiration to work.

Inspire by Using Technology to Link to In Extremis People and Places

Leader developers often assemble panels of experts—highly successful CEOs, political leaders, and combat veterans—to share their experiences and inspirational stories. An example is the World Business Forum, a traveling assemblage of the world's most successful leaders who speak on leadership and leader development. Such an approach has some merit, but it uses role models that show young leaders what we want them to be in ten or twenty years. People need to be inspired about what they'll be this year, as we see in the next example.

How the USMA Connects Cadets with Soldiers

Instructors at the USMA arrange two-way videoconferences between cadets and new lieutenants serving as leaders in Afghanistan, Kosovo, and Iraq. These unscripted videoconferences provide students the ability to communicate directly with the people who are living and working in in extremis settings. The discussion has powerful meaning for the developing leaders, because the only questions asked are those the audience themselves compose.

★ Why This Is Important for All Leaders

Young, ambitious people are inspired by seeing their in extremis futures, even if only for an hour or so. In most organizations, retention of personnel, especially highly trained leaders, is a challenge. One of the principal reasons for turnover is that people find their expectations unmet. Using videoconferences to transport leaders to their future fosters dialogue that creates realistic expectations about what service as an in extremis leader really means. The USMA is not the only organization doing this, as we can see in the next two examples.

How One Company Connects Its Leaders in a Worldwide Discussion

Systems integration giant EDS, a progressive company with more than 130,000 employees, understands the value of leveraging lateral communication among leaders and employees. The company recently contacted me to speak in its online Community of Thought Leaders' Forum, an online dialogue among five hundred leaders in EDS worldwide. Leaders must apply and be selected to participate in the forum, conducted in two live sessions: one timed for the Western Hemisphere and one for the Eastern Hemisphere.

During each session, which lasted almost two hours, I spoke for about an hour in a worldwide, streaming teleconference. Immediately after the presentation, while the leaders were still connected, questions were posed telephonically to the presenter and others who commented or asked questions. Subsequent to such sessions, EDS online reviews and carefully constructed white papers carry the creativity and new ideas into the rank and file of the organization.

How the U.S. Army Improves
Leaders by Peer-to-Peer Mentoring

Despite stereotypes that may exist to the contrary, peer-to-peer mentoring is popular and effective in both the tactical and more administrative portions of the Army. In the tactical Army, an after-action review process was developed more than fifteen years ago to allow peers and subordinates to give feedback to leaders about why military tactical operations (for training or actual fights) went right or wrong. Over time, leaders build a learning culture where everyone in an operation comes together at the end to discuss what was supposed to happen, what actually happened, and what could be done in the future to permit more effective operations.

In the portion of the Army not engaged directly in fighting, peer-to-peer mentoring was established in the fall of 2006 through an online system for rating peers. Every colonel in the Army is now given the opportunity to rate the peers of his or her choosing in October and November and to have that feedback sent anonymously to those peers later that year. Like the after-action review process, this information will increase the level of self-awareness among leaders and add to the ability of individuals to adjust their own developmental paths.

★ Why This Is Important for All Leaders

Companies like GE and IBM use similar peer-to-peer mentoring processes designed partly on the Army's model. Interestingly, however, the technique has not gained traction in Asia and in other armies where saving face and impression management are important individual values.

Inspire by Fusing Reality and Development

Leaders in in extremis settings must learn how to use lateral and hierarchical communication to share knowledge and learn rapidly because unshared knowledge is the basis for unnecessary deaths in combat. Consider the following two examples of leaders who have done this effectively.

How One Teacher of Leadership Used Her Experiences in Afghanistan to Illustrate Organizational Change

Recently the director of the Academy's principal leadership course, Colonel Donna Brazil, deployed to Afghanistan to assist in the establishment and development of a national military academy for Afghanistan. She returned with experience that took her academic class beyond the classic work by scholars of organizational change and created a classroom drama about her struggle to assist a country in its own rebirth. In this same class, the application of knowledge management principles fused with reality to form an important lesson in change.

How Another Teacher of Leadership Used His Deployment to Iraq to Teach in Real Time

Major Pat Michaelis is the instructor for the USMA's Leading Organizations Through Change course. Rather than leave the principles of knowledge management untested and only loosely tied to current events, he deployed to Iraq, with the headquarters of the Army's First Cavalry Division. His mission—assigned as an emergency, separate from his teaching role—was to design and implement a secure electronic knowledge management system for this twenty-thousand-person organization in an in extremis environment.

Michaelis recognized the developmental value of his mission to his class. Over several class periods, he contacted his students at class time using satellite communications and helped guide the seminar discussion with real-time observations. In some cases, he taped combat mission briefs (removing classified information) and e-mailed them to the students as the combat played out in the streets of Baghdad.

★ Why This Is Important for All Leaders

Imagine the inspirational power of a trainee making a suggestion about knowledge management and having it tested by the organization in extremis, with feedback during the subsequent class. People are invariably inspired by the fusion of their developmental experience with the actual work of the organization. In the case of in extremis settings, abstract principles presented in a classroom or off-site are uninspiring by comparison.

In the corporate context, business and management students should not merely study historical case studies. Instead, they should connect with actual businesses, and not just during high-profile internships. Management can be learned from the written page, but leadership requires judgment and character best derived through actual environments.

Inspire by Exceeding People's Expectations

Creative, determined leaders can help span the gap between in extremis and more routine settings, and the effect is powerful. In the Academy's Leadership in Combat course, bringing the war to the classroom was daunting; no fieldwork had been done in this area since the oral histories of World War II and Korea. The solution was as simple as it was profound: send the instructor to the source, as described in the following example.

Why Two Instructors Went to War to Learn More About Combat Cohesion and Leadership

In April 2003, during combat operations to take Baghdad, four instructors deployed to Iraq: one a professor of Arabic and the others psychologists and leaders. They left the United States with what they could carry in their individual rucksacks, and their goal was to update knowledge of combat cohesion and leadership by interviewing captured Iraqi soldiers and U.S. soldiers and Marines. They departed Baghdad only after hostilities officially ended in May, and immediately on their return to the Academy, they coproduced a monograph for the course that captured the nature of cohesion and leadership in the two armies.[10]

The powerful impact of this work in the class was only partly due to the new content about in extremis leadership and the dynamics of cohesion in combat. Although the content of their work had value, an important secondary impact was inspirational: the future in extremis leaders taking the class were stunned that their professors had assumed significant personal risk to enrich learning in the classroom. Their expectations were profoundly exceeded.

★ Why This Is Important for All Leaders

This inspirational style of development works in nonmilitary settings as well. Would it not exceed the expectations of a junior associate coming to work in the morning if, without advance notice, you put that person on a corporate aircraft to visit a customer or plant that he or she had been handling electronically or over the phone? Ask yourself, "How can I inspire beyond the incremental bonus?" If people work for you, they have expectations. When you dramatically exceed those expectations, you inspire them.

Final Thoughts: Consider How to Develop Future Leaders in Your Organization

Dangerous contexts build leaders and the right leadership habits better than any other context, including higher education. To capitalize on this phenomenon, you don't have to rush to the top of a mountain or out the door of an airplane. In extremis leadership works just as well conceptually, and it has considerable utility across a broad range of circumstances.

For those of us who train and develop leaders who operate in dangerous settings, our theories and curriculum developed in business or academe, without respect to the nature of the context, are no longer sufficient. Good leader development is based on research, and research is always specific to the context in which the research was performed until it has been proven to apply across contexts. It is inadequate to provide leadership instruction without a careful and analytical accounting of how the danger inherent in the work will be important to both leaders and followers. The best way to do that is to spend time in the dangerous setting, observing and objectively analyzing what occurs; if that's not possible, the next best choice is to learn as much about it as you can.

Leading in all contexts, dangerous or not, takes a toll on leaders in terms of their physical and emotional well-being. As you might expect, there are unique physical and emotional demands placed on in extremis leaders. The next few chapters expand on the lessons learned in dangerous contexts to understand how emotions, tragedies, and other powerful experiences affect behavior under conditions of threat.

Summing Up

1. Authentic leaders aren't afraid to join in the fray. Keep in mind how Ric Olson and his aide took the place of two of his soldiers on Christmas Day: they rode on patrol in a Humvee on the roads of a remote outpost in Afghanistan, while the two soldiers enjoyed a holiday meal in safety back at headquarters. True leaders should walk the walk, not just talk the talk.

2. Make sure the leaders you're developing are truly competent. Competence is the only authentic basis for trust or loyalty, so make sure you and the future leaders you're developing are truly competent. Recall how Utah Steve, my skydiving instructor, deliberately destabilized himself and me in free-fall during a tandem skydive to show me how difficult it can be to land someone safely. He knew that if we survived that fall, I'd be fine working with novice skydivers: he tested my competence, and I passed.

3. Teach future leaders to be inherently motivated by conditions, not motivated by inappropriate levels of excitement. Be careful about firing up others: situations can get out of control quickly, often with disastrous results, including unnecessary loss of human life, if the situation poses a high-risk danger. The best leaders exhibit their calmest and most level-headed demeanors when the circumstances are most dangerous. Excitable leaders get people killed.

4. Roll up your sleeves, and do the dirty work. Prove you're willing to do anything you ask of your followers. Keep in mind the example of the first sergeant who cleaned the latrine to set an example for his division. Similarly, Jonathan Tisch, the CEO of Loews Hotels, has done every job his employees do: from working the front desk and cooking meals to making beds and cleaning bathrooms. Think about how you are willing to endure hardship or do menial tasks, and what you expect of your own followers.

5. Learn when to walk away and when to keep going, and don't be afraid to tell the truth. Don't be seduced into doing something that doesn't feel right. As Becky Kanis learned when she was training to be a skydiving teacher, if you can't see the light (literally, in her case), don't let anyone jump. The same advice works in any other situation in business and other walks of life. Real risk management requires a plan: What are the abort criteria for new projects in your organization?

6. Communicate with your people, and teach future leaders in real time. Inspire by telling true stories of real-world experiences, as recent as possible. Use electronic technology to bring leaders from around the world together using videoconferencing or other technology so they can learn from each other without having to travel, thereby saving time and other expense. Nevertheless, whenever possible, get out into the field and see for yourself what's going on—whether it's with far-flung employees, customers, or soldiers on the front lines.

4

Learning About Fear and Leadership from Dangerous Settings

Handling Emotion During In Extremis Situations

At the heart of the psychology of dangerous settings are the dark emotions that grip people who are uninitiated or unprepared—emotions such as fear, anxiety, and sometimes anger. Even experienced professionals have emotional reactions to the stark realities and permanent consequences inherent to in extremis environments.

In extremis settings are dramatic, and like any drama, the dynamics of emotion are powerful and interesting. Ever since Daniel Goleman introduced the term *emotional intelligence* to the leadership literature, writers and thinkers who ignore this important component have been missing the color and character of leadership.[1] In extremis leadership, with its richness and authenticity, illustrates leadership qualities that are deeply embedded in the character of those in charge. How might that be unique? What role might feelings play? Are the best in extremis leaders passionate and keyed up? Or are these professional leaders icy, emotionless, and mechanical? Clearly, to understand the essence of in extremis leadership requires exploring fear and emotion in the in extremis context.

Of course, there are also positive emotions associated with the triumph and self-confidence derived from the successful negotiation of a dangerous enterprise or activity. For example, the tremendous joy experienced after the first parachute jumps has been colloquially labeled "perma-smile" by skydiving instructors. The climbing term *summit*, as both a noun and a verb, has expanded to encompass any significant positive achievement. There are a host of emotions and feelings associated with the high drama inherent in danger. It would be a daunting task to explicate such a wide variety of emotions; therefore, this chapter looks at fear, the most common emotion in high-risk situations, to better understand how true danger affects emotions. And going forward, I acknowledge that fear may or may not be a good proxy for other emotions and other contexts.

Understanding emotions in in extremis situations is particularly challenging because emotions are difficult to study and understand as they occur and after the fact. For example, interview techniques don't work well, because emotions are experienced in the here and now. As I approached this problem, I considered various research strategies, all of which seemed to be inadequate for understanding emotions in these settings. The answer I came up with was to experience the phenomenon of emotion in in extremis settings firsthand, as I describe in the first example in this chapter. But before we get to that, let's take a look at how soldiers describe their fear during combat.

Plumbing the Depths of Fear in Dangerous Situations

Fear heralds the arrival of unforgiving consequences in dangerous settings. For example, consider the following account of fear captured in the best-selling book, *We Were Soldiers Once, and Young.* Journalist Joe Galloway coauthored the book with the commander of a U.S. Army unit following the famous Battle for LZ X-Ray in the Vietnam War.[2] Galloway was a reporter living with U.S. troops during the Vietnam War when officially there was no such practice. The battle itself played out on a helicopter landing zone (LZ) used by the First Squadron, Seventh Cavalry. The American air cavalry squadron of about eight hundred men landed nearly on top of a regiment of Vietnamese regular infantry, about twenty-seven hundred strong. The vicious around-the-clock fight in November 1965 was the first major battle of the Vietnam War and the basis for the movie *We Were Soldiers*. Here's how Bill Beck, an assistant machine gunner, described his emotions during that battle:

> While Doc Nall was there with me, working on Russell, fear, real fear, hit me. Fear like I had never known before. Fear comes, and once you recognize it and accept it, it passes just as fast as it comes, and you don't really think about it anymore. You just do what you have to do, but you learn the real meaning of fear and life and death. For the next two hours, I was alone on that gun, shooting at the enemy. Enemy were shooting at me and bullets were hitting the ground beside me and cracking over my head. They were attacking me and I fired as fast as I could in long bursts. My M-60 [machine gun] was cooking. I had to take a crap and leak bad, so I pulled my pants down while laying on my side and did it on my side, taking fire at the time.[3]

Similarly, many of the soldiers and Marines I interviewed in Iraq in 2003 related stories of how danger created fear, and with it the realization that something had changed, that death was present. Here's what one gunner had to say:

> I experienced fear the whole time we were in contact. I didn't want to show my fear because I didn't want it to take the best of me. . . . I wanted to get everyone home just like they wanted to get me home. That first time I experienced bullets fly by, it was like, this isn't a game anymore. We are no longer training. I would actually die now. After the first few thoughts, I was like, well I can't be scared. . . . After that, I need to get over my fear. I need to do my job, otherwise we are not going to live.
>
> *Bradley Fighting Vehicle gunner, Baghdad, Iraq*

And consider this particularly poignant example of fear from a soldier who related what it was like to be forced out of an armored vehicle by a fire inside while being shot at from outside the vehicle:

That was basically my biggest [experience of fear] I guess, as I look back, and all I could think about was all the ammunition that we had in the back and . . . picturing that going off and basically blowing us all to hell. We all had to dismount the track [track-driven vehicle] and get the fire under control. At the time . . . we had a lot of bullets firing, and we also had to jump out with very limited cover . . . get the fire out, then load back up and head out to fight again. That was probably my scariest time.

Mechanized infantryman, Baghdad, Iraq

Fear can be gripping and debilitating, a mostly psychochemical process caused by the release of pure adrenaline in near-death experiences. For example, some experienced skydivers have survived to tell about fear induced by a perceptual phenomenon known as ground rush. During most of a free-fall skydive, there is little perception of falling, because the ground is so far away that there are no perspective cues that permit the parachutist to recognize speed toward earth. It's rationally apparent that you're falling, but you can't perceive the speed because there is nothing nearby that shifts position relative to you, the falling object. Below a certain altitude (in my own unfortunate experience, this was somewhere below fifteen hundred feet, or about six seconds from the inevitable impact), your eye suddenly perceives cues in peripheral vision that signal the ground is rushing closer at tremendous speed, and the earth literally appears to close rapidly around you, like sliding into the mouth of an enormous whale. In a millisecond, a huge surge of adrenaline is released involuntarily, and even the most experienced jumper feels panic stricken and fearful. That's ground rush. I've experienced it only once, and I never want to experience it again.

Clearly fear abounds in dangerous settings. The important task for leaders is to understand how fear works, how it influences subordinates, and how to either live with it or control it in in extremis conditions. Beyond that understanding, coming to know fear has implications for settings that don't threaten life but cause fear in our own way, for our own reasons, in the more representative times of our lives. I decided to experience emotions firsthand, the way anyone with a sibling or a child or a parent will be able to understand, thus creating an example to illustrate the unique character of the emotions of in extremis leaders. At that point, how to control (or, more precisely, not control) emotions such as fear through an external focus will help all readers understand themselves and their capacity to lead through fearful, if not life-threatening, circumstances.

Facing Every Parent's Worst Fear and Anxiety: Watching Your Child Deal with a Potentially Dangerous Situation

Four months after her eighteenth birthday, my younger daughter, Kerry, approached my wife and me and asked that I arrange for her to skydive. Her request came without the usual buildup of probing questions or curiosity directed at my sport. Tension gripped the room, and I instantly realized two seemingly incompatible certainties. First, I was certain I did not want her to jump out of an airplane; second, I knew I could not refuse her request. How could I tell her no when I spent so much time telling her and her sister and her mother how careful I am and how safe free-fall parachuting can be when done properly? How could I tell her no when I spent countless hours teaching other people's children how to rig, how to fall, how to land, how to fly? When what we say and what we do matches, that unity is a gift we call integrity. My heart sank when I realized that the core of my identity, my personal integrity, was setting into motion a chain of events that would soon bring my daughter to the door of an open, moving airplane.

I initially tried to reason through my anxiety over taking my child into harm's way—here was something to be thought through or figured out. I searched for the perfect rationale—surely this activity was reasonable. But my love for my daughter made risk to her unreasonable; concern settled deep into my heart like the chill that settles into the eastern slope of a mountain at sunset. If Kerry were injured or killed, how could I, or anyone else, possibly accept whatever rationale I offered? No analysis would let me off the hook. I was literally risking my reason for being because even the safest skydive is not without significant risk.

Tandem skydiving, where the new jumper is a passenger on the front of an experienced instructor, is generally thought of as safe, and its track record is solid. But skydiving in any form is not an amusement park ride. Every year, people are injured and sometimes killed on tandem skydives. Just two weeks prior to Kerry's request, a tandem pair in Waynesville, Ohio, nearing the end of the free-fall, deployed their parachute. During the opening sequence, the freefall photographer who accompanied them managed to get above and in front of the tandem pair. When the parachute opened, it surged forward and the videographer, still in a 120 mile per hour free-fall, went through the top of the deploying chute. The collision killed the tandem instructor and seriously damaged the parachute. The passenger, injured and unable to steer the parachute, hung helplessly in front of the limp body of the tandem instructor while the parachute spiraled a half-mile from the airport and crash-landed the pair in a farmer's field. The videographer, who suffered a broken pelvis, was able to land his parachute, but he is living through the tragedy of having killed a good friend doing a sport he loves. Unquestionably, a tandem skydive carries a substantial element of risk.

I have done high-risk activities my entire life, but taking my daughter on this skydive had an emotional component I hadn't felt before. The potential for personal loss was far greater than I had ever experienced. The look in my wife's eyes told me that if anything happened to Kerry, I would also lose my partner of twenty-three years. I would lose the ability to enjoy a sport that's given me meaning for almost two decades. If my daughter were killed or badly injured with me, I was certain that the depths of my own grief would interfere with my job. Despite the fact that it was her decision, it was my lifestyle that

had clearly led her to this decision. If in extremis leaders exhibit genuine caring and concern for the people who follow them and if that
caring and concern create anxiety in them, then I was experiencing
the purest form of that emotion.

Finding Comfort in Action: Onward to the Limits of Competence

I made arrangements for the jump about four days later, and as the
jump drew near, I became increasingly anxious. I desperately continued my strategy to overcome the emotions I was feeling by being
logical. During the drive to the drop zone, I concentrated on the need
to commit myself to this skydive fully and assume all of the responsibility for it that I possibly could. I would make the weather decision.
I would inspect the gear. I would hand-pick the tandem instructor and
watch his every move on the ground, in the aircraft, and during every
inch of the free-fall. Parachute systems have an automatic activation
device on them that will deploy the reserve parachute if the jumper
passes through 750 feet at free-fall speeds. I convinced myself that
I needed to disconnect my device so that if there were any issues
with my daughter's skydive, I could literally follow her into the ground
without my own reserve activating if I were unsuccessful at fixing the
problem.

Underneath this plan to overcome risk with competence, I became deeply concerned that I might not be useful at all on the skydive. I assumed that my anxiety would continue to build, moment by
moment, and would reach a crescendo during the jump. Would I
become panicky? Using a sports psychology technique I usually
reserved for competition, I tried to visualize the action before it
occurred to see the finish of the jump, with Kerry landing relatively
softly under the canopy. I visualized myself feeling unbridled relief and
elation to see her safe and sound on the ground. As it turned out, that
vision was not to materialize. I was completely wrong on all counts.

Kerry and I pulled my gear out of the back of our car and walked
to the staging area for experienced parachutists. As I began to
compose, inspect, and organize my own gear, my anxiety started

to weaken, and the undue concern that I had for her began to fade. I thought perhaps it was the familiarity of setting up my rig or the inevitability of our upcoming jump. But for whatever reason, instead of the anxiety continuing to build during execution, it started to ease, almost imperceptibly at first and then faster and faster. Walking to the student area, I found the tandem master I had arranged to be there, as well as the two free-fall photographers who would record the event for Kerry. I had engaged one of the world's finest free-fall cameramen to film this jump, a Russian named Igor Shpino, as well as an old friend and military free-fall instructor named Mike Lanfor. Whatever was to occur, I was confident it would be digitally captured for posterity.

As Kerry was placed in her harness by the tandem master who would be her instructor for the jump, a Hungarian expatriate improbably nicknamed Danish, I carefully but discreetly inspected each stitch on the webbing and the condition of the hardware that would attach her to Danish. I strapped on my gear, and as I tightened each part of my own harness, it seemed to fit like an old, comfortable shoe. The anxiety over risk and performance continued to diminish. It was as if familiar sensations of control and mastery were filling my body with every tug on the adjusting straps of my harness.

As we strode to the idling aircraft we all—even Kerry—wore confident, comfortable smiles. I glanced over at Kerry and saw her smile at the photographers who were trying to capture her emotions as she climbed into the plane she would never land. I climbed into the jump plane first. It was a clean Swiss utility aircraft called a Pilatus Porter, small but capable of climbing rapidly with its turbocharged engine and short-field takeoff design. As nine jumpers loaded the aircraft (me, Kerry and her instructor, two photographers, and four fun jumpers), it was "game on"—a total focus on the events of the moment. My anxiety and negative feelings that characterized the preparation had been replaced by a sense of active vigilance, an outward orientation on the context, and this incredible environment that was beautiful but could turn hostile and deadly in a flash. This outward focus was familiar to me: I knew it would hang around like an old friend, keeping me focused and ready to react.

We rolled down the runway, and as the aircraft rotated off the ground, the senior instructor onboard shouted "Shawanga," the name of a local Native American princess who had leaped from a cliff with her lover, and the other experienced skydivers shouted back in unison, "Fly, baby, fly!" Kerry's eyes widened like saucers. As we climbed to altitude, I went through my own mental checklist of things that I could do to add safety to her jump. I pointed out the clouds as we passed through them at seven thousand feet—just two thousand feet above her five-thousand-foot opening altitude. I visually inspected her harness for the second time. I gave each of the photographers a nod and a smile. While Kerry was looking away, I pointed to Danish and mouthed the words, "Take care of her." He grinned and nodded.

At thirteen thousand feet, I quickly rechecked my own equipment and then focused on reading Kerry's expressions. She was still grinning widely. I stared out the window, searching for air traffic (particularly to the rear and beneath the aircraft where the pilot couldn't see). I was focused outward, scanning for unanticipated danger in the in extremis context. At 13,500 feet, one of the jumpers slid the door open, and I felt the familiar, chilly blast of air forty degrees cooler than ground temperature. One of my parachuting mentors refers to the cold blast as "the breath of dead skydivers as they whisper to us, 'Be careful.'" Kerry was still smiling and confident.

As the fun jumpers left, first the single and then a pair and then another single, I sensed that the sight of them falling away from the aircraft caused her to experience some uncertainty. My own confidence continued to build unabated, and as the photographers climbed outside the aircraft (clinging only to the door frame) and Danish slid Kerry into the open door, we were all ready to go.

Nothing Left to Do: Exit, Exit, Exit!

As Kerry and Danish tipped into free-fall, all my anxiety vanished, and I was out the door a half-second behind them, scanning their equipment for potential problems or irregularities. Two or three seconds out of the aircraft, Danish deployed a fifty-four-inch drogue parachute on a fifteen-foot bridle to slow the heavy tandem pair. Meanwhile, their speed and the separation of our exit caused the distance between us to grow uncomfortably far—more than fifty meters. I tucked my arms to my side and stood on my head. A tiny computerized altimeter in my helmet would later reveal that I dove at more than 150 miles an hour to close the gap between myself and my daughter, yet it seemed to take an eternity to catch the tandem pair, now rocketing toward the ground at more than 120 miles per hour.

I spread my arms and legs wide to arrest my high closing speed and eased up to the pair for a dock. Gently I gripped my daughter's wrist. She still had a smile on her face, although the wind was pressing her cheeks up in to an exaggerated grin, much like Batman's archnemesis, the Joker. I cocked one leg at the knee, wheeled inward using the grip as the turning axis, and kissed her on the cheek. At that point, we were passing below the seven-thousand-foot clouds that I had noted earlier during ascent, so I backed off to let Danish do his job. The critical event, the opening sequence, was about to occur.

As he pulled his rip cord, I stayed nearby until the parachute itself lifted off his back in its black deployment bag. At that point, the ability for another free-faller to assist the pair had passed. Now the carefully maintained equipment had to do its job. I flipped over onto my back and watched the parachute billow, suck air, inflate, and then form a perfectly rectangular design. Kerry and Danish appeared to spring skyward as they stopped relative to the rest of us still in free-fall. I flipped over onto my belly, located the two photographers to ensure we had adequate separation for opening, and activated my main parachute. Immediately after I was jerked to a halt, my familiar black and gold canopy blocked my view above. I grabbed one of the steering toggles and pulled down hard, starting a radical diving turn that would allow me to see the horizon (and the tandem pair) above me, over the tail of my own diving parachute. Snap-turning my head like a figure skater in the centrifugal spin, I could see Danish and Kerry lazily beginning to make their way to the open field of the airport.

I swooped out of the turn somewhat dizzy and panting because of the force of gravity on my body and gathered my thoughts. My emotions were completely counter to my intuition about how I thought I would react after seeing her in the relative safety of an open parachute. No joy. No relief. I found it impossible to experience any powerful emotions at all. The job wasn't done. I knew that I needed to get to the ground and prepare for Kerry's landing because I wanted to be there for her.

I reached up and grabbed the strap that ran to the right front lines of my parachute, pulled it almost to my waist, and started my parachute on a long, carving dive toward the drop zone. I set up my landing between the two photographers, right where I knew Danish would land with Kerry. I immediately took off my parachute harness, dropped my gear, and monitored the pair on their final approach. At thirty feet, Kerry lifted her legs in an L-shaped position just as she was trained, so her instructor's legs would take the first impact. Danish expertly flared the huge parachute to flatten the glide, and they skidded to a gentle landing on their bottoms on the grass by the target, no more than twenty feet away. Kerry was safe.

I waited impatiently for the rush of relief, for the outpouring of emotion from seeing my youngest daughter safe after being outside an airplane and off the ground for almost five minutes. It simply didn't come. I had scrutinized every element in the skydive from start to finish. Everything fit, was well managed and well planned, and well executed. I love my daughter dearly. How desperately I wanted to feel joy and relief! Those emotions just seemed hopelessly out of reach. Nonetheless, I walked briskly to her, helped her to her feet, and hugged her tightly. It felt good to have her in my arms and to know that she could better understand the appeal of free-fall that had taken me out of the house so many sunny days before.

As a research psychologist, I am used to interpreting data in order to understand human behavior. As a father and a skydiver, I have also learned that a single powerful experience can be worth a thousand data points. And in the process, on a cool August morning high above upstate New York, my daughter and I learned about the dynamics of emotion in in extremis leaders, together.

In the days following this jump, I analyzed why my feelings were so flat, why I was so emotionless both during and after Kerry's jump. And I found the answer in the work I had been doing for this book.

Why In Extremis Settings Flatten Emotions

One of my principal research findings was that in in extremis settings, the danger from the environment focuses the leader's attention outward. This phenomenon presents itself anecdotally time and time again. For example, soldiers who are wounded don't realize it until after the shooting has stopped. High-threat events create temporal distortion: the mind literally focuses so intensely on the threat that the perception of slow motion occurs; for example, when a car crashes, seconds can pass that seem like minutes. At these levels of outward orientation, emotions are difficult, if not impossible, to experience. The experience of emotion requires inward focus, a recognition of the self, and how one feels. Emotion involves reading one's own heart rate, respiration, and other physiological and psychological reactions to surrounding events.

In contrast to this inward focus, dangerous settings demand attention to the world around us, not to the world within us, and in extremis leaders become practiced at this outward focus—a learning orientation, a survival orientation. This certainly brings our puzzled fascination with the remarkable self sacrifices of some in extremis leaders (and followers) into sharper focus. They are willing to risk, or even sacrifice, themselves in moments of extreme danger, because for them, *the self ceases to exist*. It's sacrificed to the outward focus demanded by learning and trying to survive in in extremis environs. And that makes the experience of emotions, especially anxiety and fear, almost impossible.

Of course, training and acquired competence help too. In a classic study from the 1970s on the psychology of fear, skydivers were rigged with devices to monitor their heart rate, respiration, and skin conductivity to measure their physiological excitement and anxiety in the ascent to altitude and prior to the jump. For student parachutists, physiological markers continued to rise and peaked immediately prior to the jump. In contrast, however, among experienced parachutists, the same measure increased slightly, but after the aircraft ascended to above a thousand feet, the elevated physiological measures began to diminish. Interestingly, the researchers attributed this effect to the fact that skydivers can exit the aircraft after a thousand feet and have enough time to open their parachutes and survive. For these confident, experienced jumpers, the initial climb to altitude was perceived to be the most dangerous part of the skydive. Personally, I am much more anxious in commercial aircraft than I am in jump aircraft, particularly when landing, because I have many fewer landings than takeoffs.

In extremis orientation offers a different explanation for the phenomenon. The alternative explanation is that experienced jumpers are practiced at focusing outward, toward the in extremis environment. Because they are increasingly focused outward and not paying attention to the physiological cues that their bodies are providing, they become progressively less anxious as they get closer to exit, or to other predictable, threatening events. Similarly, deconstructing my own example about anxiety in (supposedly safe) commercial aircraft, my ability to focus outward has no meaning in such circumstances, because I am neither piloting nor capable of jumping out of the commercial plane. Therefore, despite rational statistical evidence to the contrary, well-maintained commercial aircraft make me more nervous than the airborne jalopies often found at drop zones. Having options is important to in extremis leaders.

Controlling Emotions: A Bad Strategy for High-Risk Leaders

Interestingly, then, as the danger inherent in the environment increases, the self-focus of experienced in extremis leaders decreases, along with their experience of emotion. What a gift to humanity.

And what an incredible life skill: rather than working to overcome emotions as they present themselves, these leaders simply fail to experience them.

★ Why This Is Important for All Leaders

Transfer this pattern to high-risk, elite businesses or to other non-life-threatening settings. People can be taught to sharpen their focus and skills, to turn outward and make sense of the environment in periods of high risk, rather than getting emotional, dysfunctionally excited, and self-absorbed. High-risk businesses have a tremendous need to develop and demand leaders who focus well enough to become progressively calm in the face of adversity.

This is not to argue that leaders must learn to control their emotions. In fact, attempting to control emotions may in some instances cause the leader to focus inward on the emotions themselves rather than continuing to address the threat. And emotions that are recognized are very hard to control and even harder to hide from followers. Emotions must be experienced as they come. It's important for leaders to understand, however, that when they feel emotions during high-risk circumstances, the reason they feel these emotions is that they have insufficient external focus. That means it's time to reconnect with the environment and deal with the threat. The phenomenon is even recognized intuitively by some in extremis professionals. My tandem mentor and friend Utah Steve Webb refers to this moment as "putting on the cowboy hat."

Leading Without Ego

The outward orientation and self-abrogation of in extremis leaders also establishes an ethical character that is critical to leadership in all walks of life. It makes sense in our culture that captains should go down with their ships, mountain guides should give their last bottle of oxygen to a client, and lieutenants should lead from the front in combat. Yet in less threatening environments, we've somehow come to tolerate, perhaps even expect, greater ego investment and selfishness from leaders. For example, when Carly Fiorina stepped down as CEO of Hewlett-Packard, she received a $42 million severance package (although information concerning the severance packages of the nearly fifteen thousand people terminated during her tenure is not readily available). And if you put "six-thousand-dollar shower curtain" into a search engine on the Web, you will uncover the story of Dennis Kozlowski, former chairman of Tyco, and his $62 million severance package.

As senior management tied perquisites to positions, the image of a leader became linked to self-indulgent levels of pampering and reward, an irony given the inescapable professional demands of most executive positions. Fueling the stereotype that leadership is all about personal success and personal rewards, the past decade has represented a painful tutorial in holding some members of the corporate elite accountable for unethical and illegal actions that hurt their organizations and advantaged themselves. The best among ordinary leaders still cultivate their own humility, still place their organizations before their own needs and comforts, still engender tremendous trust and loyalty by being loyal to followers. As the following story reveals, some captains do go down with their ships in the face of disaster that would make others cut and run.

The relationship between a leader's personal risk and ability to inspire confidence is powerful, but it cuts both ways in a dynamic business environment. One of the best examples of this comes in the tale of the rebuilding and repeated bankruptcy of Malden Mills.

How One Leader Valued the Needs of His Employees More Than Company Profits

Malden Mills was a family-owned business in Lawrence, Massachusetts, that produced Polartec and other fabrics. The story of its struggle for success reveals how CEO Aaron Feuerstein was torn by his perceived moral obligation to his employees and family legacy, but at the same time forced to balance his personal risk against volatile, uncertain, and complex financial challenges.[4]

The Malden Mills textile facilities in Lawrence burned to the ground on December 11, 1995, injuring thirty-one workers. Feuerstein rapidly made the decision to rebuild the plant, and in a matter of months he had pledged three consecutive thirty days of wages, a total of ninety days, to the plant's out-of-work employees. He made a number of decisions in support of his workers and the local community that garnered significant trust and loyalty from them during this crisis.

In an interview at the time, Feuerstein said that CEOs "bear three responsibilities: to their shareholders, for whom they must be profitable; to workers; and to the community in which they do business. . . . The shareholder, worker, and community must each be weighted in the hard decision a CEO makes, a task that takes wisdom and intelligence."[5] Feuerstein garnered considerable loyalty and attention with this stance, and he believed "we're going to win because of this," recognizing that synergies were developing among bankers, suppliers, loyal customers, and others who were paying attention to his commitment and downward loyalty to his employees. He was leading through the crisis in an ethical and morally superior fashion.

All was not well, however, in terms of the leadership and management of Malden Mills. Aaron Feuerstein's family and other stakeholders were clamoring for him to be replaced and angered over his decisions, which they viewed as excessively risky to stakeholders. The realities of debts-to-assets were being set aside in order to maintain purposeful commitment to the workers.

There was also a point where Feuerstein's willingness to share risk with his workers ceased. In 1997, BankBoston wanted to fund and rebuild a fabric brand produced by Malden Mills. In the process of negotiations, the bank insisted that Feuerstein pledge his personal assets, including his own stock in the company, to collateralize the loan. Feuerstein objected, refused to accept that level of shared risk, and eventually closed a division of the mills that he had pledged to keep open. In the end, Feuerstein rebuilt a plant that was first class and paid his employees while no cash flow was coming in, greatly exceeding what his insurance coverage would cover, but he also had to file for bankruptcy under Chapter 11.

★ Why This Is Important for All Leaders

To understand more fully the value and limitations of leadership lessons from in extremis contexts, it may be helpful to analyze the basic relationships in extreme high risk as compared to business. In the case of truly danger- ous circumstances, the dynamic is largely between leader and followers, and the threat of death borne by both sets the moral and ethical agenda on the mountainside or in combat. No one else is involved; even in the case of sponsors, the threat of death washes away the transac- tional obligation. Business is inherently more complex in that it always adds a third entity to the equation: a client or stockholder. Balancing the needs of this third entity pushes leaders to decisions that are suboptimal for some, satisfying for others.

How Leaders Should Handle and Overcome Fear

Brian Germain, a psychologist, adventurer, and in extremis leader, once wrote this about fear: "Defending peace is easier than creating peace."[6] What he meant was that it's easier to continue to stay relaxed than it is to bring fear or other emotions under control once they have begun to influence the ability to perform. Once adrena- line is flowing, heart rate and breathing have skyrocketed, and ten- sion sets in, there is momentum to the mood. Left unchecked, the mood is usually interpreted as either anger (fight) or fear (flight). The phenomenon is freshman-level psychology.

But in organizations, the same holds true. Fear is contagious, and it is enhanced by the commonly understood tendency for rumors to proliferate and grow. The in extremis interpretation of that idea is that it's easier to remain in an outward orientation through relaxation and focus than it is to shake the self-absorption and fear once emotions have taken over and one's focus is inward. It's about maintaining. Outward orientation is incompatible with the self-preserving psychobiology that fuels fear and panic—the ultimate collapse into the self.

Current therapists, as well as early classical psychologists like William James, understand that if you can establish certain conditions in the individual, such as relaxation, these conditions are incompatible with fear. The majority of behavioral therapies to cure anxiety and fear are based on progressive relaxation. When the effects of fear make themselves known in a way that's distracting, one word should enter the consciousness of in extremis leaders and followers: *breathe.* Of all the autonomic responses to an adrenaline rush—including heart rate, respiration, skin conductivity, and muscle tension—the one that we can best control consciously is respiration. Deep, controlled breathing is largely incompatible with the other elements of the fear response. Physical relaxation can get you to the point where mental relaxation, and therefore outward focus, can be reestablished and maintained.

Take a full, deep breath, bring the air under pressure in your lungs, and exhale slowly with the air still under pressure. In yoga, such breathing, called *ujaia,* assists both the mental and physical states by increasing oxygen absorption into the blood. Make this a habit when you experience fear or anxiety or when you're under moderate stress. You'll be well on the way to in extremis leadership when you begin to do it automatically, no matter how significant the threat. Fear is incompatible with functioning. Slow respiration and relaxation are incompatible with fear. Breathe.

We all know it's important to stay calm in an emergency; here's an example of how effective it is for the leader to stay cool and guide his followers to safety.

How Staying Calm and Relaxed Can Help You Survive a Life-Threatening Situation

I recently witnessed the crash of a small aircraft just off the end of the runway at the municipal airport in Lake Wales, Florida. It was fully laden with skydivers and was piloted by Jim West, an extraordinary in extremis leader with almost fifty years of experience including tens of thousands of hours flying jumpers and thousands of skydives himself. The Cessna 206 had just rotated into flight, but at four hundred feet off the end of the runway, when it was too low for the skydivers to survive an emergency exit, the engine abruptly quit. There was a deafening, sickening silence. It was every skydiver's nightmare: a failed aircraft too high to survive if it crashed but too low to allow parachutes to open.

It was a moment of truth for the jumpers in the plane. Would they sit tight in the heavily loaded aluminum shell, hoping to survive what lay ahead? Would they try a panicked escape regardless of the circumstances, destabilizing the plane by scrambling out and hoping for a quick opening?

The skydivers stayed with the aircraft and walked away from a crash landing. Returning to the drop zone, they told an incredible story of how their in extremis leader instantaneously maintained relaxation and control of their group. At the moment the engine seized, Jim turned around in his seat, smiled at the jumpers from behind his sunglasses, and said in his classic Ohio drawl, "You'll want to keep your eyes open, boys, 'cause this is going to be a good one." At that instant, the jumpers focused on the correct procedure—staying put—and were pulled out of their self-focus (that is, their inward focus) by Jim's confidence and the dry humor he injected into the life-or-death situation. It was authentic and instantaneous transformational leadership, focused on the way ahead, and delivered with comedic poise.

Although the aircraft was a total loss because of the crash landing, Jim brought himself and everyone else back alive. He told me it was his seventh airplane crash, a shocking statistic to most of us, but this barnstorming aviator has been around hard-working, crop-dusting, often experimental aircraft his whole life. To survive seven crash landings is not an indictment of competence but a testimony to a steady hand and the ability to wring the last measure of control out of an airplane with a dead stick.

★ Why This Is Important for All Leaders

The lesson is clear: leaders have to maintain relaxation and stability among followers, especially, and immediately, in the presence of threat. Most of us tend to view Jim West's ability and foresight as amazing. He was able to do what he did because when the crisis occurred, he focused on his people and the need to fly the aircraft instead of his own fear. With an outward orientation, there is no fear.

In many organizations, however, some people act as if the display of tension and intensity is a badge of competence or commitment. Think of the most recent crisis in your organization. Chances are that vacations were cancelled, golf games rescheduled, and taking lunch may have seemed like a reckless form of self-indulgence. Humor was abandoned, seen as out of place and inappropriate. Any form of relaxation or lack of business focus seemed to create the impression that an individual was not committed, engaged, or fully aware of the gravity of the crisis. Tension may have been seen as the most appropriate state.

From the in extremis perspective, relaxation is not selfishness; it's the opposite: indicative of an outward focus on the organization and the environment. Leader control is lost when people begin to display the unmistakable indicators of self-focus: weakening the group through posturing, finger-pointing, and the abrogation of personal responsibility. From the in extremis perspective, that's not the way to handle a crisis. It's a part of the crisis you're handling. Jim West was committed by unforeseen circumstances, and he survived in part because he focused on his people rather than inside his self, where fear and uncertainty may have lurked.

The Perils of Blame: Finger-Pointing Is Not Effective Leadership

Anger and finger-pointing when things go wrong can undercut all leaders, particularly those in in extremis circumstances. In fact, General Pete Schoomaker, the Army's chief of staff, used the term *in extremis* in a televised conversation with President Bush in the aftermath of the 2005 Hurricane Katrina disaster in New Orleans. As the gripping tragedy played out on national television to those of us only marginally affected by the hurricane, nearly 1.5 million people along the Gulf Coast were homeless, and many more were threatened by drowning, disease, and the crushing sense of dislocation and loss. It was time for government leaders to step up. And if greed is the undoing of many corporate leaders, the tendency to finger-point and assign blame during tragedy is the increasingly characteristic failing of government leaders, as illustrated in the following example.

How Not to Respond to Disaster: Pointing Fingers Just Delays Response and Recovery

New Orleans Mayor Ray Nagin blamed the Louisiana and federal governments for the inadequate response to both evacuating and caring for his citizenry during and after Hurricane Katrina. The flames of anger were fanned not just by reaction to the disaster and the grossly inadequate response to it, but by the city leader's suggestions that racism was at the root of the poor response. Not long after the hurricane, Nagin was quoted as saying, "If it's race, fine, let's call a spade a spade, a diamond a diamond. We can never let this happen again. Even if you hate black people and you are in a leadership position, this did not help anybody."[7]

It's unclear exactly to whom Nagin was referring, whether he was lashing out at the president of the United States or the governor of Louisiana, Kathleen Blanco (who in turn blamed city and federal governments for the response), or FEMA director Michael Brown (who gave congressional testimony characterizing both the state and local governments in Louisiana as dysfunctional). Regardless of exactly whom Nagin was blaming, he did it often and publicly. My own Web searches under "Nagin blames" have returned between two thousand and eighty thousand hits, depending on the search engine.

★ Why This Is Important for All Leaders

The real tragedy behind anger and finger-pointing by leaders in dangerous or disastrous circumstances is not that it erodes their power base (which it usually does) or that it reveals a lack of control by the leader (which it always does). The tragedy is that it undermines follower confidence and makes operations or recovery much more difficult.

It can harm followers' mental health as well. In 1996, a group of researchers led by University of Kansas professor Eric Vernberg studied the emotional reactions of children, third through fifth grade, to Hurricane Andrew. Their research approach was to quantitatively measure four coping strategies among the survivors: positive, blame and anger, wishful thinking, and social withdrawal. The results, published in the prestigious *Journal of Abnormal Psychology*, revealed that anger and blame were more strongly associated with posttraumatic stress disorder (PTSD) symptoms than other forms of coping.[8] Leaders who induce or enhance feelings of blame and anger among followers, then, may be directly responsible for increased incidence of PTSD and the attendant human and economic consequences.

In dangerous circumstances, anger, finger-pointing, and blame by a leader sends an unmistakable message to followers: "I am not responsible for your lives, I am not in control; circumstances are now in control of us." In typical day-to-day leadership, blaming and finger-pointing send exactly the same message. In contrast, the best strategy is to focus the frustration and anger on a better way ahead, as illustrated in the following situation.

Giving In to Frustration
Doesn't Solve the Problem at Hand

This lesson was driven home to me one wintry night in Germany during a large-scale military exercise, typical of U.S. Army training there in the late 1980s. My artillery battery, consisting of 110 men and forty armored vehicles, had just finished a rapid fifty-mile move north. The purpose of the move was to trick the opposing force into believing that a larger unit, habitually supported by my artillery, was positioned farther north than it actually was. The plan was for my unit to conduct this feint, but then, under cover of darkness, load our armored cannons and all our gear (except rifles and chemical protective gear) onto rapid-transit trucks and reposition back to the south. My soldiers and I would follow the cannons on buses arranged by our higher headquarters.

It was a great plan. At 1:00 A.M., the trucks showed up at a prearranged location, a German rest area along the autobahn. We loaded our armored vehicles and gear, the trucks left, and we waited for the buses to arrive. By 2:30, it was apparent that the plan was off track: the buses were more than an hour late, and because we were so far north and our main communications gear had left with the trucks, it was nearly impossible to communicate with higher headquarters. The situation was dangerous because the men had no protection from the deepening German cold: the temperature was ten degrees Fahrenheit and dropping rapidly. Our sleeping bags and heavy clothing were all on the trucks. I was worried about my men developing frostbite and livid with the higher headquarters staff that I felt was responsible for what I considered to be a debacle.

My first sergeant, a tough leader named Smith, asked me what I intended to do, and he immediately read my frustration and anger. I was ready to call the men together and tell them the truth: that our higher headquarters had screwed up and that this disastrous circumstance was somebody else's fault. It would have been a huge mistake as a leader, and my sergeant saved me: "Sir, no need to get the men angry too. You're mad enough for all of us. This cold is just another enemy. We fight."

He then issued the order to the men to go to full chemical protective gear: charcoal-impregnated overgarments, gas masks, rubber gloves, and boots. Soldiers hate chemical protective gear because it is uncomfortable and hot. Once suited up, he gave each of our three platoons a mission: one was to find firewood, one was to consolidate all the frozen food and water that soldiers had with them, and the third was to do light physical training. Imagine how strange this would have looked to a passing German at 3:00 A.M.: U.S. troops in chemical gear doing calisthenics and building fires at a rest stop.

But it got the job done: the men were busy, no one got frostbite, and eventually our headquarters straightened out the buses. Shortly after daybreak, we were on our way. At our destination, I gave my jeep driver money to go to a German bakery in the nearby town and buy enough hot, fresh-baked breakfast rolls and butter to give the soldiers a little extra treat with their morning Army chow—which, of course, turned up cold. And the first sergeant got two rolls for focusing on responding to the situation rather than just laying blame.

The Perils of Defeatism: Giving Up Is Not Good Leadership

Much like anger and blame, defeatist attitudes erode the capability of both the leader and the team. Recently at Duke University, a group of executives were engaging a panel that included mountain climber and consultant Alison Levine (introduced in Chapter Three). Part of Levine's leadership message is that personal responsibility is absolutely required of leaders in dangerous circumstances and that such willingness to accept responsibility is key even in safer business settings. Levine is a former Goldman Sachs employee and saw the same need there, expressing it as, "people have to be able to step up" when talking of climbing teams, and in the business context, "everyone at Goldman Sachs has to walk the walk and talk the talk." Levine is tenacious on this point—a tenacity perhaps born of clinging to the side of a mountain.

One African American seminar participant in the rear of the room, in response to what the panel was saying about leadership, argued that racist perceptions had to be fixed before a leader could lead in a diverse environment. Paraphrasing, the commenter said it didn't matter what culture one was from, because race is a limiter. "My family has been rich forever," he said, adding without humility that he was on the boards of several Fortune 500 companies. "It doesn't matter what your background is or where you are. Even at the White House, dressed in a suit, I've had people hand me their car keys and tell me to park their car. Here in Durham, when my kids shop, security follows them through the store."

Levine didn't miss a beat. She immediately shouted, "Take their car!" Peals of nervous laughter rang through the room, but her point was clear: good leaders don't ever absolve themselves of personal responsibility or personal control over their destiny; a defeatist attitude is really just abdication of responsibility and control. It's unleadership.

Later Levine commented on her frustration with people who can't get beyond the situation: "People say 'our company sucks, our business sucks, my home life sucks.' I tell them, 'No, it's 'cause you suck.'"

★ Why This Is Important for All Leaders

The lesson about attitude from dangerous circumstances is this: negativity is a luxury that can be indulged only in safe and secure places. In dangerous contexts, personal responsibility is in such profound demand that you can't use time or energy to complain about the environment that's trying to kill you. You simply have to fix it. And you can do that only by taking responsibility for your own self and your actions.

Final Thoughts: Consider How You Handle Emotion During In Extremis Situations

In *We Were Soldiers Once, and Young*, journalist Joe Galloway recalls transcending fear in the presence of a selfless and inspiring in extremis leader. Assuming the almost absurdly calm example set by a tough, battle-hardened sergeant, he was able to take photographs even as the American position was about to be overrun by North Vietnamese soldiers:

> The incoming fire was only a couple of feet off the ground and I was down as flat as I could get when I felt the toe of a combat boot in my ribs. I turned my head sideways and looked up. There, standing tall, was Sergeant Major Basil Plumley. Plumley leaned down and shouted over the noise of the guns: "You can't take no pictures lay-ing down there on the ground, sonny. " He was calm, fearless, and grinning. I thought: "He's right. We're all going to die anyway, so I might as well take mine standing up. " I got up and began taking a few photographs. Plumley moved over to the aid station, pulled out his .45 pistol, chambered a round, and informed Dr. Carrara and his medics: "Gentlemen, prepare to defend yourselves!"[9]

Leaders must avoid the temptation of encouraging followers to engage in destructive impression management or other forms of fak-ing, panic, or paralysis when things are going wrong. Instead, take a deep breath, focus outward, let the situation develop, and act on the environment. Behaving as if something is wrong leads follow-ers to feel that something is wrong. It simply makes it harder to deal with the problem at hand.

You and I are able to learn from the experiences described in this chapter: my experience skydiving with my teenage daughter, Jim West's adroit piloting of his stricken aircraft to a safe landing, and soldiers and photographers focusing outward to deal with the envi-ronment instead of their emotions. What these experiences revealed is that the lessons of leadership in dangerous contexts are somewhat counterintuitive yet useful. And whether your organization is recov-ering from a mill fire or you're keeping your followers from spinning out of control when your plan fails and you're all stranded on a cold highway in the middle of the night, remember that emotions are part of the leader's medium as much as clay is central to the potter's art. In extremis leaders learn that focus on emotions has a time and a place—but the time is after the crisis and the place is safe. Until then, the focus is outward.

In the next chapter, we look at situations where leader confidence was misplaced somewhat, where follower concern that leader behavior could influence their physical well-being or survival was warranted. We'll explore what happens when people actually die.

Summing Up

1. Learn how to handle your own fear so you can manage others' fears, too. Fear is mostly a chemical reaction to a situation: adrenaline is released in near-death situations. Regardless of what causes it, however, fear can be gripping and debilitating, and it abounds in dangerous settings. Leaders need to understand how fear works, how it influences subordinates, and how to live by focusing outward in in extremis conditions.

2. Recognize that extreme situations, properly handled, will often flatten the emotions you expect to have. I found this out when I went skydiving with my teenage daughter: I was anxious and fearful that my daughter would be harmed or even killed. I battled my fear with logic and preparation, making as sure as I could that nothing would go wrong with Kerry's equipment or the people accompanying her on her skydive. I thought my anxiety would increase as the time for Kerry to jump approached, but the opposite happened because I had been trained to focus outward during in extremis situations. Instead of being more anxious, I became more vigilant. And when she landed safely, I found that I was almost completely emotionless: I didn't feel relief because in extremis situations flatten emotions—a fact that all leaders need to understand.

3. Focus outward on the environment, not inward on your emotions. Dangerous settings demand attention to the world around us, not to the world within us, and in extremis leaders become practiced

at this outward focus. This is a learning orientation, a survival orientation. And it is why some in extremis leaders (and followers) are willing to risk, or even sacrifice, themselves in moments of extreme danger because for them, the self ceases to exist. It's sacrificed to the outward focus demanded by learning and trying to survive in in extremis environs. And that makes the experience of emotions, especially anxiety and fear, almost impossible.

4. Don't try to control your emotions. Attempting to control them may cause you to focus inward on the emotions themselves rather than continuing to address the threat. And once recognized, emotions are hard to control and even harder to hide from followers. You can learn to sharpen your focus and skills, to turn outward and make sense of the environment, in periods of high risk rather than getting emotional, dysfunctionally excited, and self-absorbed. High-risk businesses have a tremendous need to develop and demand leaders who focus well enough to become progressively calm in the face of adversity.

5. Lead without ego. Just as captains go down with their ships, great leaders should face the same adversity that their followers do. Unfortunately, sometimes that means the end of the organization you work for, as when Aaron Feuerstein, the CEO of textile manufacturer Malden Mills, finally had to file for bankruptcy because he stood by his employees after devastating plant fires and other setbacks crippled his business. In the end, however, leaders have no greater entitlement to security or comfort than the people they lead.

6. Stay calm, and breathe deeply in times of extreme adversity. This might sound like trivial advice, but it's not. Studies have proven that breathing and relaxation techniques help people deal with enormously difficult situations, as pilot Jim West did when he safely crash-landed his seventh plane and made sure everyone survived. If you can stay cool, you can do amazing things.

7. Don't lay blame or point fingers during the crisis. Instead, focus on dealing with recovering from the difficult dangerous situation at hand. After it's over and everyone is safe, then you can start analyzing what went wrong, who was responsible, and how to prevent such a situation from ever occurring again.

8. Don't let anger and frustration get in your way. Leaders get annoyed or even angry, but good leaders don't show it to their followers. That doesn't accomplish anything; instead, it increases the anxiety of everyone involved. Instead, focus on recovering from the situation, as my very sensible second-in-command reminded me when our battalion was stranded in Germany one night in freezing weather. He helped all of us get through that night safe and intact.

9. Don't give in to a defeatist attitude. Blaming others is the easy way out of a tough situation, but it's unleadership. Don't give in to it. Instead, good leaders do whatever is necessary to overcome the problem at hand—whether responding to racist treatment or dealing with a more dangerous situation.

5

Leading When Tragedy Strikes
Learning to Cope with Loss

I n extremis leadership holds a certain moral high ground because the consequences are recognized as potentially grave. In dangerous contexts, the best leaders know their jobs, commit to their followers, make themselves physically strong and resilient, and prepare themselves emotionally. In life's less dangerous undertakings, the same principles also hold true. Although this book focuses on in extremis leadership, fundamentally it's about helping all people live their lives with the benefit of exemplary leadership. Unfortunately, studying leadership in dangerous contexts means coming to grips with the fact that some leaders, and many who are led, will not live out their lives. All leaders need to learn to respond to death and continue to lead in the face of the most tragic circumstances. The personal nature of such circumstances makes death both a responsibility and an opportunity for serious practitioners of the leadership art.

Do you consider your organization safe and unlikely to experience the death of a member? If so, when death or a serious injury occurs, your people will be especially unprepared. Have the vision to see that as long as there are hearts beating, some will unexpectedly stop. The post-9/11 world has its own particular dangers: corporate kidnappings, always a terrorist tool, continue to be an unanticipated, profound challenge for leaders. There are a few lessons that are well developed among in extremis leaders and work well regardless of the risk threshold in any organization.

Being able to respond to death is a life skill that clearly is not limited to in extremis leadership. People who lead in dangerous contexts, however, can teach us much about the subject, because they have more experience with it. For example, in my role as a career Army officer, I have officially represented the Army in uniform at more than forty burials, crematorium interments, funeral services, and visitations. I've had the enormously difficult task of informing someone that his or her loved one had been killed. And perhaps most important of all, I've been in direct leadership roles when people have died unexpectedly and the organization had to receive the news, mourn, recognize the fallen, and move on. And the responsibility ultimately was mine.

Such experience is also common in personal life. As we raise our children, we have to assist them when they lose friends to automobile accidents and diseases. All families have to deal with the loss of close relatives. Our community recently had to make sense of the death of a twenty-eight-year-old basketball coach to a heart arrhythmia less than a month after taking her team to the National Collegiate Athletic Association (NCAA tournament). My family recently mourned the loss of a long-time friend, a mother and Army wife, to a fast-growing cancer that struck her down two months after diagnosis.

In dangerous contexts, death always walks with both the leader and the led. A classic skydiving T-shirt shows a jumper falling in a forty-five-degree, head-down position, arms swept back, legs extended, with the Grim Reaper standing on his back. The caption reads, "Surf's Up!" Experienced jumpers often watch someone narrowly escape catastrophe, or find an equipment fault on the ground, turn to each other with a smile, and say, "Surf's Up!"—eliciting puzzled looks from novices and nonjumpers. In other contexts—academic, business, public service—the Reaper seems more distant, aloof. But inevitably organizations are touched by the death of one or more of its members.

Death is a critical time for leaders, who have a brief window to influence the organization for the good—or lose the chance forever. This chapter retraces the paths of leaders through tragic circumstances involving death and reviews some practical guidelines for how to react in such circumstances. The paths explored are not as dark as you might expect, because handling death is more about celebrating life and taking care of the living than it is about the death itself. Good leaders celebrate life and take care of the living.

Learning the Lesson That Bad Things Happen: Focus Outward, It's Time to Lead the Living

My first story about death involves celebration from the start. I was celebrating Halloween 1998 with my family in Seoul, Korea. I was visiting our home in the city, a twice-monthly indulgence granted me by my second-in-command, Frank Villanueva, who covered for me in the battalion area while I was away. My wife, Kay, and our daughters were living in a small apartment on an urban military reservation called Yongsan, and I had made the nearly two-hour trek from my command, an artillery battalion situated within shelling range of the Demilitarized Zone. The kids had finished trick-or-treating and were counting their candy—the entire process an alien activity to the Koreans but embraced by them with good humor nonetheless. My wife and I had just cracked open a bottle of Shiraz when the phone rang, beginning a series of events that would change my view of leadership forever.

The first report was ambiguous but disturbing: one of our twelve forward-observer teams was working with an infantry battalion on a mission overlooking the border, and as they withdrew to the south, they somehow drove into a river. They were in a tracked fire support team vehicle. I knew that the boxy fifteen-ton aluminum armored hull was capable of floating and fording waterways, an inconsistently reliable feature that seemed to sometimes cause more problems than it solved. Yet the duty officer who called me said that there might be a fatality—every commander's nightmare. To lose a soldier to a noncombat cause is perhaps the most difficult, tragic circumstance that a leader has to face. I passed the report to my boss to keep the information flowing up the command chain, pulled on my boots, kissed everyone good-bye, and headed north.

As I passed the northern outskirts of Seoul, my cell phone rang. It was Frank. The situation was starting to unfold with unforgiving clarity. The heavy tracked vehicle went out of control on a four-lane bridge over a river and crashed through the concrete and steel side barrier, flipping end over end, sixty feet, into twenty feet of cold, rushing water. Two bodies had been recovered.

I was stunned. These men were from the Steel Battalion, well trained, completely focused. Stuff like this didn't happen to us. I called Colonel Jim Church, my commander, who arranged for a helicopter to rush us to the site. While I was finalizing the plan, another call rang in: three dead for sure and at least two survivors. I couldn't sort out whether I could feel good about the survivors, because almost nothing could seem positive in the face of three deaths in the battalion. Then the phone rang again: five dead, two survivors.

As the helicopter flared to land near the bridge, I could see searchlights, medical evacuation helicopters, ambulances, soldiers moving about, and a few Koreans from a nearby village who were willing to leave their beds at 2:00 A.M. to witness the activity. As I walked across the bridge to the gaping hole in the concrete wall, I saw a camouflaged entourage of staff officers walking to the same place. Centered in the throng was the Second Infantry Division commander, Major General Bob Dees. He was responsible for more than seventeen thousand soldiers, five of whom had drawn their last breath. I saluted, and we exchanged the greeting of the division:

"Second to none, Sir." After rendering a report with the information I had, I looked him in the eye, took a deep breath, and sighed. An accident of this magnitude would be on CNN in an hour, and five families would soon open their doors on Halloween eve, candy in hand, to find a casualty notification officer and an Army chaplain on their step. It was unquestionably the lowest point in my life thus far.

General Dees looked back at me and without hesitation said, "You know, Tom, it's not whether bad things happen that makes or breaks a commander. It's what he does with the hand he's dealt that really matters." His message was characteristic of a leader who had lost people in the past, and knew that more would be lost in the future. Leading is about respecting the dead and helping the organization grieve, not about how the leader feels. Death announces to good leaders that it's time to lead the living. Bob Dees is an in extremis leader.

Leading Around Death Is Symbolic: Demonstrate Respect

A leader, especially one in a dangerous or high-risk enterprise where trust is important, has to demonstrate to the members of the organization that he or she respects them and holds their well-being in high regard. People watch leaders in the presence of the dead very carefully, because the dead are the most vulnerable members of any organization: they can't defend themselves, and they project the innocence of the human soul. They no longer have the ability to contribute, so there is no transactional purpose associated with their treatment. Therefore, how the leader treats them and the surviving members carries important transformational messages that can't be driven home in other contexts. You reach every member of your organization by the way you treat your dead.

Handling the Death Event

It is important to look at how leaders demonstrate respect for their followers and peers, so let's look at some specific ways to prepare for a death event, respond to tragedy, and recognize the dead so that the living can move on. As we work through these principles and examples, put yourself in the shoes of the leader. Assume that the tragedy has struck your organization and that you need to respond. Visualize yourself in these circumstances, and your ability to lead will grow. The first principle is that you can't lead if you're in the dark about your people's life events.

Tell People in Your Organization What You Need to Know

The first step in ensuring that you can lead your organization through tragedy is ensuring that you hear about it. Events surrounding a death or hospitalization move rapidly. Imagine returning to your office after a four-day weekend and asking your secretary, "Where is everyone?" She answers, "At the funeral." You have to make clear what you require as information and how fast you need it. In the military, such knowledge is labeled the commander's critical information requirements. Typically leaders need to be told immediately whenever any of the following occurs:

- Death or hospitalization of an organization member or immediate family member

- A life-threatening, lost-time accident occurring within the organization

- Major theft or felony crime committed in the organization

- Significant threat to the organization's core mission

- Legal action or credible exposure to legal action, such as damages caused by an employee in the conduct of duties

- Organizational exposure in the media, such as a positive or negative newspaper story mentioning the organization, or a visit to the organization by a journalist

Perhaps you are responding incredulously to this, as in, "Surely you don't mean the CEO of a thirty-thousand-person organization has to know these things immediately?" Well, yes, that's exactly what I mean. It's a common practice in organizations where people risk their lives, but it should be more broadly applied. In some organizations, it is thought to be good enough for direct-level leaders to know critical information about people and then decide for themselves what the pinnacle leader does or does not need to know. That approach does not work because the information will never get to the senior leader. Every general I know in charge of Army divisions—some more than twenty thousand strong—had the critical information requirements listed above brought to their personal attention within twenty-four hours—and not just in wartime. This personal information flow connected them with their organizations in several key ways.

First, it reminds the senior leader that he or she is in charge of human beings, a point that can be lost in the dizzying array of managerial responsibilities that leaders of medium-large organizations (those with fewer than thirty thousand people) must execute. Second, it drives the right behaviors by subordinate leaders. If they know that the boss knows that the Smith family lost a child in an auto accident, they may be more likely to execute the appropriate direct-level leader responsibilities with respect to followers in need. If the boss knows, everyone knows. That is a healthy organizational dynamic when it comes to responding to personal tragedies. Finally, there are times when decisions that influence the organization have to be made from the top. Not all the information reported as serious or critical requires that senior leadership take action, but it should be the senior leadership that makes that decision.

Serious leaders should take a lesson from in extremis leaders and be very specific, and aggressively detailed, about being personally informed when tragedy or other critical incidents occur. It's easy for staff to put the information in an executive summary, rapidly readable in the morning, with follow-up as required. Don't be aloof. In extremis leaders can't afford it, and neither can good leaders in more representative enterprises.

Make Sure Nobody Gets Left Behind, Ever

The Army chief of staff, General Pete Schoomaker, presents "challenge" or "excellence" coins to many of the soldiers he encounters in his continuous travel throughout the force. I have one. It's oblong, the unmistakable racetrack shape of a soldier's identification tag, or dog tag (though much too heavy to be worn around the neck). Four simple first-person statements are listed on the back of the coin, taken from the Army's statement of the in extremis art—the Warrior Ethos:

> "I will always place the mission first."
>
> "I will never accept defeat."
>
> "I will never quit."
>
> "I will never leave a fallen comrade."

The Warrior Ethos is sacred to those in the profession of arms: soldiers really do live and die by these words. Amazingly, however, the ethos symbolizes how soldiers in assignments that do not expose them to increased risk should nevertheless apply in extremis principles to their own daily lives. Placing the mission first, never quitting, and never accepting defeat are key principles for any person in any role, particularly leaders. The last promise, "I will never leave a fallen comrade," is perhaps the most organizationally focused, unique element of the ethos. It sends an important message to peers and followers: you count, even in death.

What is the equivalent in organizations that are not warrior class? First, any death or hospitalization requires acknowledgment by the leader—ideally by a personal visit, but by phone or card if circumstances prevent the visit. By "any death or hospitalization," I mean exactly that: if it happens to anyone in the organization, it requires recognition by the CEO or designated representative. In an earlier chapter, I made the point that inspiration is achieved by exceeding people's expectations. There is no better time to exceed expectations than when an employee or follower is grieving and at perhaps the saddest point in their lives.

Whether a death or tragedy is acknowledged has little to do with where an individual works in the organization: the recognition and respect should be evident. There is no status hierarchy for fallen comrades, from the lowest wage-grade worker to professional peers. To attempt to delineate hierarchically whom the leader does or does not recognize when tragedy strikes is doomed to fail. It's organizational poison. In in extremis conditions, risk, however slim, is shared. Common lifestyle (and a basic understanding of morality) means that the janitor's wife's life is worth as much as that of a promising corporate vice president's. Tie your organization together top to bottom, and lead so that tragedy makes it stronger. Learn from the Warrior Ethos, and never leave a fallen comrade.

Take the Lead by Staying Humble

As leaders engage followers during tragedy, it is critically important that they remain humble and unassuming in all aspects of the process. It seems simple, but many of us are accustomed to being in charge and visible in most aspects of our organization's work. When others die or are badly injured, their honor and well-being have to remain the focus, and it's almost a zero-sum game. The leader has to be small so the focus of the activity can make the decedent or the hospitalized person big. I learned this lesson most poignantly during a funeral following an air disaster that claimed the lives of almost 250 soldiers. I watched the biggest man I knew become very small in the face of the family of a young soldier who had met his rendezvous with destiny.

How One Leader Handled Tragedy by Focusing on the Family and the Fallen, Not the Funeral

The crash of a chartered airliner in Gander, Newfoundland, in December 1985 represents the largest single-incident loss to a U.S. Army battalion in history. An airliner chartered by the Army had stopped at Gander for refueling. The flight was carrying 248 soldiers home to Fort Campbell, Kentucky, following six months in the Sinai on peace-keeping duty. It was one of three flights transporting soldiers back to their homes and families just prior to the Christmas holidays. After refueling in icy conditions, the DC-8 departed for Fort Campbell, the final leg of the flight. Shortly after the aircraft rotated off the end of the runway, it stalled and rolled violently to the right, crashing into heavily forested terrain. In a second, the aircraft disintegrated and the fuel tanks exploded, scattering bodies, body parts, and debris over the snow-covered Canadian forest. Subsequent fires burned for a day as the ongoing blizzard blanketed the smoldering crash site with snow and ice.

At Fort Campbell, the soldiers' families had already gone to the airfield to welcome their loved ones home. Word of the tragedy reached the unit's senior leadership at Fort Campbell about an hour after the plane went down. During the next several hours, staff officers worked feverishly to confirm the flight manifest, a document compiled in Egypt. Families were asked to assemble in the brigade gymnasium, where the brigade commander announced that while the report was still unconfirmed, the plane had apparently crashed, and there were no survivors. The Army death toll included one-third of the infantry peacekeeping battalion, plus some support personnel from other units. Approximately two-thirds of the dead were not married and therefore had family to notify across the United States. Thirty-six children were left fatherless.

The Gander disaster was a stunning blow to the 101st Airborne Division, an organization composed of some of the toughest in extremis leaders in the Army. Unlike other plane crashes in which the victims don't know one another and hail from different locations, these men had served together at Fort Campbell for several years. Among everyone in the Army, there was a close affinity and identification with the division's lost soldiers derived from shared occupation, values, lifestyle, and organizational commitment.

The Army leadership revealed corporate-level care and concern by quietly issuing an order that every funeral of every soldier would be attended by a general officer, regardless of the timing or location of the funeral. This move by the senior leadership set the tone for all of the recognition ceremonies to follow. The task sounds daunting, and it was—but this level of commitment is not merely for in extremis leaders; it is a way of committing everyone in any organization touched similarly by tragedy. Such times are not improved by efficiency, and senior leader presence is a must. In another example, following the collapse of the World Trade Center buildings on September 11, 2001, Howard Lutnick, chairman and CEO of Cantor Fitzgerald, went to twenty funerals every day for thirty-five days.

The Casualty Affairs Office in the Pentagon coordinated with the generals' offices to ensure appropriate coverage of Gander-related funerals. At the time, I was the aide to the chief of field artillery at Fort Sill, in southwest Oklahoma. My boss, a major general named Gene Korpal, was asked to attend the funeral of a young infantry sergeant who would be laid to rest outside his small town in the Texas Panhandle.

The general, his wife, Lil, and I flew out of Fort Sill and headed for Texas. It was extraordinarily rare for a general officer's spouse to be granted permission to fly on Army aircraft, another indication of the unique level of organizational commitment to the surviving families of the Gander crash. As we flew around the usual south Oklahoma thunderheads, everyone aboard had the Gander crash and its lesson of aircraft fallibility foremost in their minds. We landed uneventfully at a tiny municipal airport and were met by a van I had arranged with the burial detail: a group of eight soldiers and one officer from the 101st. This group had come to perform the funeral instead of the generic military honor guard ordinarily dispatched from a regional post. Great organizations bury their own dead.

The service for the soldier was held at a small, whitewashed country Baptist church on the outskirts of town. I recall the family as stoic and proud. The congregation and friends of the family spilled out of the church foyer, and the open doors let a dry Texas breeze move through the pews, the constant fanning of the attendees methodically suspended during prayer and the reading of scripture. Celebratory music resounded as the military pallbearers took the flag-draped coffin from the church and placed it respectfully in the hearse, beginning the eleven-mile journey on dusty, white gravel to the family cemetery.

The details of military funerals have become familiar to most of us: a grieving family in a row of chairs, the crisp dress uniforms of the burial detail, the firing of the rifle salute, a bugler playing taps, the folding of the American flag, and the gentle but official presentation of the flag to the next of kin. Military honors are an entitlement for soldiers killed in the line of duty and retired soldiers on their death. Fellow soldiers, however, are seldom seen at military funerals because they are usually still serving abroad. This made the presence of the soldiers from the 101st even more meaningful, and their duty was well received by the family and friends of the deceased. To put it bluntly, however, their performance at the funeral was well below par.

One of the soldiers bearing the casket stumbled and almost went down, an extremely rare occurrence in military funerals and one that can usually be avoided through rehearsal. As the detail folded the flag above the coffin, the usual tight creases buckled and the flag began to bulge in the middle. Some of the red and white was visible after the final fold. The sergeant at the head of the detail refused to take the colors, commanding, "Refold the flag." The second ceremonial fold turned out fine, but when the folded flag was passed over the coffin, along with an empty cartridge case from the rifle salute placed in the final fold, the shell casing dislodged and hit the top of the metal coffin with a clang. As the horrified soldiers froze, the two-inch brass casing rolled from the top of the coffin and proceeded to tumble through the space between the casket and the burial vault, hitting several times, all the way to the bottom.

I looked at my boss, seated with the family, and he was absolutely emotionless. This afternoon, I thought, was not going to be good for the burial detail from the 101st. My general's operating style was typical of an artilleryman who had spent a lifetime computing gunnery solutions to less than a tenth of a degree of direction and elevation: he had a penchant for detail and a well-developed lack of tolerance for error. I knew he was aware of every deficiency in the service, and for the people of this patriotic Texas town, there would be no "do-overs." This would be their image of the Army. I thought to myself, "Give him room. He's seething underneath."

General Korpal received the flag from the burial detail and knelt before the proud, grieving family: "This flag is presented on behalf of a grateful nation, in recognition of the honorable and faithful service rendered by your son." The family seemed unaware of, or maybe unconcerned about, the blemishes in the graveside service, and after some refreshments back at the church, we were on our way. Just before leaving, the general had me give challenge coins to each military member of the burial detail, a move that puzzled me. I was frankly waiting for a low-yield nuclear explosion that would mark the unvarnished assessment of how the service went. Lil Korpal wept quietly for a while on the way home, a reflection of her empathy and authenticity.

As we entered the office, I was met by the secretary, who looked at me and winced: "The chief of staff of the 101st Division is on the phone about the unsatisfactory funeral." The lieutenant in charge of the detail had apparently called back to the division headquarters in

Kentucky to accept responsibility for the performance of his detail. As I entered the general's office, he was removing his tie, and I explained that a colonel from the 101st was on the line to discuss the way the burial detail performed. He looked at me and said, "He doesn't need to talk to me. Tell him the lieutenant and his men did their job, and the family was pleased and grateful. The 101st just needs to bury their dead."

As I turned to leave, he looked up and said, "When soldiers honor soldiers, there is no such thing as a bad funeral."

★ Why This Is Important for All Leaders

My general got small, and by doing so, he kept the focus on constructive grieving for the 101st Airborne Division and the family of the dead soldier. Readers should do the same. It's a foreign concept to the world outside the military, and it may seem like a sacrifice for a well-known CEO or corporate leader to be so focused on the family that both their identity and standards appear set aside. But just the opposite is true: by letting go and getting small, people show how big they really are.

Once the basics are covered with respect to leader presence at services or in other symbolic ways that affect the family, it becomes time for the organization to begin healing and move on. It is a critical time: some grief can be shared at the same time that the family is grieving, but the leader has to look specifically at the needs of the organization. Sometimes the organization itself needs to grieve. Sometimes even if the organization does not need a mourning period, it's useful as a way of bonding, of creating social cohesion, for an organization to recognize its loss. The story in the next section shows how one organization did just that—and made itself stronger in the process.

Accept That Recognition Is a Required Part of Moving On

Recognizing the dead is a key step to moving on, and in dangerous settings, it's seldom possible to use a classic funeral to accomplish the recognition and grieving. In military settings, comrades are frequently deployed overseas and therefore are long distances from the graveside services of their dead peer. Traditions have developed to honor the dead with rituals without the presence of the deceased or their family. Such traditions are unique and mostly unfamiliar to the public.

Thus, in organizations where death seldom occurs, the same principle holds true—members may be buried at home afar, or the distributed nature of the organization may simply preclude a traditional gathering. In such circumstances, it is important for leaders to support some form of recognition. The example below may pique the creativity of organizational leaders who want to recognize a loss without getting into actual funerals or, in some cases, the physical presence of bereaved loved ones. With tailoring and taste, the same principles may be applied by leaders in most organizations.

Death Rituals: How the U.S. Army Respects the Deceased and Renews Its Organization

When the five soldiers in my battalion, an 850-member multinational organization, died in the bridge accident described earlier in the chapter, their bodies were quickly transported to the American Army hospital in Seoul and then on to the United States, each under the escort of a soldier who had known them. Subordinate commanders aligned the soldiers of the battalion in a formation on a large, paved area where our vehicles were parked. Rumors had already begun to move from soldier to soldier, but most had no idea of the magnitude of the disaster. I explained to the 850 men that they had lost five brothers—four were American, and one was a Korean soldier assigned to us. There was an audible groan—a rare but understandable breach of discipline by a battalion known for its superb bearing. As I announced the names of the deceased, there was no audible reaction, only the sound of the wind blowing the American flag and the regimental colors in front of the men. Following the formation, throughout the battalion area, the mood was palpably somber. Soldiers have a hard time understanding how fate visits death on some but not others.

It was apparent that a service was necessary and appropriate, and even before I spoke to the soldiers, a service was being planned jointly between our chaplain and our senior sergeant, Command Sergeant Major Charles Cabrera. The service, in classic combat arms tradition, had three consistent rituals: representations of the bodies, recognition of the deceased, and acceptance of death. These three aspects of in extremis death rituals can be found and expressed in different ways among police officers, skydivers, firefighters, climbers, and others, but the concrete examples in the Steel Battalion services clearly illustrate the three aspects of ritual.[1]

Representation of the Bodies of the Deceased

Because my soldiers' bodies had been immediately transported to their next of kin, the sergeant major supervised the construction of a representation using the equipment that was formerly in the dead soldiers' possession. A hollow wooden platform was built and painted in branch colors to match the soldiers' assigned military specialty. In this case, the color representing our field artillery unit was scarlet. Five slots were cut in the top of the platform, into which the soldiers' bayoneted rifles were inserted vertically. The soldiers' helmets, each with a camouflage band bearing the soldier's name, were set atop the rifle buttstocks. Each soldier's black combat boots, cleaned and shined, were set in front of the display. Finally, the soldiers' single identification tag (the dog tag) hung on the display, from the rifle stock or the shank of the boots. The single tag bore meaning: commonly carried around soldiers' necks in pairs, in this case the second tag was accompanying the remains in transit.

The elaborate display, created in the gymnasium that would be the site of the memorial service, was a ritual representation of the fallen soldiers: boots at the bottom, helmet atop, identification tags and personalized helmet band, and the rifle, always the soldier's inseparable companion. Had we been in combat or deployed for training, the display would have been identical, although the rifles would have been simply stuck into the ground.

Recognition of the Deceased

The battalion assembled for the ceremony, standing in the rows and columns of a military formation, with about fifty or so visitors taking seats in the gymnasium. The dead soldiers were recognized in a number of ways. Eulogies were rendered, in this case by their immediate commander, an army captain, and several of the soldiers' buddies whom the command sergeant major had engaged. The words were both touching and tragic. They recognized the soldiers' selflessness and professionalism, and they were punctuated with personal anecdotes and even a few comic stories. One story described the reaction of one of the decedents when he discovered that an Asian girl he had been admiring from afar and had spoken to in Hangul (Korean) only appeared to be a Korean native. She was actually a Canadian schoolteacher of Asian heritage who enjoyed the chase, giving in only after an hour of conversation in broken Hangul. Another story described a weekend bender when an entire squad of eight grown men spent nearly twelve hours lost in the Seoul subway system. Once the stories were complete, the throng sang the classic hymn "Amazing Grace" a cappella, chosen for its balanced, nonsectarian lyrics and its familiar tune.

Acceptance of the Death

It was important that the soldiers accept their comrades' death so that their grief could progress beyond the immediate sense of loss. To heighten their awareness, a ritual known as the last roll call was used. Following the recognition portion of the ceremony, all were asked to stand, and the soldiers' immediate commander gave the order for the senior sergeant (the first sergeant) to conduct roll call—under normal circumstances a daily ritual for the men. The names of several members of the soldiers' unit were called, and each answered, "Here, First Sergeant." After five to seven names were called, a dead soldier's name was called, and no one answered. The first sergeant called the name three times, and each time there was only silence. Several other names were read, each with a living response, and in turn each dead soldier's name was called, without response. Following the last call for a deceased soldier during this painful but cathartic process, a traditional rifle salute was cued during the ensuing silence that followed. On completion of the salute, our organized recognition of the soldiers concluded.

As attendees filed out, there were individual farewells to the deceased. Most of the 850 soldiers and visitors filed spontaneously, one by one, past the display, rendered a hand salute, and offered brief words of farewell. Succinct phrases such as, "Vaya con Dios, Bro," "Dude, you rocked!" and other contemporary expressions of close association and affection typified the moment. Officers who commanded units that have adopted custom-minted coins presented as tokens of excellence and known as commander's coins left five coins on the platform by the boots, to be sent to the soldiers' families along with personal effects. These coins have enormous traditional significance among soldiers. Each unit has a crest registered with the Army's Institute of Heraldry and is worn on the shoulders of the dress uniform. Each soldier's gifts included dozens of our battalion crests, left as a symbol of eternal association with the unit.

As a final gesture of respect and memorialization, toasts were offered for our departed that evening by soldiers in dozens of Korean bars just outside the gate of the military cantonment. The first toast I recall was simply the word that represented our battalion and all it stood for: "Steel!" I also recall a toast to "going home forever." We also recognized the soldiers at the annual winter formal celebration of the patron saint of the artillery, Saint Barbara, a black-tie dinner for more than 250 artillery officers in Uijongbu, Korea (featured as the hangout of Hawkeye Pierce on the television series *M*A*S*H*). In the Saint Barbara's dinner, the traditional wine toast, "To our fallen comrades," was offered, and as is the case at most formal military affairs, it did not specify the deceased soldiers by name. Despite the official Army policy seeking to deglamorize the consumption of alcohol, these toasts continue to serve as a final acknowledgment that fallen peers will never be forgotten.

★ Why This Is Important for All Leaders

The ceremonial techniques recognizing the deceased should be tailored to each organization, and the best will have the three distinct characteristics noted: there should be a representation of the body, they should recognize and celebrate the lives of the dead, and they should gently orient mourners on the organization and its future. For example, following the loss of 658 employees on 9/11, Cantor Fitzgerald established and currently maintains a Web site with pages for each fallen employee. The decedents are represented with photographs, and there are postings by friends and family that celebrate and recognize their lives. The Web site also has a constructive and appropriate future orientation, with ways to add other recognitions, a link to a growing Cantor Relief Fund to aid families and survivors, and a link to Cantor itself.

The element of scale present in the Gander disaster and the deaths at the Pentagon, the World Trade Center, and in a Pennsylvania field on September 11, 2001, should not establish some sort of threshold for recognition. Any large organization will lose these same numbers of employees over time. As time passes, the proper recognition and remembrance will add resilience and character to the organization far beyond similar groups that do nothing or minimally acknowledge the losses. As young people die in high schools and universities, they should be remembered with permanence in some fashion, such as yearbook recognitions (following the three character-istics of representation, recognition, and future orienta-tion), and also included in more transient recognition, such as a moment of silence at graduation. Companies should do the same and send the unmistakable message that people count and that leaders are authentically touched by such loss. This leader message is invaluable in establishing loyalty and cohesion within a firm.

The Value of Good Leadership in Times of Tragedy

Such value is priceless to those who have organizations with a core of in extremis leaders and followers. For Army leaders, especially commanders, there is no event more important to the preservation of unit morale than a soldier's memorial service. Commanders at all tactical levels—from two-star division commander to lieutenant platoon leaders—attend memorials and participate when appropri-ate. Rank-and-file soldiers unquestionably identify with the de-ceased. It is an officer's solemn duty to preserve the memory of a fallen comrade and in doing so communicate respect and concern for the living soldiers in the unit. Far from being mere spotlighting or image management, the common expectation is that the com-mander is personally involved and deeply and emotionally moved. The shedding of tears is accepted and not viewed as a form of weak-ness. Soldiers are adept at recognizing the difference between super-ficiality and genuine concern. They also know that only the latter will be expressed on the battlefield, making the memorialization of soldier sacrifice among the most significant leadership responsibili-ties for Army leaders.

The presidential memorial service four days after the Gander crash provided additional examples of a phenomenon that has been described as grief leadership: behaviors and statements by key community leaders that serve to facilitate healthy coping with loss and grief among members of the group.[2] In confronting grief associated with group loss, effective leaders take actions that have the effect of unifying the community in the mourning process. For example, President and Mrs. Reagan joined the division commander and his wife in a televised memorial service at Fort Campbell, Kentucky. The division commander noted the value of the president's "sharing our sorrow," and he walked with the president to greet and console bereaved families. Reagan indicated he represented the concerns of the American people and that "the entire nation was grieving" along with Fort Campbell.

One important benefit of effective leadership in such crisis situations is to help reestablish a sense of control, predictability, and hope in the midst of confusion, chaos, and fear. Leaders at Fort Campbell tried to focus community attention on the opportunities to learn and grow provided by the disaster. A common theme was that by having suffered through this tragedy together, soldiers and their families will be stronger and even better prepared for the national defense mission.

This quality of positive leadership through disaster can be lacking in community crises. This can occur even when good leaders are available within the unit or community, but external and political factors make it difficult for recognized leaders to perform their leadership role. For example, the fear of litigation stifles many great leaders from communicating freely during a disaster, and while such fears are well founded, leaders still have to get out front. Jack Bovender, the CEO of Hospital Corporation of America that evacuated Tulane Hospital during Hurricane Katrina (described in Chapter Two), who gave numerous public interviews during the disaster, said to a group that October, "I'd rather lose the lawsuits and come out with people respecting me and the institution [of HCA]." It's a strong values-based message. Frankly, I've never heard of litigation-based leadership.

The response to the terror attacks of September 11, 2001, included many examples of highly effective leadership. For example, researchers have formally documented the critical role of leaders at the Pentagon site in facilitating healthy responses and making spot decisions about how to handle bodies and survivors, which saved lives and maintained a relative sense of order.[3] And New York Mayor Rudolph Giuliani was widely praised in the media for his highly effective leadership following the attacks on the World Trade Center, blowing through red tape, being visible to the entire city, being personally present at the attack site, and immediately focusing the city on a vision of resilience, recovery, and the famous Gotham tenacity.

These leaders focused the group on shared values, common goals, and the mutual experience of loss and bereavement. This perspective was reinforced through a series of memorial services that united their various communities, fostering a sense of integration and solidarity. Also important are clear (and nonconflicting) lines of authority and leaders who can focus group attention on the work of recovery as well as the ongoing task responsibilities of the organization.

The most recent and famous example of this was Lieutenant General Russ Honore, who blew into the Katrina crisis at the president's request. When Honore arrived in New Orleans, Mayor Ray Nagin was quoted on CNN as referring to him as a "John Wayne dude" who can "get some stuff done." Quoted further on a local radio station, Nagin said, "He came off the doggone chopper, and he started cussing and people started moving." Honore's specific actions included aggressively marshaling resources, forcefully orienting troops onto the intricacies of the humanitarian response mission (such as lowering their weapons), and pointedly dealing with the media. His admonition to a reporter who persistently asked for information not constructive to the relief effort, "Look, you're stuck on stupid," flashed around the world in a matter of minutes on video and audio clips.

Such leaders are instrumental in imparting a sense of control amid an atmosphere of chaos, coherence in the midst of confusion, and hope instead of despair. They help the community direct its energy toward rising to the challenge offered by the disaster and in learning useful lessons from the experience. Within ongoing disasters, hasty but earnest memorials can solidify the community in the grieving process. For example, the family reception at the brigade gym at Fort Campbell on the morning of the Gander airplane crash was the first and most spontaneous of these memorials. Under the leadership of the brigade commander, the value of grieving together as a community was reinforced. The same theme was played out in other memorial services held over the next few weeks.

In the early aftermath of the crash, the Fort Campbell community seemed to revert to a flatter form of social organization in which normal functional boundaries seemed unimportant. For example, organizations that usually worked out of separate buildings—such as psychologists, lawyers, personnel administrators, and chaplains—all colocated themselves into a family assistance center to eliminate the need for families in need of help to be shuttled around the usual bureaucracy. Among the grieving and those supporting, rank had no meaning; people simply helped other people, and the usual military social hierarchy was hardly noticed. Commanders waived, amended, or ignored Army regulations on their own authority if it made sense and helped families. Often these regulations dealt with the ability to extend their stay in government homes for longer than ordinarily allowed or permitted the expeditious processing of death benefits by friends or coworkers.

The lesson is that leaders must not only allow but encourage and demand as much administrative flexibility as possible in organizations that are grieving or otherwise dealing with tragedy. Far from being out of control, such flexibility allows people in lower levels of the organization the freedom to do the right things. The organization can adapt to the shock and challenge, with the leadership in the role of facilitator and role model. For example, in the months following the Gander crash, the reconstituted battalion healed. It received several performance awards for collective physical training and marksmanship, won in competition with other units across the division. Although a variety of symptoms were reported by soldiers over time, including sleep disturbances, guilt, and alcohol abuse, these were usually short term and resolved favorably. The unit and the community were free of lasting ill effects. Those who were left behind retained a generalized sense of strengthened social cohesion and group solidarity.

Final Thoughts: How to Lead When Tragedy Strikes in Your Organization

In extremis leaders live with death, and they become expert in recognizing the fallen and grieving with their organizations. It is a brutal truth that in dangerous contexts, the unfortunate or incompetent die. Those more fortunate or more capable watch others die. In the process, these leaders learn to value life and recognize that value in ways that have meaning to those left behind. In doing so, they respect not just the dead but the living. Their rituals, recognitions, and leader actions result in a tightly knit, cohesive group of survivors.

Leaders across broader contexts can learn from the tragic reality of soldiers, police officers, skydivers, high-risk mountain climbers, and other professionals who recognize their dead as a part of their professions and dangerous avocations. People are remarkably consistent in their needs and reactions around tragedy. Death is a great equalizer, and grief comes to the rich and famous, and the poor and insignificant, in exactly the same way. Leading is about people, and death presents both an obligation and an opportunity to lead. The obligation and opportunity are fleeting, though, so leaders must be ready to step up without hesitation. Both organizational practices and the leader's intent have to be in place continuously, or the event passes unrecognized.

After I started doing physically and mentally demanding military training with tough sergeants, I was exposed to the colloquial expression, "What doesn't kill you makes you stronger." The saying is supposed to inspire individuals to work through pain. The same principle holds for well-led organizations. Death, loss, tragedy: all will be visited on any organization of any significant size or longevity. The right leader preparation and action not only gets the organization through its collective pain, grief, and anger but takes the organization to a higher level of cohesion and solidarity. Be prepared to do this for your loyal followers. Your time will come.

Summing Up

1. Focus outward during and after a tragedy: lead the living. I learned this lesson when five of my soldiers died in a noncombat accident, and it's a valuable lesson for all leaders in any life-and-death situation. Don't get caught up in your own emotions when dealing with a crisis or tragedy. Leading is about respecting the dead and helping your organization grieve, not about how you as the leader feel.

2. Make sure your staff keeps you informed in times of tragedy. Many people think their leaders do not want to be bothered with the details of the dire illness, injury, or death of every employee or employee's immediate family. In fact, great leaders are involved in their followers' lives, especially when people are handling life-and-death situations or grieving. Remember, you're leading human beings, and you should lead and be there when you're truly needed.

3. Establish rituals for handling death in your organization. Even if you're not leading people in dangerous situations, death occurs in every organization: from natural causes, illness, accident, and even crime. People in your organization will need to recognize the passing of their colleagues so that they can mourn and grieve and live and work. The military has established death rituals that suit

the nature of their work, but all organizations can develop their own ways of dealing with their tragedies that are suitable to each environment.

4. Don't wait for tragedy to strike to decide how you're going to address it in your organization. Proper recognition and remembrance of colleagues who have died will add resilience and character to your organization. Send an unmistakable message that people count and that the leaders in your organization are authentically touched by the loss. Such a leader message is invaluable in establishing loyalty and cohesion in any organization.

6

Building Teams That Build Leaders
An In Extremis Case Study

In extremis circumstances tend to develop leadership qualities in those who frequent them. Dangerous contexts demand, and indeed elicit, characteristics such as authenticity and transparency that are superb traits. Such contexts call for specific mental, physical, and emotional preparation, all tailored to the unforgiving elements of environmental threat and all contributing to the development of reliable leaders across many contexts. Behaviors that are practiced in dangerous contexts help define constructive behaviors in many, if not most, leadership settings, even in the tragic circumstances surrounding death. Professional leaders, once developed in their dangerous avocation or profession, continue to apply their particular brand of leadership in ways that inspire and motivate others.

This final chapter, a case study of the U.S. Military Academy sport parachute team, shows how placing a group or team in an in extremis context develops superior leaders. The chapter uses concrete circumstances that develop leaders—a substantive focus on the "what" and the "how," elaborated in considerable detail. How does one select team members, coaches, and advisers for such a task? What are the effects of dangerous circumstances on the team and its leaders? Does the in extremis context actually produce a leader development benefit? Will such leaders excel in other leadership settings?

A collegiate parachute team is an example with high utility. If you are developing leaders in dangerous contexts, such as the police, fire departments, military trainers, and adventure schools, you can apply elements of the case directly to their training requirements. Perhaps even more important, some of the approaches taken with the in extremis team can be applied to other teams: interdepartmental work groups, youth groups, and boards of directors, for example. In extremis leadership and development produces heroes in crisis and great community leaders along the broader path of life. Such an idea, well refined, points to service in the public sector as a national wellspring of capable, engaged leaders for our organizations, communities, and government.

Teams Are Uniquely Valuable in Developing Future Leaders

Teams, in and of themselves, do not necessarily develop leaders or even positive individual qualities. Associations can develop for the wrong reasons, as gangs do. Associations may also form for the right reasons but be built around the wrong values. For example, the cult of individualism surrounding the sports marketing technique of all-star teams has produced some decidedly mediocre game play. It's best, then, if leadership is the desired outcome, with leader development a stated goal of a team or organization. And it's best to state that goal whether or not the core mission of the organization is producing widgets, winning lacrosse games, or fighting crime. All groups, teams, organizations, and communities need people who are willing to step up.

All team activities, such as youth or adult sports programs, have the potential to add to the development of individual leaders. But when you deliberately build in a leadership development function with a team and add an element of risk or danger, it's not just a team anymore: it's a superteam, developing its leaders and people along with its core mission or goals. There is no better way to develop leaders.

USMA cadets are selected in March of their freshman year for the parachute team and thus spend forty of their forty-seven months at the Academy on the team. The development that occurs in those forty months is profound and is unquestionably enhanced by the seriousness inherent in the everyday danger of parachuting. As an initial testament to how the developmental path ascends for these cadets, consider the following list of leader achievements by team members:

- Of the last six cadet first captains, who are appointed in their senior year to lead the entire Corps of Cadets, four have been parachute team members.

- In 2006 and 2007, the majority of the pinnacle command slots in the U.S. Corps of Cadets were held by sport parachute team leaders.

- Since 1999, and while taking only ten to twelve cadets each year in their freshman year, the team has produced two Rhodes Scholars and, almost every year, several Truman and Marshall Scholarship winners. In 2006, one member, Charlie Eadie, won both a Truman and a Marshall Scholarship.

- Colonel Jeff Williams, West Point class of 1978, was the cadet leader in charge of the parachute team during his tenure at the Military Academy. As I write this, he is working in the international space station.

- Ten cadets per year, picked with no parachuting experience, are turned into nationally competitive parachutists and world-class leaders.

The phenomenon surpasses anecdotal—the indicators of leadership excellence among the team members who graduate are so evident that further statistical validation seems superfluous—although in the next pages, I describe the selection and development of these men and women.

Learning Leadership on Teams: Beyond Fair Play to In Extremis Lessons

There are no do-overs in dangerous contexts. Second chances are not granted by a referee, but are instead handed down by the frivolous dictates of chance or, if you prefer, fate. This element of conscience and the threat of immediate irreversible consequences make teams in dangerous contexts a rich developmental wellspring for great leaders. Given the points made in earlier chapters, a dangerous context adds the following characteristics to the development of leaders in teams:

- Inherent motivation. Team leaders and followers pay less attention to motivation because the context is exciting and demands their full attention. This develops good leaders because they learn to be motivated by the environment, not by cheerleader or sales-type leaders. They learn a quiet, confident form of leadership.

- An orientation to learning. Team members directing energy to surviving a dangerous environment learn rapidly and spend less time distracted or self-absorbed. The team is united against a common threat: the danger without.

- Shared risk. Everyone must look out for everyone else. Although individual spotlighting and selfishness are also moderately consequential in sports with insignificant risk, in high-risk endeavors, the egoists and self-focused people unwilling to take risk alongside their peers are likely to be ostracized immediately. High-risk teams learn that no one is left behind. It's everyone's job to take care of each other—a powerful lesson.

- Common lifestyle. Teammates in dangerous environments commit to life sharing the same equipment and facing the greatest equalizer of all: the laws of chance.

The USMA sport parachute team exemplifies a team that adds an element of danger to the other positive aspects of leader development. The composition, development, and performance of this one-of-a-kind team reveal much in general about what it takes to develop winners. This chapter walks through the team's history and its in extremis character, looks at the leader development outcomes, and examines details about the selection process for cadets. Then the focus turns to the leader developers: coaches, team captains, and others who help move the team from an organization that is simply competitive to one that is profoundly developmental.

Collegiate Parachuting: A Lab for In Extremis Leadership

The U.S. Military Academy sport parachute team is a cadet club founded in 1958 in the early years of recreational skydiving. Its founding member, Henmar "Gabe" Gabriel, West Point Class of 1961, was an enlisted soldier who earned his candidacy at the Academy, and after spending a year as a cadet, went to Fort Bragg, North Carolina, for the summer of 1958 for the express purpose of learning free-fall parachuting and exporting the skill to West Point. Other paratroopers were leaving the Army with educational benefits that took them to other colleges and universities, and these former soldiers had started jump clubs at several Ivy League colleges.

The idea that parachuting at the Academy could be developmental is relatively new. In fact, the concept of individual development as the Academy's strategic model is relatively new. In 2002, the Academy formally adopted an approach titled the cadet leader development system, which eliminated the concept of attrition as a tool for shaping the Academy and took the stand that cadets who had made it through the admissions process (including the first summer's "Beast Barracks"—so named because life in the barracks for newcomers is made beastly by upperclass students) were capable of developing into superb lieutenants. The target of development is to produce a well-educated adult prepared for a career in the Army, possessing a unique identity: that of a professional officer and leader. Such individuals willingly accept responsibility for their own behavior and the behavior of the people who work for them. The best athletic teams not only win in their respective sports, but also reinforce the Academy's approach to cadet leader development by helping cadets internalize a leader self-image.

Cadets on the parachute team are responsible for themselves and for each other, and they know it. This is not true of all other club teams. Recent concerns about safety and decorum across the club sport program at the Academy have led to an institutional emphasis on officer volunteers, not cadets, who are responsible for everything the team does or fails to do. It's an operational rather than developmental mind-set that, if applied literally, interferes with the development of cadets. The risk is that such policies, instead of demanding leadership from cadets, can diffuse the leadership and management of the team to Army officers. But whereas officer leader developers for the parachute team acknowledge the commitment to safety, the in extremis nature of skydiving forces individual responsibility onto the cadets themselves.

For example, cadets pack their own parachutes, because federal aviation regulations require that main parachutes be packed by a certificated parachute rigger (an impossible standard in sport jumping) or by "the person making the next jump with that parachute." The net effect is that parachutists must be individually responsible for their own lifesaving gear. Officers associated with the team risk personal and professional criticism by accepting responsibility for cadet actions, while also allowing cadets to act independently, and sometimes fail. In in extremis conditions, when failure occurs, only redundant supervision, equipment design, or emergency training will prevent a disaster. There are no do-overs.

Common safety practices in skydiving require an individual (usually termed the jumpmaster) to ensure that the individual equipment skydivers wear is inspected prior to boarding the aircraft. Cadets are required to perform this inspection on each other, and the sergeants and officers who help with the team merely teach the procedures and observe from a distance. On the parachute team, then, cadets are personally and routinely afforded the opportunity to be responsible for preventing the horrific death of a classmate and friend. This is the developmental magic inherent in in extremis teams.

If coaches or others take on the responsibility for individual safety from cadets, little leader development or learning could take place, and neither would the operation be significantly safer. Instead, the role of coaches and leader developers is to ensure that cadets know the proper procedures and to spot-check them to reinforce the necessary standards, but the cadets themselves remain in charge of both the standards and the process by which the standards are met. In this way, they will be readier to understand and accept the responsibilities of leadership in Army units, particularly in combat units.

The process is not without error, however, as the following example illustrates.

How a Near-Death Experience
Taught a Valuable Leadership Lesson

In 2004, a cadet who was the jumpmaster (and therefore responsible for supervising both himself and the eight other jumpers on the aircraft) inspected others but failed to receive his own inspection prior to boarding the aircraft. After the other skydivers had exited, the experienced cadet leaped from the helicopter and prepared to execute a planned series of turns and back loops. As he began the first turn in the series, he felt an unfamiliar tapping on the left side of his body during free-fall. It was the chest strap of his harness: he had not fastened it through its buckle, and it was undone and flapping loosely at his side. He felt an enormous rush of adrenaline when he realized that the harness was open across his chest. Without the chest strap, the opening shock of the parachute would pull the top of the back-pack off his shoulders to the rear, and eject him forward out of the harness at 120 miles per hour, still more than a half-mile high, with nothing left to do but claw at the air and wait for impact.

Because he had noticed the strap flapping about, he had one chance to save himself: he was able to grasp the end of the strap, pull it across his body, crudely loop it around the opposite side of the harness and, tightly holding the free end, deploy his parachute. As the parachute jerked open, the harness put some load on the strap, but he remained contained. Once under canopy, he rerouted his chest strap properly through its buckle and completed the jump, eyes wide, mouth open, chest pounding, and soaked with sweat. A hundred preachy lectures with a thousand PowerPoint slides about values and personal responsibility could not do as good a job of driving home the importance of the concept as that single near-death experience did.

★ Why This Is Important for All Leaders

Part of the problem is that our lives are so insulated from routine danger that we can do the wrong thing, the irresponsible thing, repeatedly and perhaps never be held accountable. Be honest. Have you ever driven when you had too much to drink? How many times when you were borderline impaired did you think, "What's the chance of my getting caught or getting in an accident?" In in extremis settings, however, it is likely that a person will pay for his or her mistakes the first time they are made. That threat causes leaders to acquire habits of discipline and responsibility rather than give in to recklessness and allow chance to blindly protect their indiscretions. How ironic that taking deliberate risk might develop discipline and responsibility, while others who take needless chances are taught, falsely, that the odds are in their favor and that probability will never hold them accountable.

How West Point Selects Cadet Leaders

Skeptics about the development of cadets on the parachute team might immediately wonder if there is some advantage to cadet parachutists that leads to an increased selection for leadership assignments. It's important to understand that cadet parachutists are in no way administratively advantaged to be selected for leadership slots in the Corps of Cadets. This section describes that process. West Point's system of choosing leaders may have lessons that apply to other organizations seeking to hire potential leaders.

Selection of cadet leaders in the Corps of Cadets at West Point is a deliberate and fair process, involving the considered judgment of seasoned Army officers, significant amounts of peer input, a candidate's proven track record at the Academy, and recent firsthand observation of the cadet leaders in action.

Approximately ten cadets out of more than a thousand in each entering class are chosen for the parachute team. If all other qualities were held constant, parachute team members would be represented among the forty-eight cadet leaders selected by the Academy's key leader selection board at a rate of approximately one cadet every other year. The pinnacle first captain is the top cadet among the forty-eight. By chance, then, a parachutist would be selected as first captain with a one in ninety-six chance. Yet four of the last six cadet first captains have been selected and developed by the sport parachute team. The fact that three cadets from the team were chosen among the top five cadet leaders for 2006–2007 also defies probability by a wide margin. Either the team selection process is amazingly prescient, or something developmental is occurring on the team (or perhaps both).

All of this success at choosing and developing leaders ushers forth the common question: Are these pinnacle leaders simply being cherry-picked from the best of the freshman class? Or is there something special about training and development on the parachute team, particularly the in extremis aspect, that creates great leaders? In other words, are leaders born, or are they made? The answer to that question is the same as the USMA's department of admissions would give to those who ask why service academies are able to consistently produce quality leaders for the military: select promising leaders to begin with, then professionally develop them into extraordinary leaders who are willing and able to lead soldiers into in extremis contexts.

Interviews of Potential Cadet Leaders

Selections of cadet leaders are done by a formally conducted board of Army officers assigned to the supervisory staff at West Point that is convened every February. The board, known formally as the key leader board, includes an Army colonel whose job places him in charge of the Corps of Cadets (essentially the equivalent of a vice dean for student life at a civilian institution). His position is called the brigade tactical officer (BTO). Because the corps is divided into four regiments of about a thousand cadets each, the Army officers in charge of each of those regiments also sit on the board. Board membership is rounded out with the serving cadet first captain, as well as two sergeants major—the senior Army sergeants at West Point. Prior to the key leader board, each regiment conducts a similar mixed board of officers and cadets, and it narrows the candidate list of key leaders to about twelve cadets per regiment. Therefore, the key leader board considers about forty-eight cadets for the pinnacle first captain assignment, the four regimental commanders, and other important staff jobs.

Prior to the board meeting, each panel member provides the president of the board one question that will be asked. The colonel who chairs the board screens the questions and makes sure there is no duplication. He has his staff prepare a binder ahead of time of each cadet's record: grades in the academic program; physical fitness grades; estimates of military development, which include multiple peer assessments of performance as both follower and leader; and a questionnaire about leadership preferences and ambitions that each candidate fills out. Each cadet interviews with the key leader board, with each board member asking the exact same question of all candidates.

Field Training: Validation for Emerging Cadet Leaders

After each cadet interview, each member of the panel provides individual evaluations of the candidate based on a standardized grading sheet to the board president. Based on these scores, the key positions for leaders during the cadet's summer field training activities are determined. These summer activities provide the Academy rich firsthand knowledge of the leadership ability of cadets. The activities also provide cadets additional practice and development as leaders in a dynamic training environment.

After the officer leadership watches the cadets perform a variety of leadership roles during summer training, a second key leaders board is held in July to determine the year's final cadet chain of command, based on the summer performance of each cadet who attended the original key leaders board. This second key leader board does not include the serving cadet first captain because he or she graduated at the start of summer and is serving as a lieutenant in the Army. Therefore, the officer board uses the cadets' records, cadet interviews, and demonstrated leadership performance during summer training to select the cadet chain of command. This approach of "board-perform-board" (a board review, followed by evaluation of actual performance, followed by another board review) results in accurate and objective decisions about who should lead the Corps.

Composition of the cadet leader team is based not only on performance but also on diversity. The board seeks to build a cadet command chain that is reflective of the Corps of Cadets with respect to gender, ethnicity, inclusive of NCAA athletes, cadets who first attended preparatory school, and a representative balance among the four regiments. These results are then presented to the one-star and three-star generals in command of West Point for their personal approval.

An ideal end state for parachute team members, then, would be to serve the corps in leadership roles, having been chosen through the process. They are selected to serve as leaders at an extraordinarily high rate. Unquestionably, some of their success is because they "had the right stuff"—promising young people are chosen for the team when they are freshmen. That process, described in the next section, can serve as a model for finding emerging talent in any organization.

How to Compose a High-Performing Team

Selection of the people who will make up a superb high-performing team is a critical first step toward success in any organization. One important rule of selection is not to focus exclusively on composing a team with the very best individuals you can find. If you select a team primarily on individual prowess, you can easily overlook or minimize the critical elements that take an average team to a superteam: cohesion, stability of the group, positive team culture, and diversity. People with top-tier potential who work together well form the core of a truly high-performing developmental team. The rest is leadership and hard work.

It's relatively easy to find people with top-tier potential: just look for excellence across a broad range of competencies. For example, the Military Academy's sport parachute team is the only team that declines fall tryouts and instead selects cadets in late winter, after they have already had a semester at the Academy. The delay means that they have established a track record in all three developmental programs at the Academy: academic, physical, and military. If they were chosen in the fall, most of the cadets' qualities could be assessed only by reviewing their high school records.

By evaluating cadets in the winter, the sport parachute team is able to assess the cadets' ability to make good grades, their physical fitness grades and coordination in physical education classes, and their capacity to train in the military development program. Individuals with high potential for dangerous, demanding sports always score high across all three areas because in the end, physical coordination and ability are never enough. Top-tier performance on an elite team in a dangerous environment also calls for good judgment and the ability to analyze conditions rapidly.

The road to selection as a member of the cadet parachute team begins with an informational meeting, attended by more than a hundred cadets interested in competing for the ten to twelve slots that are open. It's a remarkable turnout, given that each cadet is already associated with some intramural or NCAA team because participation is mandatory even in their first semester at the Academy. Therefore, these cadets are all willing to stop what they're doing for a chance to jump with the Black Knights.

★ Why This Is Important for All Leaders

The lesson for all leader developers is never to compose a high-performing team without solid assessment of actual performance in the critical setting. Also, high-performing organizations should always choose people who are broadly competent: fit, smart, and internally motivated. Excessive focus on a single dimension may uncover performers but not necessarily leaders.

The Application Process

Following the organizational meeting, the cadets submit organized application files to the team. The files consist of standard academic and physical information about the candidate, revealing grades in all subjects, physical fitness thus far, and information about their current activities and interests. The packet also includes three letters of recommendation from peers or superiors or other supportive persons, with one exception: no current team member or coach may write a letter for an applicant. This is to minimize the "who you know, not what you know" effect that could otherwise work counter to an objective assessment of competence and goodness of fit. Finally, the packet includes a statement of why the cadets are interested in parachuting or the parachute team.

★ Why This Is Important for All Leaders

Does your organization or business choose applicants because of who they know or because of what they know? On the parachute team, the challenge and danger of the sport place a focus on competence, but in many other organizations or businesses, that focus must be actively maintained by the leader. Do you require applicants to explain in detail why they want to be on your team? If not, perhaps such a requirement would help reveal which applicants merely want a job and which applicants want a job on your team.

Assessing Potential Team Members

Once the cadets have submitted an application packet, each candidate is assigned a parachute team member who meets the candidate, coaches the cadet through the administrative aspects of the application process, and uncovers as much as possible about the candidate that may not be reflected on paper. The team member asks peers and acquaintances about the candidate cadet. They and other members of the team watch the cadet discreetly, looking to see how he or she treats other people, particularly civilian support staff and cadet subordinates. They spend enough time with the candidates to assess their judgment across a range of situations and assess their ability to express themselves. Most important, the parachute team member forms an assessment of how well the cadet will fit with members of the existing team and the team culture.

The assessment of goodness of fit is highly subjective, but it's an important part of building a team that will remain cohesive. Questions abound:

> "Is this person aware of the commitment it takes to be on the parachute team: to jump six afternoons per week, eight hours on Saturdays and Sundays, to deploy to the collegiate nationals over Christmas?"
>
> "Is this person hesitant, or clumsy, or inattentive to detail?"
>
> "Does this person talk too much (especially about himself or herself), curse too much, pray too much, drink too much, complain too much, or is otherwise over the top?"
>
> "Does this person curry favor from superiors or take advantage of subordinates?"
>
> "Is this a person I would trust with my sibling—or with my life?"

Such questions are intensely personal, but teams are composed of persons.

★ Why This Is Important for All Leaders

Ask yourself those questions about the people in the organization in which you currently work. Do the members of your team pass this test? If not, why not? The in extremis focus drives the parachute team to look at a prospective teammate and ask, "Would I trust this person with my life?" It's a useful standard to apply to applicants in more ordinary contexts as well if you want to accept the sort of team member who won't let anyone down.

Assessing Cadets' Physical Condition and Preparedness

Following several weeks of getting to know cadet candidates, the team conducts a standard army physical fitness test: number of push-ups in two minutes, number of sit-ups in two minutes, and a two-mile run.

The purpose of the test is not to test candidates' physical fitness for skydiving. Sport parachuting is not exceptionally physically demanding—it's about like diving, and much easier than gymnastics or soccer in terms of strength and stamina required. Instead, the test helps the team measure candidates' willingness to prepare (because the test is objective and announced months in advance). It is also used to see if cadets are fit enough to continue to maintain their physical condition when jumping begins to take up much of their time. Finally, it permits the team to pick cadets who are the least likely to be injured when a jump doesn't go as planned and there is a midair collision, a hard or awkward landing, or some other physically punishing mishap.

★ Why This Is Important for All Leaders

Although most organizations have a limited ability to screen applicants for physical ability, the lesson is that among those selected from within an organization to lead, determination, discipline, and stamina are unquestionably key characteristics for all leaders. There are other ways besides counting push-ups to determine if people have these qualities; the physically challenged can possess them too. The point is that leader assessments for all organizations should take them into account and form assessments to support such an accounting. You want to hire people with heart.

Narrowing the Field of Candidates

Once the hefty application files are complete with physical fitness scores and the full range of recommendations and information, a team board is convened with six team members, with representatives from each class. They review the files and select approximately thirty cadets to interview to compose the freshman team cohort. Those chosen to interview represent the top files among those who fit well with the team, and careful consideration is given to ensure that women and minority applicants are included. Although some events do have men's and women's categories, collegiate skydiving (like business and most other organizations) is coeducational. A team goal is to include women and minority cadets in the final selection as a key element in setting the tone of the team culture.

It is important to recognize the value of diversity in team composition and understand why including women and minority cadets is an important part of team selection. It's true that the team is highly visible at the mostly white male Academy and that it might be politically advantageous to have female and minority representation. Yet no Academy leader or official has ever, to my knowledge, insisted or even suggested that the team diversify.

On a developmentally oriented team, diversity is not about political correctness. The reason the team is so interested in women and minorities is that such diversity has unquestionably balanced the team culture and added creativity and breadth to its activities. Skydiving and other in extremis activities tend to be male dominated and have a tradition of bravado and machismo. It's easy for the intensity and swagger to get out of control in a pitched, competitive environment or outside the context of competitive activities when teammates are socializing. It is common to read about gender-exclusive athletic teams that collapse in scandals involving sex, alcohol or drugs, or some form of criminal activity. In contrast, diverse teams are more resistant to such catastrophic self-destruction. A small, elite team can't afford to lose any members to alcohol or other offenses or to develop cliques or other destructive group dynamics.

★ Why This Is Important for All Leaders

The nearly universal lesson to organizational leaders is that a diverse membership adds a degree of civility and mutual respect to everything a team does. Diverse teams are stable teams.

The Interview Process

Each cadet to be interviewed reports to the team board in a prescribed military uniform; the board scrutinizes the cadet for incorrect or sloppy uniform standards. The board members view skydiving as a sport where attention to detail is a life-or-death matter, and they view their team as the object of their own commitment of time and effort. Any lack of effort in the interview is seen as an indication that the cadet lacks commitment. Therefore, team tryouts themselves are a developmental process for cadets. For leaders in all organizations, the same holds true in job interviews: attention to detail in appearance is a form of communication.

To see how the cadet prepared and how he or she works under pressure, each candidate is given a set of four small cut-out forms of free-falling jumpers and is required to compose them in linked formations—having been given a sheet of sixteen such formations as preparation for the interview. The task combines memorization and spatial ability, important characteristics for skydivers, who execute complex sequences of four- and eight-person formations under tremendous time pressure in free-fall.

Each cadet is also asked to tell a joke, and frequently they are asked to role-play a challenging situation, such as, "Pretend the board is a girl [or guy] you just met and want to date. Role-play how you would impress her [or him]."

Choosing the Members of the Team

After all the interviews, the files are sorted by ratings given on simple rating sheets, and the array is placed in order of merit. Coaches are involved with deciding the exact number who may be trained. The team members themselves decide who will be taken onto the team. It's not always done in perfect numerical order of merit. Decisions with respect to who will fit with the team as a whole dominate all the way to the end of the process. Any team—in skydiving, business, or other endeavors—has to stay together in order to function as a leader development laboratory, an entity where teammates are comfortable learning together.

The process by which people are notified whether they were or were not selected is also important to the team. Each unsuccessful cadet has a personal visit from a team member who explains how difficult the competition was for the team and thanks the candidate for his or her interest. The intent is for the team to be viewed as small, excellent, and representative of the Corps of Cadets, not arrogant elitists. The in extremis context demands a self-sacrificing respect for followers, and on the parachute team, that respect extends to those not chosen.

★ Why This Is Important for All Leaders

How does your organization treat the applicants it does not select for hiring or membership? The answer to that question is a reflection of the value your organization places on people.

Leader Developers for High-Performing Teams

Deciding the players for a superteam is a necessary but not sufficient part of the process. Whether the high-performing team you're composing is an operational team for special military or police work, an extreme sport team, or a group going to work on an elite business or engineering project, you need both coaches and leader developers to make the team develop and learn as an entity and produce leaders in the end. Let's take a look at the characteristics of developers and coaches who can take a team beyond being a competitive avocation and diversion, to the point where the team is an engine for developing leaders.

Find a great team, and you'll always find an outstanding leader or leaders in charge of it. The two most commonly observed leaders are performance coaches and team captains. The most important, however, are leader developers. The best teams always have them. Sometimes they are sports psychologists or technical consultants in a sport. Sometimes they are athletic "greybeards"—older former team members—who don't have the primary responsibility for the team but assist and advise the coach and team members. Sometimes they are parents of team members, heavily involved in the support and culture of the team. Whether a coach, a captain, or someone just hanging around, the point is that someone has to focus the competitive activity of a high-performing team onto the development of the teammates.

Coach Mike Kzryzewski, the current coach of the Duke basketball team as well as the U.S. Olympic men's team, and his former coach and mentor Bobby Knight, are masters at building high-performing teams with a focus on development. Their teams win at basketball and enjoy exceptionally high four-year graduation success rates in college sports. Instead of adopting a myopic, unidimensional focus on basketball itself, they insist that their players are also winners academically and that their behavior off the court is in keeping with team standards. Both men coached basketball at West Point, and their style is part of the tradition of balanced excellence that crosses team boundaries and is evident on the parachute team as well.

The point is broadly applicable: someone on the team, whether a coach, team captain, or other person, has to pay attention to individual development. In extremis sports lend themselves to this because injuries and fatalities manifest at the individual level. But even in ordinary sports like basketball or soccer, there is high payoff from a developmental focus, and someone has to embed that focus into the habits and operating style of the team. Consider the highest-performing group of people with whom you are personally familiar. In many cases, there are people focused on more than just team performance. Those are the team developers.

Performance Coaches

Performance coaches focus on developing team skills and a winning spirit. Their focus is most intense when the team is engaging in its sport, achieving its goals, and developing capability. A track record of achievement and a winning tradition are the keys to selecting a performance coach. Let's take a look at an example.

A Model Performance Coach: Talented, Experienced, and Engaged in Performing Well

Eric Heinsheimer, the 2004–2007 head coach of the West Point parachute team, served as a competitive skydiver on the Army Recruiting Command's Golden Knights for nine years, amassing more than ten thousand formation skydiving jumps. He's a winner, and his responsibility is to transfer that skill and ability to people with less talent and experience. His myriad connections in the skydiving industry have brought more coaches to assist and have enabled the team to connect with the best equipment manufacturers and distributors. There is no substitute for a successful, engaged performance coach on a competitive team.

But Eric Heinsheimer is also an Army sergeant, and so are the other coaches formally charged with team supervision. They continuously work to develop cadets into high-performing Army officers in the context of team practices.

★ Why This Is Important for All Leaders

To develop leaders through teams, the same must hold true in other teams, groups, or organizations. Performance coaches have to blend team performance with development. Is this happening on your daughter's soccer team or your son's youth group? Is this happening among air traffic controllers in the control tower or among sales teams? If not, a significant leader development opportunity is being lost.

Team Captains

Team captains are focused on peer-to-peer relationships on the team and often on the daily conduct of team activities. They help the coach run the show and establish peer-to-peer dynamics that keep the team focused on performance and commitment. Most team captains are elected to their position, giving them some referent authority and power. Team captains are also (but not always) among the very best athletes on their respective teams. The combination of popular mandate and recognized competence gives them a leadership edge that has the potential to make teams better, as illustrated by one of West Point's parachute team captains.

A Model Team Captain:
Skilled, Well Liked, Smart, and Mature

The team captain of the West Point parachute team is Kathryn Hillegass, Katie to her teammates. She is supremely competent and universally liked. Her grade-point average in her challenging Arabic and French double major is above 3.9. She's thoughtful and mature: talking to this twenty-one year old is like conversing with an accomplished woman of thirty or thirty-five. Her integrity, character, and judgment are above reproach. Hillegass's Army physical fitness test scores are above 330—and 300 is usually reported as the maximum score, Army-wide; her score is higher than the maximum because West Point constructs an extended scale to measure the ability of cadets with unusually strong athletic performance.

Hillegass competes with three male teammates in four-person formation skydiving. The group "chunks" into its dive—that is, the four teammates exit the helicopter by taking their initial leg and arm grips in the doorway and then springing together out the door into the outside airstream as a 650-pound unit. Hillegass can hang with her male peers at fourteen thousand feet and 120 mph, and her peers respect her. Her integrity, character, and judgment add meaningfully to the development of the team's culture and climate. Hillegass, as a team captain, is the exact representation of what "right" looks like.

★ Why This Is Important for All Leaders

By assuming the example and being "what right looks like," Katie Hillegass serves an important developmental function on the West Point skydiving team. If outsiders like coaches merely preach what should be team standards, the message often falls on deaf ears or, worse, creates a form of rebellion or resistance among the membership. In contrast, when peers lead by example and with no preaching, the message is authentic and much more accepted. The in extremis character of the parachute team demands authentic leadership, but all other organizations and teams will benefit from authentic role models. Find them, and keep them in the organization. They develop more leaders like themselves.

Leader Developers

The roles of a performance coach and a peer-elected team captain are decidedly complementary. A performance coach leads with pull, using raw ability and experience to demand better and better outcomes from the team. A team captain leads with push, working together with peers to keep the group cohesive, focused, and committed to excellence. For a team to maximize its leader development potential, however, coaching and captaining are not enough. For example, as good as Eric Heinsheimer and Katie Hillegass are as team coach and team captain, respectively, their jobs are not entirely focused on the development of every individual, using the team as a context; instead, they are mainly responsible for fielding a safe and winning team. Therefore, designated leader developers are needed. Leader developers should be experienced at leadership, be visible as role models, be trained to reinforce the attitudes and behaviors required of leaders, and fill out the supervisory staff of a truly developmental team.

It is the ability to add such a dimension of individual leader development to each competitor's experience as a team member that creates the conditions for a team to become a leadership lab—that is, an engine of leader development. People must be dedicated, committing their time and personal safety to this special leader development role. Most of us know parents who fulfill this role in youth groups, chiming in, helping with motivation and attitude, and teaching the team members to get along. This role can be formalized, and it has been on the athletic teams at the Academy. Whether formal or not, all who want to help develop individuals through teams can benefit from thinking through how this is done for USMA's jump team.

Officer Representatives

Staff and faculty from the USMA volunteer to occupy this special role for both NCAA sports and more informal club sports at the Academy. Commonly referred to as officer representatives (ORs), they perform the leader development function on teams above and beyond the dedicated athletic coaching staff. In the case of the parachute team, the ORs are commissioned officers (COs) or noncommissioned officers (NCOs) assigned to West Point who, as an additional duty, volunteer as participant role models for cadet skydivers and soldiers assigned to the parachute team. Their duties are voluntary but authorized by military regulations. As leader developers and role models, they are usually not assigned specific responsibilities in training management (the coaches are there for that). Instead, the functions of the ORs are to facilitate training and operations, lead, mentor, accompany the team during travel, and coach cadets in the conduct of team administration. These are the mechanisms by which ORs gain access to the team and begin performing their leader development function.

In the context of leader development, participation is an enormous advantage. It gives ORs access, credibility, and the ability to supervise cadets on the ground and in the air. Therefore, ORs with skydiving experience may provide assistance specific to the sport, such as helping to supervise packing, drop zone operations, air-to-air and ground-to-air videography, and skills training.

Parachute team duty is one of the most time-intensive, physically demanding support roles at the Academy: the team trains six days a week and takes competitive trips over several major holidays, including Christmas and New Year's. It is, however, highly rewarding to those willing and able to make the commitment to serve the team. Although previous military and civilian jump experience is valued in the context of the team, prior jump experience of any kind or quantity does not guarantee selection and participation; neither is prior jump experience required for appointment as an OR.

Selection of the Officer in Charge

The officer in charge (OIC) leads and organizes the team of military ORs and the team captain and his or her staff. In principle, it makes sense for a team to have a single person in charge of leader developers to help organize the common effort. In other organizations, there might be a senior training developer or simply a person who has been around the longest whom people turn to for guidance and direction. On the USMA sport parachute team, someone is on the hook to organize and set the climate among leader developers.

Among all officers working with the parachute team, the most senior in grade who is also an experienced sport parachutist occupies the role of the parachute team OIC. The term *officer in charge* is really a misnomer, because the head coach is in charge of a team. The OIC is actually just an adviser and leader developer.

Competence does matter, to a degree. Ideally, the OIC should be a leader of senior military or academic rank assigned to duties at West Point and should possess a Class D (Expert) license issued by the U.S. Parachute Association (USPA). Other instructional ratings and rigger qualifications are important because power in in extremis settings is based on competence, not authority.

In developmentally focused organizations, there is a formal hierarchy of developmentally focused supervisors. In most organizations, however, such responsibilities fall on the existing leadership, which may be hierarchical or even among peers. The broader point, exemplified by the OIC of the parachute team, is that leader developers can benefit from organization and leadership. It's all about manifesting the developmental function into team activities, which usually requires a group effort, and groups perform their functions better with a little leadership.

Selection of Additional Officer Representatives

Staff and faculty who wish to participate as ORs usually contact the parachute team for information and an interview, and formally request appointment. The OIC and head coach jointly assess the need for additional leader developers, and they consider the leadership ability, skydiving qualifications, and desires of each applicant. ORs are appointed in writing by the OIC on a semiannual basis, acting on the recommendation of the head coach.

Competent skydiving skills add to a representative's credibility. Incompetence in the air, as in any other in extremis context, is leadership poison and in this case a direct physical threat to cadets. To assist the prospective OR in the decision on whether to participate in jumping, the team uses a two-phase sequence to bring ORs into their proper role.

Phase 1: Preparation and Familiarization with Team Operations. In the first four months of association with the team, new ORs operate as leader developers on a few trips, and if they wish to jump, they become licensed skydivers. Prospective ORs who are already licensed skydivers may jump with cadets and take trips as a way of familiarizing themselves with the time demands and character of the team. For those unfamiliar with skydiving but possessing exceptional leader development skills, the coaching staff and other experienced ORs provide training to build the newcomers' credibility and legitimacy with cadets. In addition to training at USMA with the team, aspiring ORs must augment their skydiving experience at a civilian parachute center (at their own expense) as a way of maintaining adequate progression and familiarizing themselves with the sport. There is no substitute for showing cadets that the leader developers are both willing and able to put themselves at risk and that they have a similar love for the sport of skydiving.

At the end of four months, all prospective leader developers understand the time demands and character of the team and decide if they want to be a participant in jump operations, remain a non-jumping contributor, or leave the team to pursue other cadet development activities. This also marks the point where the OIC and head coach can jointly determine the prospective OR's goodness of fit to the team and its mission and determine whether to continue that leader developer's association with the team. ORs who intend to continue skydiving with cadets will have earned a skydiving license by the end of phase 1 and exhibit good leader development skills and an enthusiasm for skydiving over all other avocations and outside interests.

★ **Why This Is Important for All Leaders**

When engaging leader developers in any organization, it's best to use a trial period to see if the role is a good fit. There are many high performers and dedicated volunteers who are not good at developing others. The easiest way to find out if they are good at it is to let them try.

Phase 2: Commitment and Service to the Parachute Team. This phase covers the remainder of the OIC/assistant OIC's association with the team, and it begins with a decision either to jump regularly or remain in a nonjumping capacity. Both roles require a significant commitment of personal time, which the team appreciates. The

ORs who jump must enjoy skydiving and be willing to invest the time and money that the sport demands. All ORs, as leader developers, must be passionate about cadet development and be willing to donate their time, including a significant number of holidays and weekends, to the purpose of developing the individuals who comprise the team.

★ **Why This Is Important for All Leaders**

The secret to developing leaders from teams may rest in part with the dedication and sense of purpose brought to the team by those who want to develop its members. It is common to find heroes in communities serving on Little League teams, in the Boy Scouts and Girl Scouts and other developmentally focused youth organizations, or in churches and social service organizations who give much of their time and energy to develop others. This spirit of development can be fostered among other volunteers. Perhaps as important, it can also be fostered in businesses and other occupational settings as well. Coaches, captains, and developers can exist in principle on all teams, not just competitive sports teams. Leaders across a spectrum of organizations should look to build this feature into the operations and training of their teams and work groups.

Relationship of Officer Representatives to Assigned Coaching Staff

One of the most interesting and rewarding elements of service as an OR in an extreme sport is that it requires high-quality officers and sergeants to work as a team. Regardless of rank, ORs and coaches assigned to the team (coaches are usually sergeants) maintain a supportive relationship respectful of rank but based on competence and ability. Civilian organizations can benefit from this focus on ability that pervades in extremis contexts. Even when risk is minimal, simply respecting experience and competence tends to flatten the organization in constructive ways. In risky endeavors, it is even more essential that rank take a backseat to professional competence in matters of judgment. It is a delicate balance, but it's comfortable and not at all odd when the decisions being made involve people's lives.

For example, when deciding if winds are too turbulent for a safe demonstration jump into a football stadium, the coach present with the most experience in skydiving makes the determination to jump or not to jump. Others, including those of greater military rank, support the decision and carry out the operation or endorse the cancellation. Although ORs are usually senior to the sergeant-coaches in grade, the officer's role is to support and reinforce the coaching staff's decisions. Furthermore, the function of their rank is also to take responsibility for the decision and to serve as "top cover" (military slang for protecting subordinates) when things go wrong. It should be made clear, however, that in matters of safety, anyone present at operations—sergeant, officer, or cadet—is duty-bound to call operations to a halt until an issue of unnecessary risk is resolved.

It's not that formal rank among officers and sergeants on the parachute team is unimportant: courtesy and military bearing are in fact very much intact and important to teach cadets. It is simply that there are aspects of leadership and decision making in dangerous settings to which rank and authority must defer. For all the individuals who supervise the team in any way, the most important characteristic is that they model the attitudes, intentions, and behaviors that reflect what leaders and the team should be, know, and do. The "Be, Know, Do" framework from Army leadership doctrine is responsible for the focus on developing leaders of character at the Academy (the "be" component), rather than leaders with mere knowledge and ability:

- Be. In driving leader development with a team, leaders are expected to role-model proper conduct on- and off-duty. Leaders who jump with the USMA sport parachute team, for example, are expected to have assumed the identity of both professional soldiers and skydivers. Proper conduct includes absolute adherence to Federal Aviation Administration (FAA) and USPA safety regulations and guidelines. It also includes the willingness to coach cadets on their attitudes, behavior, and decisions. Parachute team supervisors must be what cadets on the team aspire to become.

• Know. ORs are expected to maintain personal familiarity with the cadets on the parachute team, as well as with the team's interested parents and supporters. Leaders who jump are expected to know the contents of USPA basic safety regulations and the team standard operating procedures verbatim, without reference. ORs must also be familiar with instructional procedures listed in the various parachuting publication, as well as all FAA regulations that pertain to jumping—and there are several. All volunteers are also expected to have enough familiarity with the jumping gear so that they can safely inspect cadets and otherwise contribute to safety during operations.

• Do. Leaders have to walk the talk. That being said, the developmental role on a super team takes a toll of time and commitment from the leader developers. ORs who choose to participate in jump operations are responsible for maintaining currency and proficiency as USPA-licensed parachutists. Currency depends on the type and method of jumping and the parachutist's level of experience and licensing. In all cases, achieving currency requires more than fifty jumps per year. To achieve currency and proficiency (particularly given the character of New York State weather), leaders participate in skydiving beyond the limited jump opportunities offered by the team.

Furthermore, those who receive entry-level training from the coaching staff are expected to continue progression without repeated refresher training. (Overreliance on refresher training is a drain on team resources, sends the wrong leadership message to cadets, reveals a lack of commitment to skydiving, and, most important, significantly increases risk to the volunteer.) Officer volunteers who are new to jumping have to augment their training at civilian drop zones, which includes traveling some distance in the winter months, at their own expense. No one said that maintaining a developmental position on a superteam would be easy. The nature of the commitment is reminiscent of the credo of the barefoot water-skiers: "We didn't say it was easy; we only said it was cool!"

In addition, all skydivers, from cadet to colonel, are expected to maintain their gear in airworthy condition, pack for themselves, and adhere to federal regulations by managing the 120-day reserve repack cycle—the mandated periodic refolding of the reserve parachute by a certificated FAA rigger. Role models are encouraged to develop skills that enable them to contribute expertise in parachute operations. Such skills are validated by the leaders earning various instructional ratings and the coveted professional exhibition rating. Air-to-air or ground-to-air video skills are also of significant value to the team. Most important, and regardless of ratings, leader developers who work with cadets in the air are expected to exercise extreme discretion and care when jumping with cadets, in actions on the aircraft, and in free-fall. An officer's worst nightmare is to be personally involved in a collision or incident in which a cadet was injured or killed.

★ Why This Is Important for All Leaders

To those who will never help develop leaders with a collegiate skydiving team, all this may seem daunting, even fanatical. Most organizations that develop outside dangerous contexts may not require such effort. It does, in fact, take considerable determination and effort to put one's self in a position to develop others, regardless of the organization. The best organizations, however, cultivate such a level of commitment. Recall from Chapter Three the technique of inspiring by exceeding expectations.

A developmental effort that exceeds the expectations of group members can be a powerful influence on the

effectiveness of the organization. Whether in a dangerous context or not, this sometimes takes individuals with
the guts and determination to make development a reality for team members, no matter what it takes. It's more
than a commitment to duty. It's about a commitment to
showing others their duty. There is a soul-stirring quality to leader development that requires such commitment, under conditions of life or death, with young
people as the developmental focus. It requires physical
and mental courage, personal sacrifice, and a willingness
to put development ahead of all else. My favorite illus-
trative story of such courage and commitment involves
an infantry officer and military leadership instructor
named Steve Ruth.

Prove Your Commitment to a Team: Get to Where You Need to Be, No Matter What It Takes to Get There

Steve Ruth was in some respects an unlikely officer to help with the
USMA sport parachute team: when he asked to work with the team,
he had virtually no parachuting experience and only a year left on his
tour at the Academy. A solid, square-built man with almost no body
fat, he had served as the president of his graduating class at Texas
A&M University. He's 100 percent Texan: he answers his telephone,
"Steve Ruth from Texas, can I help you?" and his initials at the bottom of correspondence were "SRT" (for "Steve Ruth from Texas"). He
was well known across the Academy and among cadets as a natural
charismatic leader, assigned to teach the Academy's core course in
military leadership. As he worked out in the gym, he routinely bench-
pressed twice his weight. When he approached the team to participate as a leader developer, we said yes, but we knew we had a
challenging training task ahead of us.

Ruth's training was rocky at best. There has never been a more fearless, aggressive student skydiver: he came to the drop zone ready to learn and pumped for success. But Steve had difficulty in finding stability in the air after leaving the skid of the helicopter. Sometimes he would tumble forward, head down, and be viciously snapped upright by the opening parachute. Other times, he would pitch backward, and lines of the deploying parachute would snake upward between his legs, dragging the main parachute on the same dangerous path, yanking Steve through a violent, involuntary front flip on opening. It was fairly clear to the instructors that this particular sport did not come easily to Ruth. As it turned out, however, Ruth's contribution as a leader of the team would be made regardless of his parachuting prowess.

We had been having some team difficulty with transportation to the drop zone. Cadets are responsible on a daily basis for getting two trucks to carry jumpers and gear the twelve miles through the Hudson highland ridgelines to Lake Frederick, an open thirty-acre area on the fringe of West Point's seventeen thousand acres of rugged terrain. Occasionally cadets would miss the trucks and be absent from practice—and being absent without leave is a big deal at West Point. Unexcused absences put the head coach into orbit; no-shows and tardiness were causing serious heat for the cadets, who couldn't seem to understand why membership on a nationally competitive sports team had to be so demanding.

One day, Ruth had decided to work on his parachuting skills, but his wife needed their car. He packed his forty pounds of gear into a duffel bag with shoulder straps and started toward Lake Frederick, comfortable that the cadets or one of the other officers would see him in the first mile or two and pick him up for the ride to the drop zone. Because afternoon practices were only three hours long, there was no sense in trying to walk all the way, and the weight of the gear would make the trip prohibitively exhausting.

Unfortunately, as a matter of safety, cadets are taught not to pick up riders, and two officers, including me, passed right by Steve without noticing. He saw his potential rides flash past on their way to the drop zone, more than ten miles off. At that point he had walked two miles, but he was only about a quarter-mile from his house. Always the devoted husband, Steve had his cell phone; perhaps his wife could come get him if he called. But it seemed to Steve that there was a valuable lesson that a leader and role model could teach in this circumstance.

We were well into our practice, and the floor of the hangar was covered with black and gold nylon, with diligent cadets carefully following the procedures to pack their canopies into the harness and containers that would save them later in the air. Alternative music thumped from an iPod with external speakers in the background, and the cadet cross-chatter was steady. The head coach and I noticed that cadets began to slow, then stop both their packing and their chatter, and look toward the open door of the hangar. Soon the entire crew had frozen in midtask, with complete silence except for the music of Counting Crows in the background. Ruth strode across the threshold of the hangar, wet from head to toe with sweat, and eased his gear bag onto the carpeted floor. The head coach looked at him and said, "Sir, did you just walk out here from the main post?" The cadets were completely bewildered. Ruth took a long draw from a liter of Evian, capped it, and replied, "No, sergeant, if I had walked, I would have missed practice. I ran the flat and downhill parts. Who is running the manifest for scheduling onto the aircraft? I really need the practice."

At that moment, issues and discussions on the team involving late trucks and excuses for not making it out to practice ceased. And although Ruth left the Academy before he had the time to develop completely as a skydiver, I count him as one of the finest leader developers to ever work with the USMA parachute team. His wife, Bettina, picked him up at the end of practice, and as they drove away, cadets seemed fixed on the car, gesturing as it negotiated the winding gravel road away from the hangar. They had noticed the license plate, a red-white-and-blue Texas tag, bearing four letters: "DUTY." Steve Ruth from Texas had made his point.

Team Development and Institutional Resistance

One might think that the payoff from developing leaders in superteams would be both appreciated and embraced by institutions. The reality is that lack of funding and volunteers place most teams in the position of operating with only a captain and perhaps a coach; the concept of someone associated with the team who is there purely for the purpose of leader development is superfluous to the competitive athletic milieu. Often teams are administratively well supported by team members or the parents of team members, the role of soccer mom having become ubiquitous in modern U.S. youth culture. The challenge is that people who help teams too often simply do things for the team rather than showing the team how to do for themselves. Support is not necessarily developmental.

Parent engagement can be constructive in terms of both support and development, although we are all familiar with examples of poor sportsmanship (and even violence) stemming from parents who get carried away with the moment. The appeal to bask in the reflected glory of a team win places them on the edge of propriety when cheering on their team, criticizing officials, or even denigrating the challenger. Winning as opposed to losing is all too often a very big deal to parents. In personal development, failing can be as important and constructive as winning.

Yet a leader developer's role goes far beyond team accomplishment, focusing more on the personal and leadership development of the individuals than the group dynamics of the team or the win-loss record. Tailored coaching of individuals on a team is a relatively unique role, found mostly in Division 1 and professional athletic teams that can afford large coaching staffs. These trainers and coaches may focus on individuals, but they are interested in making them better team members and athletic competitors.

In contrast, a developmentally oriented high-performing team requires leader developers, like the Academy's officer representatives, to focus on producing better leaders, not just better athletes. This entails all of the following:

- Focusing on competitors one at a time and being attentive to all aspects of the team members' lives

- Engaging in their lives both on and off the playing field

- Paying attention to the values the athletes purport to endorse and whether those values are also expressed in behavior

- Being a leadership role model, resisting the urge to lead for the developing young leader, and instead coaching them on what they need to be, know, and do in the context of the team in order to learn to lead

The National Association of Intercollegiate Athletics (NAIA) recognizes the need for sports to serve as a character development function. Its Champions of Character program is designed to create in athletes an understanding of character values in sport. The program also provides practical tools for student athletes, coaches, and parents to use in modeling exemplary character traits, but the focus is on character, not solely leadership. The fact that NAIA has instituted such a program sends an important message: sports and athletic team activities, in and of themselves, do not necessarily develop character or leadership characteristics among team members. More effort is required. The use of leader developers in groups and teams, and ORs at the Military Academy, is based on the same fundamental assumption. Sports don't develop leaders. Leaders develop leaders, and sports are a great way to bring the process together.

Launched by the NAIA in 2000, the Champions of Character program claims to address character issues more comprehensively than any other national program for youth (an enthusiastic statement that would probably be challenged by Boy and Girl Scout programs). Whatever its scope, the program has been enacted on nearly three hundred college and university campuses in North America.

The nature of the program is such that the surrounding communities are engaged with reinforcing the appreciation of values among athletes. The espoused values are respect, responsibility, integrity, servant leadership, and sportsmanship. Rather than leaving character development in sports to chance, the program gives development roles and responsibilities to coaches, parents, administrators, and community partners.

Final Thoughts: Building Developmental Teams on the In Extremis Model

This chapter makes two fundamental points. First, groups and teams can be superb contexts in which to develop leaders. Although these forms of organizations are not inherently developmental, the right interventions made by the right people can turn all groups into leader development laboratories. It's up to senior leadership to staff and organize a leader development function into otherwise merely task-oriented groups to enable development and reap the benefits.

Second, dangerous contexts energize a team to even higher levels of development. This effect goes beyond the value to the individual, where the dangerous environment causes them to focus outward, be inherently motivated, and otherwise be intensely engaged. The team aspect brings to bear the interpersonal dimensions of leadership, including responsibility for others, an awareness of other people as possible organizational contributors or threats, and the presence of others as a social conscience holding all leader actions to scrutiny.

Together, these fundamental points have considerable meaning for public sector trainers and leader developers in organizations like police and fire departments and governmental agencies like the Drug Enforcement Agency, the FBI, and the military. Although such organizations have always trained in teams, the emphasis on safety and accident accountability has caused significant limitations in the willingness of those organizations to gain the benefit of training in dangerous contexts. During the cold war, Army commanders would often say, "Nothing we do in peacetime is worth the death or serious injury of a soldier." It's true that accidents can be tragic and should be avoided, but dangerous contexts are a part of training and should be carefully crafted and developed rather than eliminated. In extremis leadership can't be taught as a cluster of sterile skill sets that can be learned in safe and predictable settings. Training in dangerous settings produces augmented value in leader development, and the extent of that value needs to be actively and increasingly examined.

★ Why This Is Important for All Leaders

In broader, more usual contexts, the real lesson is that development takes effort and is not merely a by-product of team membership or group activity. Some thought and purpose should go into what role supportive parents lend to their children's teams and other groups and what sort of team leaders businesses select and develop. If leader development occurred without effort, everyone would have superb leader qualities. As leaders and developers ourselves, it's up to us to bring these qualities to people, organizations, and a world desperately in need of better leadership.

Summing Up

1. Make developing future leaders one of your organization's goals. Teams, in and of themselves, do not necessarily develop leaders or even positive individual qualities. Therefore, if strong leadership is the desired outcome, leader development should become a stated goal of your team or organization. And it's best to state that goal whether or not the core mission of your organization is producing widgets, winning lacrosse games, or fighting crime. All

groups, teams, organizations, and communities need people who are willing to step up.

2. Don't compose a team with the very best individuals you can find. Selecting the right people who will make up a superb, high-performing team is a critical first step toward success in any organization. But if you select a team solely on individual prowess, you can easily overlook or minimize the critical elements that take an average team to a superteam: cohesion, stability of the group, positive team culture, and diversity. People with top-tier potential who work together well form the core of a truly high-performing, developmental team. The rest is leadership and hard work. Also, never compose a high-performing team without solid assessment of actual performance in the critical setting. Finally, choose people who are broadly competent: fit, smart, and internally motivated. Excessive focus on a single dimension may uncover performers but not necessarily leaders.

3. Recognize that determination, discipline, and stamina are key characteristics for all leaders. There are other ways besides counting push-ups to determine if people have these qualities, and even those who are physically challenged can possess them. The point is that all organizations should take these characteristics into account and form assessments of future leaders based on these qualities. You want to hire people with heart.

4. Keep in mind that diverse teams are stable teams. A diverse organization adds a degree of civility and mutual respect to everything that organization does.

5. Make sure new members of your organization will fit in. In skydiving, business, or any other endeavor, the members of the organization need to work well together in order to function as a leader development laboratory, an entity where teammates are comfortable learning together.

6. Look for leader developers in your organization: the very best have them. They can be psychologists, technical consultants, or "greybeards" who don't have primary responsibility for the team but assist and advise the leader and team members.

7. Have team captains who are focused on the daily conduct of team activities. Good team captains should help leaders run the show and establish peer-to-peer relationships that keep the team focused on performance and commitment. Team captains are also (but not always) among the best members of their teams. If outsiders like coaches merely preach what should be team standards, the message often falls on deaf ears or, worse, creates a form of rebellion or resistance among the membership. In contrast, when peers lead without preaching but by example, the message is authentic, and it will be much more readily accepted.

8. Designate leader developers in your organization. These people should be experienced at leadership, be visible as role models, be trained to reinforce the attitudes and behaviors required of leaders, and fill out the supervisory staff of a truly developmental team. Also, establish a trial period to see if the role is a good fit: many high performers and dedicated volunteers are not good at developing others. The easiest way to find out if they are good at it is to let them try.

9. Keep in mind that good leaders "be, know, and do." This is the U.S. Army's leadership doctrine, and it can be applied to any other organization. It means that good leaders should be role models of proper conduct on the job and off; they should know the people, systems, procedures, and equipment in their organizations so that their followers recognize that their leaders are competent; and they should do the job—that is, walk the walk.

10. Focus on the personal and leadership development of individuals. Good leader developers should be more concerned with devel-

oping future leaders than on the group dynamics of the team or the win-loss record: there should be other people in the organization who focus on these factors.

11. Recognize that leader development takes effort. It is not merely a by-product of being a member of a team or organization. After all, if leader development occurred without effort, everyone would have superb leader qualities. As leaders and developers ourselves, it's up to us to bring these qualities to people, organizations, and a world desperately in need of better leadership.

Conclusion

The study of in extremis leadership leads the curious up the sides of mountains, out the door of flying aircraft, on the desert floor of warring countries, into the jungles ruled by feline kings, and through the doors of urban apartments fraught with fire and crime. This book has been about the people who live and work in exceptional places. In these exceptional places, people will die. But from these same places, incredible leaders will be born, their emergence crafted in a crucible of life-and-death outcomes.

The in extremis crucible is unique, and it produces unique outcomes. Authentic challenges produce authentic leaders. Settings that betray selfish people produce selfless leaders. Conditions intolerant of incompetence or inattentiveness produce attentive, competent leaders. Places where material wealth and social power have no value produce leaders driven by moral obligation and social conscience. A universe that doesn't allow do-overs creates a world where people get things done right the first time.

Social and behavioral science, the academic foundation of modern leader development, has rested comfortably on an empirical bed derived principally from studying people in idyllic denial of their own mortality and in settings where that mortality was seldom, if ever, threatened. Few scientists have been able to articulate the power of a context that harbors death, and still fewer have been able to do any research to look into the meaning or relevance of such contexts.

No more. The in extremis concept gives legitimacy and form to the idea that significant changes occur in the psychology of both the leader and the led in dangerous settings. Tenets of good science demand that researchers replicate and extend studies and theories about leadership into dangerous contexts. Until they do, their work is limited to conditions outside the in extremis obligations of soldiers, sailors, police officers, firefighters, extreme athletes, and others who lead in similar venues. For researchers with a little spunk, this opens up wide horizons for learning about leadership.

The courage and intensity of leadership scholars and leader developers must match the courage and intensity of their subjects. Leader developers in particular need to recognize the unique demands placed on leaders in crisis and in extremis circumstances. Training developers in the tough and dangerous public service jobs should gain motivation, direction, and inspiration from the understanding that their task is unique. Realism in training is no longer good enough. The in extremis lesson is that reality in training—that is, real challenges—is the key to maximum developmental gain.

I began this work with the insight that learning about leadership in dangerous contexts was a moral obligation incurred by my having responsibility to teach leadership to young people who would become Army officers and lead troops in dangerous settings. Since beginning the work in 2003, more than fifty graduates of the U.S. Military Academy have been killed in the global war on terror; twenty of them were students here during my tenure. The obligation to study and understand leadership in dangerous contexts is as compelling as ever before.

★ Why This Is Important for All Leaders

The value of understanding in extremis leadership is compelling beyond the moral imperative generated by the immediate threat to life. Not only great people emerge from great challenges; great lessons emerge as well. The lessons of leading in dangerous contexts are core lessons for leaders everywhere. If you can come to understand the value of authenticity, of sharing everything from risk to shelter with followers, of a focus on the organization and its challenges placed above selfish interests, then the rest of learning about leadership can be found elsewhere. Transactional management techniques should rest on a foundation of the type of leadership we see in in extremis settings. Today in American business, we try to insert principles of leadership into fundamentally managerial situations as if leadership were some sort of organizational or managerial effectiveness tool. We've really got it backward. We need leaders whom we can train as managers because it's much harder to train managers to be leaders.

There are glimpses of recognition already in evidence. In 2005, a group of executives from Citigroup Global Wealth Management came to West Point to hold a leadership meeting and left having successfully negotiated a leadership obstacle course with camouflage paint on their faces. Later, in the fall of 2006, Citigroup invited M.B.A. students who were also graduates of service academies (and had therefore served at least five years on active duty; many were still serving) to come to its New York headquarters. Senior leaders at Citigroup recognize the value of the sequence of leader first, manager second and want an advantage in hiring such people. Although this is a headache for the services in terms of the retention of some of their best and most highly educated officers, it's clearly a recognition by a major organization that management training over a foundation of leadership, often in extremis leadership, is a powerful advantage. In extremis leadership promises much for businesses and organizations in safe and secure venues.

That leadership in dangerous contexts has unique elements that can be researched, studied, articulated, and taught deliberately to others across contexts is a novel idea. The importance of the idea, however, lies not in its novelty but in its practicality. Whether you are a practicing leader, a motivated follower, or just a curious independent actor, powerful models of leadership in dangerous contexts can inform your safer life.

Where the Concept of In Extremis Leadership Really Comes From

Only an egoist or a genius takes sole credit for novel ideas. Insights come from the complexity, freedom, and joy of human interaction. The experiences, insights, and character of a number of in extremis leaders have helped me understand more about the elusive art and science of leadership in dangerous circumstances. The cast of mentors, study participants, peers, prisoners, and visitors is an exceptionally diverse array of men and women; blacks and whites; pacifists, soldiers, and civilians; Muslims, Christians, and Jews. Though a diverse group, each of them has risked his or her life to lead people in places where death waits, holding court in continuous judgment of their in extremis leadership. Their visits to West Point, discussions in our Black and Gold Leadership Forum and the Department of Behavioral Sciences and Leadership, their patient telephone conversations, and their candor and willingness to share their stories are what created the in extremis concept and the idea that leading under physical threat has unique characteristics.

The following biographical sketches of the leaders are not offered as an acknowledgment of assistance; statements of gratitude are elsewhere in this book. I offer them instead as a concluding depiction of why someone who came to know these people might have started thinking about leadership in dangerous contexts. They represent the totality of experience that generated the recognition of the value of in extremis leadership. The personal histories of these incredible people reflect the authenticity that resides, always, at the point of death:

- *Carol Amore*, explorer and friend, an award-winning wildlife photographer, high-definition digital videographer, and executive producer. She leads teams into remote and dangerous parts of the world and returns with outstanding images of wildlife. Her efforts are increasing the amount of time we'll be able to enjoy tigers in the wild.

- *Christian Santelices*, professional mountain guide. Christian works for Exum Guides in Jackson Hole, Wyoming, and spends part of each year in Patagonia, Chile, riding horses near the Andes with his Chilean father. As the founder and director of Global Community Project, a nonprofit organization based in Victor, Idaho, he encourages environmental stewardship in high school students by leading them in outdoor experiences. His interview taught me a lot about the spirituality of climbing.

- *Tyson Bradley*, professional mountain guide. Tyson grew up climbing and skiing in Idaho and Wyoming. He began guiding in 1994 with Alaska Mountaineering School on Denali, Timberline Mountain Guides (in Oregon), and Exum Utah. Tyson's passion is ski mountaineering, and he has made Alaskan first ski descents of Denali's fourteen-thousand-foot Wickersham Wall (1994), Foraker's Sultana Ridge (1995), and Mount Fairweather (1996). He has led four expeditions to the Himalaya and two to the Andes.

- *Dena Braeger*, Captain, U.S. Army. Dena took a 350-person maintenance company to combat in Iraq and then went to Columbia University to learn about counseling and organizational psychology. She joined my teaching team at West Point and is my point person for understanding the worldview of women in dangerous settings.

- *Alison Levine*, M.B.A. from Duke University. Mountain climber, entrepreneur, consultant, and speaker. Cured of a heart ailment at age thirty that had limited her activity, Alison became an elite athlete and nationally recognized climbing guide. She's an expert on high-performing teams in in extremis contexts.

• *David Petraeus*, General, U.S. Army, commander of the Multi-National Force in Iraq, and the former commander of the 101st Airborne Division (Air Assault); Ph.D. from Princeton University and an honor graduate from Ranger School. When he was a lieutenant colonel, I worked for him as his artillery planner, and his training standards drove home the necessity of competence in dangerous operations. He is a superior mentor, combat leader, skydiver, and friend.

• *Dick Cavazos*, General, U.S. Army (retired), Texan, heavily decorated veteran of Korea and Vietnam. He is the archetypal selfless leader, devoted to his followers and the Army.

• *Bob Dees*, Major General, U.S. Army (retired). He was my commander in the Second Infantry Division in 1999 in the Republic of Korea. A steady, unflappable leader, he counseled and mentored me following the training deaths of five of my soldiers and taught me the value and necessity of leading through tragedy. He is currently the director of military ministries for the Campus Crusade for Christ organization.

• *Clay Lyle*, Major, U.S. Army, former commander of Alpha Troop, First Squadron, Seventh Cavalry, and the first officer commander to roll his tank into Baghdad in 2003. Clay came to speak to me and our leadership course and brought his wife and new baby. We laugh about the fact that most of the questions were for his wife.

• *Eric Heinsheimer*, Sergeant First Class, U.S. Army. He is head coach of the USMA sport parachute team and has accumulated thirteen thousand jumps. He was my wingman at Military Freefall School. He is an internationally recognized formation skydiving coach, most recently coaching the Norwegian women's formation skydiving team.

• *Jack Jacobs*, Colonel, U.S. Army (retired), recipient of the Congressional Medal of Honor, on-camera military and political analyst for NBC, and the McDermott Professor of Politics at the U.S. Military Academy. His belief that nothing can prepare a person for combat is one of the reasons that I find the study of in extremis conditions so fascinating.

• *Eric Olson*, Major General, U.S. Army, formerly the Commandant of the U.S. Military Academy, who commanded the Twenty-Fifth Infantry Division in Hawaii and Afghanistan. He is a leader who would never ask his followers to do something he couldn't or wouldn't, one defining characteristic of an in extremis leader.

• *Chris Moore*, Sergeant First Class, U.S. Army, U.S. Army Parachute Team (Golden Knights). He coached me to land on target and was my inspiration to attain a professional exhibition rating as a skydiver.

• *Eric Schoomaker*, Major General, U.S. Army, chief of the Army Medical Corps. A medical doctor with a doctorate in genetics, he is a mentor and friend and the first person to connect the in extremis concept to medical professionals. He commands Walter Reed Army Medical Center.

• *Pete Schoomaker*, former Commander of U.S. Special Operations Command and the Army's Chief of Staff. I introduced him to my cadets as General Peter Schoomaker and he said, "Only my mother calls me Peter." He offered his insights as a combat commander and special operations soldier to cadets in the Black and Gold Leadership Forum.

• *Pat Sweeney*, Colonel, U.S. Army, my deputy in the Department of Behavioral Sciences and Leadership. He voluntarily left graduate school in Chapel Hill, North Carolina, when the Iraq War started in order to study trust in combat with the 101st Airborne Division. He returned to finish his doctorate and serves the Army as its expert on trust in combat.

• *Franklin "Buster" Hagenback*, Lieutenant General, U.S. Army. As superintendent of the U.S. Military Academy, he is both a college president leading a faculty and the pinnacle trainer and role model at the Academy. His personal experience commanding the Tenth Mountain Division in Afghanistan has informed his ability to prepare cadets and faculty for the physical and mental demands of combat.

- *Leonard Wong*, Lieutenant Colonel, U.S. Army (retired), a Ranger, with a Ph.D. in industrial/organizational psychology. He is a brilliant researcher and lifelong friend who convinced me that we really could do research in a combat zone. He taught leadership at the Military Academy in the 1990s.

- *Terry Potter*, Colonel, U.S. Army (retired), former professor of Arabic languages at West Point. A superb soldier, he had already announced his retirement, yet he selflessly accompanied Lenny Wong, Ray Millen, and me to combat to support our research. He was our translator in Iraq and Kuwait and befriended sick and wounded prisoners in the waiting area of the camp hospital so that they would talk to us.

- *Ray Millen*, Lieutenant Colonel in the infantry, U.S. Army, Ranger, writer, author, expert in urban warfare who was part of the Kuwait/Iraq expedition with Wong and me in 2003. Ray was the glue that held our research team together when we didn't know where our next helicopter was coming from or weren't really sure where our next meal was coming from.

- *Emily Perez*, Second Lieutenant, U.S. Army, a West Point graduate and sociology student in my department, an incredible leader and socially conscious, spiritual person. She died in the detonation of an improvised explosive device in Iraq on September 12, 2006. I was the Academy's representative to her parents at her burial at West Point.

- *Dennis Zilinski*, First Lieutenant, U.S. Army, a West Point graduate and former member of my seminar in Leadership in Combat. He died from combat wounds suffered in Iraq. I was the Academy's representative to his parents at his burial at West Point.

- *Andy Blickhahn*, Captain, U.S. Army, a great young Army officer, former cadet first captain at West Point, and the cadet captain of the Academy's sport parachute team. He was in Iraq fighting as a platoon leader seventeen days after reporting to his unit.

- *Bill Lutz*, an agent with the Drug Enforcement Agency and the director of its leadership development programs. He was one of the first people to encourage me to capture my ideas about in extremis leadership in a book.

- *Steve Ruth*, Major, U.S. Army, president of his class at Texas A&M. He was trained in industrial/organizational psychology and taught leadership in the Department of Behavioral Sciences and Leadership at the Academy. He voluntarily deployed to combat over the Christmas and New Year's holidays to study in extremis leadership and negotiations in dangerous settings. Steve is the most duty-focused, charismatic leader I have ever known.

- *Frank Wierczynski*, Colonel, U.S. Army. A tremendous soldier and leader, he spoke to the Academy's combat leadership class about the Battle of Takur Gur in Afghanistan.

- *Nate Self*, former U.S. Army Ranger, led his men through a bloody fight on Robert's Ridge in Afghanistan to recover the body of a fallen Navy SEAL, Neil Roberts. Nate was honored by President Bush at the White House in 2003 and awarded a Silver Star for his heroism in battle. He honored the Academy's Department of Behavioral Sciences and Leadership with a visit in 2006.

- *Sean Hannah*, Lieutenant Colonel, U.S. Army, Ph.D. in leadership from the University of Nebraska Gallup Institute. He is in charge of the Leadership and Management Studies program at West Point and teaches leadership courses in the Department of Behavioral Sciences and Leadership. A veteran of Desert Storm, Sean is without a doubt the best leadership theoretician in the department and my finest critic.

- *James Halterman*, Sergeant First Class, U.S. Army, senior parachute rigger for the U.S. Military Academy Sport Parachute Team, and one of the finest sergeants I have ever known. He gave this priceless advice to cadets on actions they were to take in the event of a broken leg on a demonstration skydive: "Shut up, take the pain, and wave to the crowd. You were acting like a hero; now you get to be one."

- *Tom Buchanan*, professional skydiver with five thousand jumps, and safety and training adviser for the Blue Sky Ranch in Gardiner, New York. The Ranch (a place so famous it is a proper noun in skydiving circles) is famous for "no rule," yet has a remarkable safety record. The skydiving culture there is superficially crazy, yet to the trained eye, there is continuous attention to detail in safety. Buchanan has, as much as anyone else, set the tone of safety culture at the Ranch and has been my mentor on how to keep my jumpers safe. There are people who are alive today because of Tom Buchanan's persistent efforts.

• *Guy Wright*, professional skydiver and organizer of large skydiving formations. He is a no-nonsense leader who taught me that in some endeavors, "you have to fire someone right before the first time they screw up."

• *Joseph W. Pfeifer*, deputy assistant chief, chief of counterterrorism and emergency preparedness, Fire Department of New York. One of New York City's experts on leadership in dangerous circumstances, the first chief on the scene at the World Trade Center on September 11, 2001. I'd follow Joe down any hallway.

• *H. Norman Schwarzkopf*, General, U.S. Army (retired), West Point graduate, Vietnam veteran, commander of combined forces in the First Gulf War. A tough warrior leader, generous with his time in the Department of Behavioral Sciences and Leadership, who spoke to a small group of cadets in the Black and Gold Leadership Forum.

• *Howard Prince*, Brigadier General, U.S. Army (retired), my predecessor in the Department of Behavioral Sciences and Leadership from 1978 to 1990, distinguished combat veteran, clinical psychologist, founder of the Jepson School of Leadership at the University of Richmond and the Center for Ethical Leadership at the University of Texas.

• *John "Doc" Bahnsen*, Brigadier General, U.S. Army (retired), Vietnam veteran air cavalryman. Doc Bahnsen is a colorful, outspoken warrior. When invited to speak to my combat leadership course, he spoke to cadets about the challenges of developing a team that was mentally prepared to kill aggressively and professionally, while at the same time risking their own lives for their country. He talked to them like professional peers—typical of people who have spent large amounts of time in environments where rank is less important than competence.

• *Robert Scales*, Major General, U.S. Army (retired), former commandant of the Army's War College in Carlisle Barracks, Pennsylvania. An accomplished author, he is a friend and one of the world's most serious thinkers on the human dimension of combat. He is also a prolific author.

• *Tony Nadal*, Colonel, U.S. Army (retired), one of the company commanders in the first major battle of the Vietnam War, made famous in the movie *We Were Soldiers*. Subsequent to the fight, Tony returned to West Point to teach leadership in our department. He has been generous with his time, helping to teach cadets the rigors of combat and the demands that are placed on leaders in dangerous contexts.

• *Ric Shinseki*, General, U.S. Army (retired), former Army Chief of Staff, Class of 1951 Chair for the Study of Leadership in the Department of Behavioral Sciences and Leadership, West Point. He spent two years helping my cadets, my faculty, and me understand leadership. He has the most personal integrity of any man I have ever known. He was fond of calling me "boss," which, of course, I really wasn't.

• *Dave Corderman*, supervisory special agent and chief of the Leadership Development Institute, Federal Bureau of Investigations. Dave not only understands the idea of in extremis leadership, but he understands how to develop leaders for whatever contexts they may face. His work with me on the Gallup Leadership Summit in Washington, D.C., in 2006 was a high point of my year.

• *Greg*, Special Operations Command (security concerns precluded my knowing either his rank or his surname). Trained as a sniper and military free-fall parachutist, he has more than thirty direct action missions completed in his career thus far.

• *Casper*, Special Operations Command (security concerns precluded my knowing either his rank or his surname). Trained as a military free-fall parachutist and in multiple military skills as well, he has more direct action missions "than he could count."

• *Rebecca (Becky) Kanis*, West Point graduate, director of innovation for Common Ground, a nonprofit dedicated to eliminating homelessness in New York City. She is a former Army signal officer in special mission units and is tough but with a huge heart.

• *Kathryn Hillegass*, senior at West Point, captain of the Academy's sport parachute team, and Arabic/French double major. The Academy's best skydiving videos feature jumpers dressed identically in black, gracefully crafting various formations in free-fall, and one with a red ponytail dancing out the back of a shiny black helmet. That's Katie.

• *"Utah" Steve Webb*, professional skydiver with ten thousand jumps, my tandem examiner and mentor. An inflexible, demanding, yet patient and kind human being. If you are on the front of Utah Steve in free-fall, you are considerably safer than you were when you were riding in the airplane.

• *Curtis "Mike" Scapparotti*, Brigadier General, U.S. Army, formerly the Commandant of Cadets at West Point. He talked about leading in combat to my students and me and explained why he kept the pictures of his soldiers who were killed in action in his pocket throughout his tour in combat. I now do the same with photos of cadets I've helped graduate who have died fighting in the global war on terror.

• *Matt Densmore*, Major, U.S. Army, currently in psychological operations at Fort Bragg, North Carolina. Matt taught in the Department of Behavioral Sciences and Leadership and became so fascinated with the topic of in extremis leadership that he went to Iraq to collect data with special operations units. He worked through the frustration of having all his hard-earned data wiped clean on his hard drive when he left the top-secret assignment but returned to West Point to write about in extremis leadership.

• *Everett Spain*, Major, U.S. Army, M.B.A. from Duke University. Ev taught leadership in USMA's Department of Behavioral

Sciences and Leadership and took a break to go to Iraq to experience in extremis contexts firsthand. He was the first of my faculty to be wounded—thankfully by just a few small mortar fragments—while studying in Iraq. He is currently serving in Iraq as the aide-de-camp for General David Petraeus.

- *Donna Brazil*, Colonel, U.S. Army, permanent professor at West Point, course director for the Academy's only core course in military leadership. She volunteered to leave her husband and three children to go to Afghanistan, where she helped the Afghan Army create the National Military Academy of Afghanistan, modeled after West Point and its leadership instructional techniques.

- *Pat Michaelis*, Major, U.S. Army. I took a chewing from our dean for bringing Pat to teach leadership in the Department of Behavioral Sciences and Leadership prematurely. Pat had an M.B.A. from Harvard and had just been withdrawn from Senator John McCain's staff by the Army congressional liaison for working the summer on Capitol Hill "without permission." Pat taught brilliantly for a semester, then continued to teach his students by satellite from Iraq while he composed a lateral electronic communications network to support the entire First Cavalry Division in a combat community of practice.

- *Jack Jefferies*, intense skydiver and elite athlete, with fifteen thousand jumps—probably the most accomplished formation skydiver in history. He possesses two qualities at their extreme limits: talent and humility. A brilliant and effective consultant in organizational dynamics, he has adjunct professor status at West Point and teaches the high-performing teams portion of the leadership curriculum.

- *Bob Carter*, Major General, U.S. Army (retired), sociologist, formerly the commissioner of the San Francisco Crime Commission. He taught in the USMA's Department of Behavioral Sciences and Leadership for many years and brought in extremis contexts to life for many cadets and for me.

- *Steve Carter*, special agent, Federal Bureau of Investigation, San Francisco office. He is Bob Carter's son and a superb public servant.

- *James Gagliano*, Special Agent, Federal Bureau of Investigation, New York City office. He is intensely dedicated to his men and the Special Weapons and Tactics mission.

- The free-fall instructors of the Military Freefall School, Yuma, Arizona. They train in an unforgiving environment without respect to rank or authority. Their function defines in extremis development.

- Thirty-six Iraqi prisoners detained in Um Qasr, Iraq, in April 2003. My interviews with them taught me much about the inhumanity of war and the price of failed in extremis leadership.

- Fifty-four U.S. soldiers interviewed in the vicinity of Baghdad, Iraq, in May 2003. Proud of you. Thanks for your sacrifice.

- Sixteen U.S. Marines interviewed in the vicinity of al Hillah, Iraq, in April 2003. Proud of you too, and thanks for the helicopter ride to Baghdad.

- Sixty-two cadet skydivers on the U.S. Military Academy Sport Parachute Team, 2001–2007. Develop the mind; discipline the body; own the edge.

Resource
Physical Development for In Extremis Leaders

Danger makes it important for in extremis leaders to maintain exceptional cardiovascular fitness and muscular strength. My fitness icon when I was younger was Lieutenant Colonel Dave Petraeus, currently serving as a four-star general, and charged with command of the Multinational Forces in Iraq. He could run farther and faster than most of his men and was fond of demonstrating a rope climb without the use of his legs, ascending a twenty-five-foot climbing rope hand over hand in an L-shaped pike position. Fitness was a huge part of Petraeus's leadership style, and of his life.

In 1991, just prior to my arrival in the 101st Airborne Division (Air Assault), Petraeus was commanding an infantry battalion, the 3rd Battalion, 187th Infantry, known as the physically toughest out-fit in a physically tough division. He was supervising a machine-gun range at Fort Campbell in Kentucky, and he happened to be stand-ing next to the division's commander, Major General Jack Keane.

One of Petraeus's machine gunners was firing belt after belt of ammunition down range, and in the middle of a long burst, he expe-rienced a jam. The cartridge was stuck in the chamber, but the bolt had not come forward with enough energy to fire the round. The gun-ner was pulling his weapon off-line for maintenance and carelessly pointed it in the direction of Petraeus and Keane. At that moment, the heat from the barrel ignited the powder in the cartridge, "cook-ing off" the round, which fired out the end of the barrel at more than three thousand feet per second. It struck Petraeus just above his name tape on his uniform shirt, penetrating his body armor front and back, a through and through wound to the chest cavity.

The division commander and the medics on site worked to stabilize the commander and control the bleeding from the wound. A medical evacuation helicopter was called immediately and flew him to Vanderbilt Medical Center in Nashville, where thoracic surgeon Bill Frist performed emergency surgery.

Frist attributed the fact that Petraeus survived such a gunshot wound to his incredible level of personal fitness. Petraeus astonished his men with his quick recovery, running and finishing the Army 10 miler just a few months after being shot. Following severe injury, one's original level of fitness counts in terms of both survivability and recovery time.

Even beyond recovery from injury, in extremis settings place an additional physical demand on leaders. The special demand is unabated functionality. In extremis leaders working in the presence of threat cannot afford an immediately debilitating injury such as a dislocation or even a torn muscle or ligament. Depending on the exact circumstances, fatigue can be managed. Leaders manage fatigue among their subordinates all the time, and if they're smart, they accurately gauge and manage their own fatigue as well. Weakness can be mitigated with rest—in military terms, this is a tactical pause. Insufficient strength may be overcome with teamwork or even tools. But an immediately debilitating injury can be fatal to the individual leader and place impossible demands on a team of followers. In military slang, the word *turf* is used as a verb: "to turf" means to hit the ground due to complete exhaustion or a debilitating injury. Elite leaders require unabated functionality. They can't afford to turf.

Debilitating injury is a possibility that can never be eliminated. For elite leaders, it's a disastrous outcome worthy of deliberate mitigation. Just as succession planning is important for unpredictable catastrophic loss of a business leader, just as chain of command is critical in military, police, and fire department operations, fitness activities that help prevent debilitating injury are a necessary—even obligatory—form of preparation to lead. In extremis leaders are characterized by the routine expectation of danger and stress. Unlike more reactive crisis leaders, they prepare for and assume that the toughest possible demands will challenge them. Most leadership training has some mental or even emotional preparation. Elite leaders also prepare physically, and in specific ways, to maximize the chances of survival and success.

Threatening settings place unique fitness demands on those who navigate dangerous space. This resource acknowledges such fitness demands and specifically addresses physical preparation for in extremis leaders. There are exercises far outside the usual routine of most athletes that are particularly useful to people who work in dangerous settings. Joint stability, balance, and flexibility are much more important in dangerous contexts than on the fields of friendly strife found in common sports. But the lesson goes much further than that. It also explains why a fitness regimen for in extremis leaders might apply to those who live more routine lives, because certain types of exercise can protect all of us from the frustration and annoyance and physical debilitation of physical injury.

Being in Good Physical Condition Is a Benefit to Leadership

Across the spectrum of in extremis leaders, fitness seems universally valued, and it makes intuitive sense that tough environments demand physically tough people. Elites, whether successful business executives, professional actors, or Army Rangers, place physical and mental demands on their bodies that are best met when they are in good physical condition. In terms of a public image, elites unquestionably benefit from a healthful, trim appearance. Leaders project competence in order to build trust and loyalty, and fitness is a publicly apparent form of personal competence.

Perceptions of a leader's overall health matter greatly. When a leader is not fit or is exposed to injury, a perception may develop that the organization is similarly debilitated. This is most apparent in instances where the injury or physical malady of the leader results in death. In the recent past, several organizations experienced the unexpected death of their CEO, with measurable negative consequences to perceptions about the organization. For example, following the April 2004 death of sixty-year-old CEO Jim Cantalupo, McDonald's shares fell 42 cents to $27.04 in morning trading on the New York Stock Exchange. More than the death of a CEO can cause instability. Apple rode out share price adjustments based on CEO Steve Jobs's cancer surgery. Despite gloomy predictions for these companies and some pessimism on the part of analysts, both organizations recovered using strategies to negate public and shareholder perceptions of instability in the leadership of the company. The point is that perceptions of the leader's health affect perceptions of the entire organization.

As with most other values, however, there is a wide gap between principle and practice with fitness. Most of us are not elites and have a demanding schedule that makes workout time somewhat fungible. For the typical leader, working out is a stress release and a functional endeavor, focused on improving both appearance and health. And make no mistake: many great leaders have been less-than-perfect physical specimens, from Winston Churchill, who smoked cigars and was fond of Boodle's gin, to Dave Thomas, the congenial and highly successful founder of Wendy's fast food restaurants.

The gap between principle and practice in physical fitness will probably exist forever. One way to close the gap is to ensure that exercises not only add to general fitness and well-being but also tend to prevent injury. It's not that every exercise need be done. It's that every exercise matters in the search for better fitness.

In Extremis Leaders Need to Be
Physically Functional at All Times

Most training approaches to personal fitness are characterized by the development of strength and stamina. Running, fast walking, swimming, and other cardiovascular activities help keep excess weight off and make the heart and lungs healthy and efficient. Such training gives individuals the speed and stamina to perform faster and longer at whatever they do. Strength training benefits active people in a number of important ways: better definition and functioning of the muscles, increased bone density, and resistance to injury, to name a few.

Scientists at the U.S. Army Research Institute of Environmental Medicine (USARIEM) acknowledge the continuous physical demands of in extremis environments. USARIEM is working to improve both leader and follower performance by focusing on the prevention of musculoskeletal injuries, one of the major premises behind the joint stabilization strategy for leaders. It is also conducting research on the effects of nonsteroidal anti-inflammatory drugs on the body.

Maintaining physical function in dangerous environments is worthy of study. Soldiers, fire department personnel, and others in dangerous professions have extreme physical demands placed on their bodies, including the need to move rapidly while carrying heavy loads over rugged and dangerous terrain. As a result, musculoskeletal injuries (which include injuries of bones, joints, ligaments, tendons, muscles, and other soft tissues) are common among those who operate in dangerous and demanding environments. In fact, Colonel Paul Amoroso, an Army doctor and USARIEM research epidemiologist, maintains that musculoskeletal injuries are the top cause of disability discharge in the Army.

Although the most profound consequences for injury occur in dangerous environments, problems with musculoskeletal training injuries have been studied most frequently during basic training because of the size of the subject pools and the ease of access to soldiers in the predictably regimented training centers. According to USARIEM scientists, typically 25 percent of men and 50 percent of women in basic training experience some form of musculoskeletal injury. The U.S. Army Center for Health Promotion and Preventive Medicine at Aberdeen Proving Ground in Maryland, in collaboration with USARIEM, has been studying musculoskeletal injuries among Army trainees for more than twenty years.

The payoff is significant not only in keeping soldiers and their leaders free of injury, but in minimizing the use of nonsteroidal anti-inflammatory drugs (NSAIDs) such as aspirin, ibuprofen, and naproxen. Soldiers tend to use a lot of these drugs to cope with their frequent musculoskeletal injuries. Using such pain relievers is okay if the doses are kept small, but if taken too frequently at too high a dosage, they can cause problems. For example, prostaglandins help protect the lining of the stomach from acid. Therefore, injured leaders who take large doses of NSAIDs are setting themselves up for gastrointestinal problems, including ulcers, because NSAIDs block prostaglandins. Other side effects include problems with blood flow to the kidneys and even damage to the liver (especially when combined with heavy alcohol use).

For leaders, the ability to maintain flexibility, stabilize joints, and avoid injury goes beyond avoiding the inconvenience of limited mobility or the public perception of weakness or vulnerability. It means avoiding painkilling drugs and their side effects, which seem to combine destructively with the stressful lifestyle typical of many leaders.

Three Qualities of Elite Leader Fitness

In extremis leaders, as well as elite business leaders, need a fitness program in order to maximize functionality and minimize the chance of a debilitating injury at a critical time. The distance-running, fitness-trained executive has become stereotypical among the corporate elite. But distance runners, for all their cardiovascular development, are among the most routinely injured amateur athletes in the world. Most firehouses and military gyms have weight-lifting equipment, yet back injury is one of the most common health insurance claims for these groups. Common exercise routines underplay the value of activities that stabilize joints from dislocation, minimize the falls that lead to broken bones, and protect muscles from tearing—catastrophic failures in in extremis settings. It's the addition of these three protective goals that separates elite leader fitness from mere conditioning. The three goals are joint stability, balance, and flexibility.

Joint Stability

Do your fitness activities involve walking or running on a predictable, stable surface such as paved streets or a treadmill? Do you use strength machines that isolate muscles by lifting weights with cables or pivoting weights around a mechanically fixed axis? If so, you may be preparing yourself to be an exceptionally fit but injured person. To understand why this is the case requires understanding how joints function and remain stable, how they fail, and how they are rehabilitated after failure.

The primary stabilizers of joints are passive structures—the bones and the ligaments that join otherwise separate body parts into a functional joint. They are considered passive because their basic physical characteristics and relationships cannot be changed. The exception involves injury: ligaments can be torn; bones can be broken. By themselves, these passive structures are insufficient for joint stability during motion.

Joints also require secondary stabilizers—muscles—in order to maintain stability through movement. Unlike the passive bones and ligaments, these muscles can be trained in ways that make it less likely that a joint will dislocate, providing the functionality required in in extremis settings and the resistance to injury sought by all leaders whose absence due to injury can have organizational consequences.

The muscles that stabilize joints work rapidly to stabilize the joint in response to two perceptions: the ability to sense movement (kinesthetic perception, or kinesthesia) and the ability to sense the position of a joint in space (proprioception).

There are complex arrays of mechanoreceptors in both the passive structures (ligaments) and the secondary stabilizers (muscles) that speed information to the central nervous system and coordinate the muscular stabilization of the joint. These mechanoreceptors are most active at the end ranges of motion, and they work the muscles in concert with bones and ligaments to prevent hyperextension or other damaging joint movements.

But some actions occur faster than muscles have been trained to stabilize the joint, and in those circumstances, only the ligaments and other passive structures offer stability. When the movement of a joint occurs beyond the ability of the body to stabilize it through primary or secondary means, injuries such as torn muscles, strained or torn ligaments, and sometimes broken bones may occur. The leader is then out of the picture, and an in extremis leader may be in the gravest of circumstances. For elite business leaders, relearning normal functional movements and timing can cost several months of normal joint use, notwithstanding time spent in physical therapy and rehabilitative exercise. Such an outcome may be unnecessary. Muscles respond to training, and trained muscles react faster to stabilize joints.

Exercise physiologists have not spent a lot of time figuring out how to stabilize the joints of in extremis leaders. They have, however, learned to stabilize the joints of injured people, and the principles are the same. Rehabilitative training illustrates this process of stabilizing joints. To reestablish stability as a part of a nonsurgical healing process, trainers follow three steps:

1. Range of motion is resumed, either on the individual's own power or by gently guiding the affected limb through the proper range of motion.

2. Strength and proprioception are restored by adding weight while carefully controlling range of motion.

3. Ballistic movement without weight on the joint and then with weight finishes the training.

This constructive sequence forms the basis for the design of a protective, injury-preventing workout for leaders.

★ **Why This Is Important for All Leaders**

All leaders, whether in physically demanding, dangerous jobs or office environments, can spend more time working and less time healing if they recognize the value of deliberately stabilizing their joints.

Strength and cardiovascular workouts can be modified to create joint stability by introducing deliberate instability into the activity. The joints are required to counter the unstable weight and thereby increase both the ability to sense movement and the position of joints in space (again, kinesthesia and proprioception, respectively). Muscles develop in ways that better stabilize joints.

As you transform your normal workout to one that will maximally increase joint stability, it's best to be patient when developing stability throughout the range of motion. First, perform the movement without bearing any weight on the joint—what trainers call an open kinetic chain. Next, close the kinetic chain by using the floor or a wall to push against and bear weight on the joint. Finally, add velocity to the motion, using free weights, pulley systems, or rubber sheeting of various thicknesses designed for exercise.

The wisdom of introducing instability as an exercise technique reaches beyond the design of the perfect in extremis workout or the creation of an action-hero physique. Most of life's activities occur on an unstable surface. Leaders who want to stay uninjured and in the game need to pay attention to their workouts.

Balance

Most of us take balance for granted. When standing upright, our center of gravity is within its base of support. When we move, our center of gravity can extend beyond that base of support, exceeding the limits of stability and necessitating a step or stumble to prevent a fall. In running, we deliberately extend the center of gravity forward, beyond the base of support, and therefore cannot stop instantly without a step or two to regain balance. Even when standing still, our muscles, especially the core muscles of the torso, work automatically and reflexively to keep us upright. Most of us take balance for granted. Leaders who wish to avoid injury cannot.

In a peaceful, safe environment, our sense of balance is seldom in our conscious thought. The occasional stumble is barely noticed; even a few weeks on crutches can be overcome with a little attitude. In an in extremis setting, however, a fall can be fatal, and it can put an entire team at risk. And for elite business or political leaders, a physical fall can mark a power decline. Serious leaders need to stay on their feet or be willing to pay the price in credibility and image.

You can learn balance through the practice of balancing. Several devices are available to assist in developing an enhanced sense of balance. The voodoo board is a straight board slightly longer than a skateboard, equipped with a roller about six inches in circumference and about as wide as the board. The user must develop the skill to balance on the board atop the roller and then progress to the ability to sway from side to side, rolling the roller underneath the board. It trains the muscles of both the legs and core to react instantaneously to shifts in the center of gravity. The BAPS (Biomechanical Ankle Platform System) board is a disc about three feet in diameter, with a dome underneath in the center. The user stands on the board and must continuously work to maintain balance and level the board. In addition, dance classes, skating, and skateboarding are exceptionally good activities for developing balance.

Another element of balance to consider in an elite fitness regimen is the balanced development of opposing muscles—for example, the quadriceps on the front of the thigh and the hamstrings on the back of the thigh, or the pectoral muscles of the chest and the opposing back muscles. If one or more muscle groups is underdeveloped relative to opposing groups, muscular injuries can occur even with proper warm-up and stretching.

This point was driven home during a softball game when a sprinting base runner who appeared to be fit (that would be me) turfed because of an excruciating hamstring tear. My entire team had jogged for fifteen minutes prior to the game as a warm-up, and we did a collective stretching routine that loosened the hamstrings considerably. But at the time, my fitness routine included primarily distance running, so my weak hamstrings and overdeveloped quadriceps were hopelessly out of balance. The muscle was so badly torn that the injured limb had seventeen degrees' greater range of motion than the uninjured leg, and the external bruising ran from just below my buttock to my midcalf. Three months of recovery was a weighty price to pay for an unbalanced exercise routine. In the softball game, I was out. In an in extremis setting, I might have been down for the count.

Flexibility

The third aspect of in extremis fitness that merges with joint stability and balance is flexibility—an important element in the conditioning of leaders. The reason that flexibility is important to leaders, especially those who work in dangerous environments, is the maintenance of unabated, continuous capability—the ability to continue without a debilitating injury in in extremis conditions. From a leader perspective, stretching to improve flexibility is a prophylactic for disaster. A soft tissue injury such as a bad sprain or muscle tear can quickly relegate leader or follower to the role of excess baggage, literally carried by others.

Three principles govern the strategy that must underpin stretching to maintain flexibility and prevent injury in dangerous contexts— or in the case of leaders who simply cannot afford to be laid up:

1. Concentrate your stretching on muscle groups based on the consequences of their failure or injury. All injuries are not created equal. Under most circumstances, a sprained or broken wrist, for example, is only moderately annoying when compared to a torn hamstring or a back injury. Leaders should do a quick analysis of their work environment and answer two questions. First, what is the most likely form of injury to occur in your environment? Second, what is the most dangerous form of injury likely to occur? The first question is common sense and used by most athletes, but in some respects, the second question is even more relevant—and certainly so in in extremis environments.

2. Stretch where and when you can. "Green Ramp" is the Army term for the place where paratroopers wait, geared up, prior to boarding an aircraft for training or combat jumps. Soldiers, once checked by their jumpmaster and other leaders, are often seen napping or otherwise playing the inevitable "hurry up and wait" game ubiquitous in the experience of soldiers at war. As they board the running aircraft, several in most large-scale airborne insertions will fall victim to soft tissue injuries on the drop zone, particularly at night. Green Ramp is a superb place to go through stretches, particularly for the critical lower extremities like hamstrings, knees, and ankles. What is your Green Ramp? Are there places where you could make better use of your time by loosening your muscles rather than sitting idle? Learn to stretch as a matter of habit. It is easier to accomplish it that way than trying to set aside specific times to stretch. Of course, prior to exercise, stretching is a must.

3. Ensure that your stretching matches the equipment and conditions that place specific demands on your body. There are general-purpose stretches, but those of us who use equipment such as weapons, firefighting tools, axes, and other implements have to take their weight, function, and required range of motion into consideration from the start. Stretches need to pattern after the demand. My personal favorite stretching strategy is to stretch when I'm already geared up for a sport parachute jump and waiting for the aircraft. Stretches made when I'm harnessed up and weighted down with equipment are guaranteed to be constructive to my activity.

Here is a simple example of how this in extremis analysis of flexibility requirements can work in a common setting. Assume that your primary piece of equipment is a laptop. The most likely injury is a strain caused by tension, and your most dangerous or threatening injury would be loss of work due to a spasm in your neck or back. This analysis suggests that you need to stretch your shoulders, upper back, and neck to prevent the annoyance of muscle spasms and headaches. This is particularly true if you routinely carry your laptop through airports or in and out of vehicles. Because such work often includes sitting, which can put pressure on the lower back over time, you should consider standing at a drafting table to work or simply take periodic breaks. To build this into your lifestyle, do a quick upper back stretch each time you leave your workstation for a break. Discreetly place a blank sticky note or other reminder at the water cooler or coffee pot to remind you until the stretch becomes a habit.

Combine Strength, Balance, and Flexibility to Complete Your Workout

Probably the finest activity to hone and maintain balance and flexibility is yoga. Yoga combines meditative breathing with stretches and positions that continuously develop the body's ability to lengthen and center the core—that is, all the muscles of the torso and spine.

Breathing through the exercise is systematic and deep, enabling the shoulders to open, the back muscles to relax, and the vertebrae to stack with the least strain on discs and connective tissues. Yoga positions often use one limb against another, so that body awareness increases markedly. Endurance yoga uses positions that are held for one to two minutes, and power yoga variations may use positions for only ten seconds or so in rapid succession.

The other important characteristic of yoga is the mental benefits that accrue from disciplined breathing, stretching, and balance. Yoga can be an intensely meditative state, resulting in feelings of inner peace and satisfaction. The breathing is deep and cleansing, and it results in relaxation. Stretching reduces muscle tension and restores alignment and balance to primary stabilizers, the joints and the spine.

How to Extend Your Tenure by Improving Your Physical Flexibility: Kareem Abdul-Jabbar's Twenty Years as a Star Player

Kareem Abdul-Jabbar, the legendary basketball center, is a superb example of how flexibility and stretching through yoga and other deliberate training outside the usual cardiovascular and weight routines can prevent injury and keep a leader in the game. His professional basketball career is recognized as one of the longest-running professional athletic tours in history: twenty seasons as a professional basketball player. He retired at age forty-two, twice the age of some other NBA players.

Abdul-Jabbar played college basketball at UCLA under famed coach John Wooden. Coach Wooden had structured Abdul-Jabbar's training program around cardiovascular fitness, with little or no weight training. The focus on cardiovascular fitness was to match the UCLA fast break style of play, keeping Abdul-Jabbar in the game as long as possible, and ensuring that he could rapidly move down court into scoring position. Wooden had little confidence that weight training would be of help to his players, especially Abdul-Jabbar. Although strength is generally thought of as good, it is commonly accepted that the changes in muscles caused by intense lifting can throw off the delicate touch essential to shooting the ball.

In the middle of his college career while working on cardiovascular fitness, Abdul-Jabbar began to study aikido, a traditional martial art that includes stretching, particularly the basic stretches involving hamstrings, groin, and lower leg muscles. His connection to martial arts and to the joint protective value of stretching deepened during the fall of his junior year, when he was introduced to martial arts expert Bruce Lee.

Lee, a fighter, fully understood the value of stretching and flexibility as a way of protecting joints and muscles. He taught Abdul-Jabbar a method of stretching that was new at the time: static stretches held for twenty to thirty seconds, as opposed to the more familiar quick, jerky, repetitive moves. It is now commonly held by athletes and trainers that static stretches prevent damage to muscles and are the best way to increase flexibility.

Abdul-Jabbar began to learn yoga while playing college ball, a decision that he would later credit with extending his career in professional basketball. Abdul-Jabbar said once in an interview, "I believe that yoga is one of the reasons that I was able to play as long and as healthy as I did. Yoga is somewhat hard to quantify in terms of benefits because you see them in all the injuries you don't get. For me I noticed improvement in my posture—that was key for me because I had been having lower back problems. After I started doing yoga positions—asanas—all that changed. My health greatly improved overall."[1]

★ Why This Is Important for All Leaders

Many approaches to leadership, most notably the military's service academy approaches, work to develop leaders on multiple dimensions: intellectual, social, emotional, and physical. For in extremis or elite leaders, the physical dimension takes on added value and meaning. Health and fitness are not just imperatives for individual development and well-being. A fitness regimen that includes the development of joint stability and balance is key to keeping leaders engaged in the challenging, nonstop work of running the world's most demanding organizations.

Notes

Introduction

1. R. Toner, *New York Times*, Feb. 15, 2004, sec. 4, p. 1.

Chapter One

1. P. Pintrich and D. H. Schunk, *Motivation in Education: Theory, Research, and Applications* (Upper Saddle River, N.J.: Merrill-Prentice Hall, 2002), p. 3.

2. J. M. Reeve, *Motivating Others* (Needham Heights, Mass.: Allyn & Bacon, 1995), p. 10.

3. J. P. Raffini, *150 Ways to Increase Intrinsic Motivation in the Classroom* (Upper Saddle River, N.J.: Pearson Professional, 1996), p. 3.

4. K. Weick, "Enacted Sensemaking in Crisis Situations," *Journal of Management Studies*, 1988, *25*, 305–317.

5. J. M. Burns, *Leadership* (New York: HarperCollins, 1978).

6. B. M. Bass, "From Transactional to Transformational Leadership: Learning to Share the Vision, " *Organizational Dynamics*, 1990, *18*, 19–31.

7. Sweeney's work is described more fully in "Trust in Combat Leadership, " in D. Crandall (ed.), *Leadership Lessons from West Point* (San Francisco: Jossey-Bass, 2006) and is under review in several scientific venues.

Chapter Two

1. J. Swartz, "Phishing Style E-mail, Tracing Software Used," *USA Today*, Sept. 28, 2006, p. 2B.

2. *Wall Street Journal*, Sept. 7, 2005; portions excerpted by Daniel Weintraub at http://www.sacbee.com/static/weblogs/insider/archives/2005_09_07.html.

3. T. Layden, "Remembering Pat Tillman, " SI.com, Apr. 23, 2004. http://sportsillustrated.cnn.com/2004/writers/tim_layden/04/23/remembering.tillman/index.html.

4. P. Savage and R. Gabriel, "Cohesion and Disintegration in the American Army," *Armed Forces and Society*, 1976, *2*, 340–376.

Chapter Three

1. G. Gray, *The Warriors: Reflections on Men in Battle* (Orlando, Fla.: Harcourt, 1970), p. 13.

2. M. Rokeach, *Understanding Human Values: Individual and Societal* (New York: Free Press, 1979).

3. Gray, pp. 119–120.

4. F. Hesselbein and E. K. Shinseki, *Be·Know·Do: Leadership the Army Way* (San Francisco: Jossey-Bass, 2004).

5. Although not formally credited in the document, as is the custom for Army doctrine writers, B. Harris was the primary author of the U.S. Army's doctrinal field manual on leadership, *FM 22-100 Military Leadership* (Washington, D.C.: U.S. Government Printing Office, 1983). Copies can be made available through special arrangement with the Department of Behavioral Sciences and Leadership, U.S. Military Academy, West Point, New York.

6. S. Stouffer and others, *The American Soldier: Combat and Its Aftermath* (Princeton, N.J.: Princeton University Press, 1949).

7. F. Cohen and others, "Fatal Attraction: The Effects of Mortality Salience on Evaluations of Charismatic, Task-Oriented, and Relationship Oriented Leaders, " *Psychological Science*, 2004, *15*, 846–851.

8. M. Landau and others, "Deliver Us from Evil: The Effects of Mortality Salience and Reminders of 9/11 on Support for President George W. Bush, " *Personality and Social Psychology Bulletin*, 2004, *30*, 1–14.

9. G. Sullivan and M. Harper, *Hope Is Not a Method: What Business Leaders Can Learn from America's Army* (New York: Random House, 1996).

10. L. Wong, T. Kolditz, R. Millen, and M. Potter, *Why They Fight: Combat Motivation in the Iraq War* (Carlisle Barracks, Pa.: Strategic Studies Institute, 2003).

Chapter Four

1. D. Goleman, "Emotional Intelligence: Why It Can Matter More Than IQ," *Learning*, 1996, *24*(6), 49–50.

2. J. Galloway and H. G. Moore, *We Were Soldiers Once, and Young* (New York: Random House, 1992).

3. Galloway and Moore, p. 118.

4. Feuerstein's decisions were portrayed in a series of *Boston Globe* articles by journalist Bruce Butterfield, Sept. 8–11, 1996.

5. A. Esposito, "Factory Owner Says His Fame Reflects Poorly on Society, " *Worchester Telegram and Gazette*, June 11, 1996, p. 1.

6. B. Germain, *Transcending Fear: Relax, Focus, and Flow* (n.p.: Brian Germain, n.d.), p. 70.

7. G. Russell, "Mayor Nagin Speaks Out, " *New Orleans Times-Picayune*, Sept. 11, 2005, p. A15.

8. E. M. Vernberg, A. M. La Greca, W. K. Silverman, and M. J. Prinstein, "Prediction of Posttraumatic Stress Symptoms in Children After Hurricane Andrew, " *Journal of Abnormal Psychology*, 1996, *105*, 237–248.

9. Galloway and Moore, p. 182.

Chapter Five

1. For a complete discussion of military death rituals, see M. Ender, P. Bartone, and T. Kolditz, "Fallen Soldiers: Death and the U.S.

Military," in C. Bryant (ed.), *The Handbook of Death and Dying* (Thousand Oaks, Calif.: Sage, 2003).

2. K. Wright (ed.), *The Human Response to the Gander Military Air Disaster: A Summary Report* (Washington, D.C.: Walter Reed Army Institute of Research, 1987.

3. M. Thomas-Lawson, J. Whitworth, and J. Doherty, "Role of Leadership in Trauma Response: The Pentagon Family Assistance Center," *Military Medicine*, 2002, *167*, 71–72.

Resource

1. K. Abdul-Jabbar and M. K. McCarthy, 1990, *Kareem* (New York: Random House, 1990), p. 60.

Index

237

Acknowledgments

I first acknowledge the committed young people who enter our military academies, colleges, universities, firefighter training courses, police academies, and other public service training and education programs knowing full well that they will lead others in life-threatening circumstances and may lose their lives as a result. My early study and writing was all about giving them, especially cadets at West Point, leadership concepts specific to their incredible challenges. They are the reason I started thinking and writing about in extremis leadership, although the book in your hand is a broader work that I hope will inspire leaders from many walks of life.

I'm profoundly grateful to Frances Hesselbein, Bob Gaylord, and the Leader to Leader Institute for their encouragement and support and for all they do to advance leadership thinking, writing, and innovation. They make a difference in the lives of millions because of the thousands of leaders who benefit from their generosity, drive, and commitment. Frances's admonition to "write every day" has filled our world with ideas about leadership and the books that carry them.

I thank my fellow faculty in the Department of Behavioral Sciences and Leadership at the U.S. Military Academy for their support and for having me on their team. This dedicated group of professional soldiers and scholars works tirelessly to produce great young leaders, most of whom take the sons and daughters of America into in extremis contexts. Many people on our busy team covered meetings for me, taught classes for me, put off consultations with me, and otherwise helped me find snippets of extra time to write this book. Although I considered writing this book my duty, I couldn't have finished without their professionalism and support.

Many people have offered comments, encouragement, and helpful criticisms to me as I thought through this book, and a few stand out as real champs: Lenny Wong, Walter Ulmer, David Campbell, Brian Barefoot, Rick Swain, Don Snider, Pat Sweeney, Howard Prince, Don Campbell, Bruce Avolio, Bernie Banks, Becky Kanis, Brian Germain, Charlie Hooker, Chris Casciato, Doug Crandall, Everett Spain, Matt Densmore, Dennis O'Neil, and Sean Hannah. I'm especially grateful to Generals Fred Franks and Ric Shinseki, two of our nation's most accomplished soldiers and experts in battle command and combat leadership, for their comments and encouragement, and for their continued service as visiting professors at West Point.

Thanks to Terry Potter at Georgetown and Adel Allouche at Yale for helping with translation. And thanks to Lazlo Andacs and Stephanie Kingston for their incredible camera work.

Collectively, this book could not have been written without the more than one hundred interviewees who agreed to share their stories. Thank you for your time, your candor, and for what you do every day.

Special thanks go to our office staff, my assistant Joanne Wright (who transcribed many scratchy, sandy tapes from Iraq), as well as Ericka Booth, Darien French, Anita Howington, Carl LaCascia, and Jennifer Trainor, all ably led by Katie Hauserman. Thanks to Lori Doughty, an attorney from the Staff Judge Advocate who kept me straight on the legal intricacies of this book project as well as dozens of other innovative (or, well, hare-brained) schemes to enliven my department's teaching and outreach responsibilities.

Ruth Mills, my developmental editor, was a superb sounding board and pricelessly blunt critic, and her efforts to broaden the work are the reason I think most readers will recognize in extremis leadership in their daily lives. Allison Brunner, Jesse Wiley, and Amie Wong are a publishing dream team. Larry Olson, also from John Wiley & Sons, has been a cheerleader, friend, consultant, mentor, and source of inspiration to me and many authors at West Point. No single person has had more of an influence on leadership writing and publishing at the Military Academy than Larry Olson. And to the late Jo-Ann Wasserman, one of the first publishing professionals to take an interest in my writing and thinking, God bless you and keep you; you left us too soon.

I couldn't publish a book about leadership without acknowledging my parents, Trish and Loren Kolditz, who were the first two leaders I knew. Their personal example to my brother, Dan, and me made leadership in our school, church, and community a way of life, an expectation, and a moral obligation.

To my wife, Kay, thanks for your love and your patient reviews of my draft work. And to our daughters, Jenna and Kerry, thank you so much for understanding when I needed to write and for the love and support you've given me in writing and in all other facets of my work and our lives together. Tradition holds that the husband and father is a source of strength and stability, but in reality these three women keep my heart beating, and I would be aimless without them.

Many people have helped make this book better than I could have made it myself, but any mistakes or omissions are mine. All of the royalties from this book go to two nonprofits—the Leader to Leader Institute and the Association of Graduates of the U.S. Military Academy—to benefit the development of future leaders.

Passages in this work have been adapted from several articles and book chapters that I authored or coauthored during the preparation of the book. They are available through their publishers or through inextremis@dropzone.com:

"Leading As If Your Life Depended on It." In D. Crandall (ed.), *Leadership Lessons from West Point*. San Francisco: Jossey-Bass, 2006.

"Research in In Extremis Settings: Expanding the Critique of 'Why They Fight.'" *Armed Forces and Society*, 2006, *32*, 655–658.

"Authentic Leadership in In Extremis Settings: A Concept for Extraordinary Leaders in Exceptional Situations" (with Donna Brazil). In W. Gardner, B. Avolio, and F. Walumbwa (eds.), *Authentic Leadership Theory and Practice: Origins, Effects and Development*. Oxford: Elsevier, 2005.

"The In Extremis Leader." In F. Hesselbein (ed.), *Leader to Leader*. Special supplement. San Francisco: Jossey-Bass, 2005.

"Leadership Lessons of the Third Verb." *Performance*, 2004, *12*(3), 17–18.

"Leadership Learnings from Iraq." *Opening Bell*, 2003, *5*(1), 1–2.

The Author

Thomas A. Kolditz, Colonel, U.S. Army, is professor and head of the Department of Behavioral Sciences and Leadership at the U.S. Military Academy at West Point, New York. Kolditz has served in an array of military tactical command and technical staff assignments worldwide and as a leadership and human resources policy analyst in the Pentagon. His department is responsible for teaching, research, and outreach activities in leadership, psychology, sociology, and management at West Point. In 2003, Kolditz and a small team of researchers traveled throughout Iraq to study cohesion for the Army's chief of personnel.

Since 2001, Kolditz has served as a coach and mentor to the U.S. Military Academy sport parachute team. An accomplished parachute instructor with more than a thousand jumps, he weaves his personal experiences and abilities as a soldier, skydiver, and scholar into the firsthand study, analysis, and practice of leadership in dangerous circumstances—in extremis leadership—and how such leadership can inform the practice of leading in more ordinary settings, across the private, public, and social sectors. His teaching and research efforts center on applied social psychology and leadership.

A frequently requested speaker, his audiences have included the World Business Forum and executive audiences from Goldman

Sachs, Anheuser-Busch, Citigroup, EDS, and the Center for Creative Leadership. As a professor, he has led academic seminars or given lectures to students from Babson, Wellesley, and Olin colleges; Columbia University; Yale University; Duke University; the Beijing International M.B.A. program; the U.S. Army War College; and the U.S. Military Academy. Kolditz has been quoted by the Associated Press, *Marine Corps Times*, *Air Force Times*, the *Atlanta Journal Constitution*, the *Toledo Blade*, *National Defense* monthly, *Psychiatric Times*, CNN.com, and CNNMoney.com, and he has been interviewed by Kirsten Cole on WCBS TV as well as John Grayson on CBS Radio. Kolditz's military and law enforcement engagements have included the DEA Group Supervisors Institute, the New York Governor's Law Enforcement Leadership Series, the Army Medical Command, and the New Jersey State Association of Chiefs of Police.

Kolditz has published more than thirty articles across a diverse array of academic, military, and leadership journals, including *Leader to Leader*, *Journal of Personality and Social Psychology*, *Journal of Personality*, *Japanese Human Resource Journal*, *Performance*, *Armed Forces and Society*, *Perception and Psychophysics*, and *Military Review*, and he serves on the editorial and advisory boards of several academic journals. He is a Fellow in the American Psychological Association and in the Inter-University Seminar on Armed Forces and Society and a member of the Academy of Management and the Society of Psychologists in Management.

He holds a B.A. in psychology and sociology from Vanderbilt University, as well as master's and Ph.D. degrees in social psychology, a master's of military arts and science, and a master's in strategic studies.